The **Art**
Teacher's
SURVIVAL GUIDE
for Secondary Schools

To art teachers everywhere. You have shared your love for art, and inspired, comforted, and given something to students that can never be taken away—an appreciation for the beauty they and other artists created.

The Art Teacher's

SURVIVAL GUIDE

for Secondary Schools

GRADES 7–12

SECOND EDITION

Helen D. Hume

JOSSEY-BASS™

A Wiley Brand

Published by Jossey-Bass
A Wiley Brand
One Montgomery Street, Suite 1200, San Francisco, CA 94104-4594—www.josseybass.com

This book was originally published by Pearson Education, Inc.

Jossey-Bass books and products are available through most bookstores. To contact Jossey-Bass directly call our Customer Care Department within the U.S. at 800-956-7739, outside the U.S. at 317-572-3986, or fax 317-572-4002.

Wiley publishes in a variety of print and electronic formats and by print-on-demand. Some material included with standard print versions of this book may not be included in e-books or in print-on-demand. If this book refers to media such as a CD or DVD that is not included in the version you purchased, you may download this material at http://booksupport.wiley.com. For more information about Wiley products, visit www.wiley.com.

Library of Congress Cataloging-in-Publication Data

Hume, Helen D.
[Survival kit for the secondary school art teacher]
    The art teacher's survival guide for secondary schools: grades 7–12 / Helen D. Hume.—
Second edition.
        pages cm.
    Includes bibliographical references and index.
    ISBN 978-1-118-44703-1 (pbk.)
        1. Art—Study and teaching (Secondary)—United States—Handbooks, manuals, etc.   I.   Title.
N363.H86 2014
707.1'2—dc23
2013028770

Printed in the United States of America
SECOND EDITION
PB Printing 10 9 8 7 6 5 4 3 2 1

CONTENTS

ABOUT THIS RESOURCE

If you are looking for fresh, imaginative ways to teach basic art skills while exploring a variety of media, this ready-to-use *Survival Guide* is for you. It presents a studio-based secondary school art program that combines art history and appreciation with how-to-do-it lessons and classroom survival skills.

This all-in-one book is written for seasoned or inexperienced teachers of secondary school art students. Others who will find it useful are artists, homeschoolers, teachers of other specialties, and institutional or recreational art coordinators.

The more than sixty-five reproducible projects and eighty alternative suggestions encourage individual creativity, while giving introductory notes and specific information for the teacher and step-by-step, clearly stated directions for students.

Each project contains a list of materials, goals, and objectives based on Visual Arts Core concepts; explicit directions; appropriate vocabulary; and illustrations. A number of projects are appropriate for group or research activities. Each project encourages an individual approach to creativity.

Overview of the Book

Chapter One gives an overview of basic survival strategies for a student-centered art program. Suggestions are given for fostering a studio atmosphere that encourages individual problem solving; getting support from administration, staff, and students; and helping students improve their skills.

Chapter Two, "The Art of Teaching Art," includes history and cultural connections. Eight timelines show connections between the visual arts and other fields such as science and mathematics, literature, and government. Information on elements of art and principles of design is given in reproducible handouts.

Chapter Three, on drawing, presents teaching skills in a variety of drawing media such as pencil, pen and ink, charcoal-eraser, and fine-line markers. Projects include contour drawing, perspective drawing, drawing from observation, portraiture, and art journaling.

Chapter Four, on painting, covers painting with most media: watercolor, ink, oil paint, soft and oil pastels, and acrylic. Projects include plein air painting, painting a large mural, watercolor exercises, and encaustic.

Chapter Five, on printmaking, covers the basics of printmaking, with projects of varying degrees of difficulty. Preprinting projects using brayer prints and paste-paper lead to basic printmaking techniques that include collagraphs, reduction prints, linocuts, and watercolor monotypes. After-the-print techniques combine drawing materials, collage, and photocopy transfers to enhance the finished print.

Chapter Six, on photography, deals with the realities of today's photography, concentrating mostly on the basics of composition, camera functions, and taking digital photos. Projects include changing color photos to black and white, a photo journalism assignment, and photo appreciation. Basic instructions for developing film and darkroom printing are included.

In Chapter Seven, on digital graphics, students are encouraged to use their own photos as a basis for some of the projects. Lettering projects can be combined with images to design a business card, an invitation to a special event, or a poster design. A group project alphabet booklet will challenge students of all levels.

Many of the projects in Chapter Eight, on fine crafts, continue enduring traditions, such as ceramic slab, coil, and thrown pots, a sculptural ceramic project, and carved clay. Fiber projects in weaving and quilt design in cloth, paper, or computer are included. Book design is also explored.

In Chapter Nine, on sculpture and architecture, students may work in a variety of found materials in papier-mâché, recycled and molded paper pulp, carved wood or stone, plaster, and clay.

Chapter Ten, on careers in art, introduces a variety of techniques that a student might experience when actually working in the field of art. These include projects in graphic design, clothing design, architectural model making, children's book illustration, and industrial design.

THE AUTHOR

Helen D. Hume taught most of her career in the Parkway School District in St. Louis County, Missouri. Courses she taught were advanced placement art history, photography, sculpture, design, crafts, and graphic design. Later she taught and supervised preservice art teachers at universities in the St. Louis area. When her husband was transferred, she taught for three years in the Antwerp, Belgium, International School, where she established the art program, and later she taught for three years at the International School of Vale do Paraiba, São Jose dos Campos, Brazil. Her degrees are from Webster University.

She is an active member of the Missouri Art Education Association, the St. Louis Artists Guild, the St. Louis Symphony Volunteer Association, and serves on the Manchester Arts board of directors. A prize-winning artist, she is a plein air painter, photographer, and graphic artist, participating in individual exhibits and group shows.

This is her ninth book for art educators. Her other books are *A Survival Kit for the Secondary School Art Teacher; Art History and Appreciation Activities Kit; American Art Appreciation Activities Kit; The Art Teacher's Book of Lists; A Survival Kit for the Elementary/ Middle School Art Teacher; The Art Lover's Almanac; The Art Teacher's Survival Guide for Elementary and Middle Schools*, 2nd edition; and *The Art Teacher's Book of Lists*, 2nd edition.

ACKNOWLEDGMENTS

My gratitude goes to Joan Larson and Marilyn Palmer, friends and art teachers extraordinaires, who agreed to act as consultants on the book. Their experience and common sense have been invaluable during the writing of this essentially new book. The professional advice these two outstanding teachers have given as they have reviewed and given input on each chapter has kept me on track and helped me realize anew how creative art students can be when turned loose to imagine. Their students are lucky to have had such wonderful, dedicated master teachers.

There is no way to ever appropriately thank the artists, arts educators, and friends whose love of creating art and teaching have enlivened the book. They have answered my questions and allowed me to use their ideas and illustrations of their work or that of their students. In particular, I wish to thank Grant Kniffen, Beth Goyer, Linda Bowers, Suzanne Walker, John Nagel, Michael Swoboda, Linda Hertelendy-Wein whose encaustic painting is on the cover, George Schweser, Beth Kathriner, Eric Ludlow, Emily Dames, Laurie Kohler, James Daniels, Daniel Raedeke, Gwyn Wahlmann, Delphine Williams, Alan Kmetz, Traci Bolda, Tracy Jay, Barbara Aydt, Christine Vodicka, John Dyess, Robert Shay and the late Bill Vann's family, Kathy Schrock, Clare Walker Leslie, Lisa Sisley-Blinn, Timothy Smith, Marceline Saphian, Elizabeth Concannon, Thirteen Squared Art Group, Charles Goolsby, Harriet Fisher Thomas, Elizabeth Cavanagh Cohen, Christine Sarra, Joanne Stremsterfer, Brian Crawford, Katy Mangrich, Tom Lutz, Clint Johnson, Johanna Prinz, Susan Hume, Helen Moore, Weavers' Guild of St. Louis, Amy Kling, William Perry, John Tiemann, Adam Long, Peggy Dunsworth, Christa Ollinger, Carrie Finnestead, and Stacey Morse.

Lynn Ezell of the National Art Education Association and NAEA President Dennis Inhulsen have given me good advice. Dr. Jennifer Allen, who spoke at the Missouri Art Education Association, was especially helpful in clarifying my understanding of the Visual Arts Core Standards.

And I wish to thank the staff at Jossey-Bass whose careful attention to detail has been so appreciated for making the book more readable. I especially want to acknowledge senior editor Marjorie McAneny, whose experience and sensible approach to writing have been invaluable; editorial program coordinator Tracy Gallagher; vice president Lesley Iura; production manager Pamela Berkman; production editor Susan Geraghty; and marketing manager Dimi Berkner. Copyeditor Sarah Miller made it easier to read and had some great suggestions. Cover designer Jeff Puda has a great understanding of what it takes to make a book appealing. They will never know how much I have appreciated their help in this and previous books.

Without the help of museum and artists' representatives, it would not have been possible to include museum prints in this book. Stacey Sherman of the Nelson-Atkins has been especially supportive in helping me to select illustrations for *all* of my books from the time I began writing books. Others whose help is deeply appreciated are Kristin Goode of the Mildred Lane Kemper Art Museum at Washington University; Shannon Sweeney of the Saint Louis Art Museum; Anita Duquette and Kiowa Hammons of the Whitney Museum of Art; Carlie Forsyth of the NewArtCenter Gallery, Salisbury, UK; Shelley Lee of The Roy Lichtenstein Foundation; Ryo Munakata of the Munakata Shikô Memorial Museum, Tokyo; Randy Smith, Jean Ponzi, and Deborah Frank of the St. Louis Botanical Garden; Jen Sweet of Citygarden, St. Louis; Maria Elena Murguia of the Artists Rights Society of New York; Kathryn Pawlik of VAGA; and Liz Kurtulik of ARTS Resource Images.

We thank the following for permission to use the works from their collections:

Mildred Lane Kemper Museum, Washington University: *The City II*
Museum of Modern Art: *Whaam!; Moon; Target with Four Faces*
Nelson-Atkins Museum of Art: *Still Life; Pablo Ruiz with Itch; End of Day Nightscape IV; The Steerage; Olive Orchard*
St. Louis Botanical Garden: *Limon S. Remi; Trash, Really? (Quilt)*
St. Louis City Garden: *Bird; Two Rabbits*
Saint Louis Museum of Art: *Clasped Hands of Robert and Elizabeth Barrett Browning; Ornament from the Scoville Building; In Praise of Flower Hunting*
Wadsworth Atheneum Museum of Art, Hartford, Connecticut: *Big Wood Island*
Whitney Museum, New York City: *Music Pink and Blue II*
ARTS Resource Images: *The Twenty Marilyns* (Private collection, Paris)

The **Art** Teacher's

SURVIVAL GUIDE

for Secondary Schools

Basic Survival Strategies

Get Off to a Good Start

Get to Know Your Students

Students are at an important stage in their lives. They are capable physically of doing almost anything an adult can do and are in the process of becoming independent thinkers and responsible members of society. You have an opportunity to contribute to their general knowledge: things that *educated* people know. This is possibly the last time the student will have a formal art course, perfect personal skills in art, and prepare for a career in art. Perhaps you are the teacher who develops in a student a lifetime appreciation of and love for art.

Friendliness and an Interest in Your Students

These will go a long way toward fostering an ongoing relationship. Avoid sarcasm, as it is often misinterpreted, although humor and an appreciation for your students' sense of humor will be a saving grace. Find out what your students are involved in (work, activities, other classes). Go to some student events in which your students participate (sports events, plays, or concerts); you will be glad you did. They also like to know that you have a life outside the day at school, and they don't mind hearing about it once in a while. Use a conversational tone while sharing problem-solving techniques as if the students were your colleagues.

Fairness to *All*

Fairness to all students should be ingrained in your teaching. It truly is important to remember that all students deserve equal time: those to whom everything comes easily deserve your attention as much as those to whom nothing comes easily. Start conversations with the in-between or nondemanding student; you will always learn something about him or her that you hadn't realized before. Be sensitive to the possibility of gender bias.

Encourage Good Decisions

Albert Burr, one of the greatest principals I've ever met, says that we are teaching high school students to become decision makers. If they show poor judgment, we need to give them greater guidance, or even make decisions *for* them, if necessary, until they learn to make better decisions. Help students develop skills, responsibility, respect, and the ability to build personal relationships. Let them know you have very high expectations for achievement in your art class, as that is the tradition in *this* school.

Think about Each Individual

Try to spend a quality few minutes with each student every class day. I found it was useful to review the class list, really reflecting on how each student was progressing and also reviewing whether that student and I had spoken about his or her work that week. Tell them that each of them is entitled to 1 ½ minutes of your time every single class period, and while they may not get exactly that amount every time, over the period of the week they will receive their 7 ½ minutes. I've had students come up and say, "I'm ready for my 1 ½ minutes today."

Mentoring

A number of school districts now include mentoring programs for new teachers. A mentor and mentee might meet up to six times a year, perhaps getting a release day to visit a school in a different district. Colleagues whose schools have such programs support them strongly, stating that it benefits both teachers. If you are a new teacher and your district does not have a formal mentoring program, seek advice from experienced teachers or your state's art education teachers' association blog.

The Day-to-Day Stuff

Arriving in Class

Keep a table next to the door on which you place handouts and art paper if needed for that day's lesson. As students pick these up on their way in, it piques their interest. Ask students to get their work in progress from the storage area and be seated and ready to work in time for attendance.

Attendance

In most schools attendance is tracked online. To make class start faster, call the names only of those you think are absent—just in case they are not seated, but are somewhere in the room.

The Seating Chart

It took me almost fifteen years of letting students seat themselves anywhere to realize that posting a seating chart on the door on the first day of class would improve my teaching. Photo rosters are available to teachers in many districts with an online database. Make a seating chart by cutting up and pasting the faces and names on paper with restickable glue stick to make strategic seating moves within the first few days. Make a copy for your convenience or that of a substitute. After a week you can leave students seated where they are and take down the chart, reserving the option to move a student or two if necessary. A colleague says that her daughter told her that allowing students to sit anywhere without a seating chart only helps kids who already have friends in the class, because they always sit together. But it isolates the kids who don't have friends in the class and makes it harder for them.

Develop a Studio Atmosphere

You've tried to make the room as functional and *artistic* as possible, and you can expect students to get out materials and be ready to work, allowing you your few minutes at the beginning of class. The perfect studio atmosphere fosters independent learning and self-motivation. Ideally your principal could walk into the room, bringing important visitors, and your students would all be working as you quietly walk around having soft conversations with individuals or small groups.

Motivation

Sometimes reality isn't too far away from this ideal if students know that you expect work to be completed within a given time period and if they are working toward a personal goal such as developing a portfolio or completing something for an exhibition. Teacher and student assessments are other motivating tools, as students are aware that you expect them to be on task while they are in the art room. Include a rubric in your lesson so students know what your expectations are. Common Core State Standards for the Arts will emphasize independence and creativity.

Getting Students' Attention and Keeping It

Consider yourself the coach. You're there to give the pep talk and get on with the game. Because you are smart enough to know that your instructions should be short and sweet, you will notice when students are not watching you. I have found that the most effective way of control is to interrupt yourself in the middle of a sentence and just look at the student who is talking or involved in something else. You can look at the ceiling; act as if you have nothing else to do in the world but stand there patiently waiting.

When he or she notices that the class has gone silent and finally looks at you, give the kindest fake smile you can summon and continue. You don't have to do this very many times for your students to get the message that you expect their attention. It is far easier to allow students to control their peers than to *demand* respect. But don't push your luck. Notice when you are beginning to lose even the most polite of students. Students of that age have about a twenty-minute attention span (as one of my students pointed out to me).

Nonverbal Discipline

Even though you may have no official rules, you still have rules (or expectations, if you like). Let students know you like secondary school students and you like teaching them.

If someone is giving you problems, *never* call him or her out in front of peers, but find a chance to get the student outside the room and ask, "What did I do wrong today?" This usually stuns them, and they realize their behavior was inappropriate. Sometimes you find out the major problem that student is having that particular day and can be of help. Sometimes you realize you'd better let it go with that student for that day.

Silent Signals

With so little time to talk with each student in a class period, there are many ways to send quick, *silent signals.* A smile, silent nod of approval, or thumbs-up lets someone know he or she is remarkable or at least is on the right track. Sometimes a raised eyebrow or widened eyes give the student the idea that you're less than pleased with behavior. It can convey the unspoken message "I can't *believe* you are doing that" or "Oh, how you have disappointed me."

Electronic Devices

Every school has different policies concerning cell phones and other electronic devices. Working within that framework is important so that students can expect the same policies from every teacher in the school. Some districts allow cell phones in class, and teachers are encouraged to develop lessons in which students can use these remarkable research tools. Some schools leave it up to the individual teacher, and you need to make a decision and clearly state it to students, abiding by what you have said you will tolerate. A conversation about the use of cell phones can be a good lesson on respect. Would you use a cell phone in church? During a stage play? A teacher deserves the same respect that is shown in these settings.

Take Advantage of Technology

Most schools have computer technology in place, and art teachers have access to labs or have computer classrooms in the art department. Many schools have interactive whiteboards and document cameras that allow the teacher to put together a slide show of large visuals to share with the students. Some of these programs offer interactive games and art-related videos. Have students take digital photos of their own work, title it, and place it in a digital folder labeled with the project name. Or you can take the photographs, placing the work on the floor or on a neutral-colored wall to record. You can use selected examples to show students if you teach this project the following year.

Original Resources

Although students can easily learn how to copy something, such as a scene from a magazine or a celebrity portrait, that process is teaching *copying* rather than teaching how to make art. They might go to the Internet or a book for research, but unless they make significant changes from images that are not their own, it neither fosters the feeling of achievement nor results in originality. Instead, encourage students to develop personal ideas from their own sketches, photographs, and interests.

Vary Your Teaching Methods

Students respond well to a variety of methods of presentation. As you select projects or techniques to explore, think of ways to present them that do not involve long lectures. Demonstrate, write on the board, present selected portions from videos, introduce them to artists through the many beautiful books available at libraries or images on the web, pose questions, host visiting artists, take them on field trips (even within the school)—anything you can think of to keep them involved in and excited about their own learning. Help students develop listening skills through good questioning techniques: "What will we do first? Then? Then?" Use adequate wait time; it may save time in the long run. Move freely around the room when you are teaching something—*proximity* is a wonderful way to keep students involved. Try not to end an introduction with "Any questions?" Most students have them, but don't want to admit ignorance. If a student asks a question about something that you thought you had already made clear, act as if it is the greatest question in the world; someone else will also appreciate the answer.

Give Open-Ended Assignments

Try to avoid "classroom" assignments in which you already know what the end result will be. Instead, teach projects that foster independence and the opportunity for divergent thinking.

The Sovereign Feline
Nicole Brawley. This cat brings a smile to the owner of any animal. Parkway North High School, St. Louis, Missouri, teacher Grant Kniffen.

If you state that you expect creative solutions, you will usually get them. If you give general expectations within such an assignment, there is still a great opportunity for personal reflection. Secondary school students are particularly introspective, and "about me" projects often yield exciting outcomes.

Each One Teach One

If you are teaching something complicated, you will need many different approaches and repetitions to get information across. Enlist your students as teachers! When they notice a classmate who might not understand the process, ask the student to be a teacher for a minute. It won't hurt them, and having to explain a process to someone else may clear up any misunderstanding they themselves have. It never hurts to have the steps written on a poster or the board and to expect students to take notes.

Students in Grant Kniffen's advanced class were challenged to do a large acrylic portrait.

Self-Portrait
Alexandria Stanley, acrylic, 48 × 60 inches. This student's portrait includes items of furniture, discarded jeans, and a favorite teddy bear. Parkway North High School, St. Louis, Missouri, teacher Grant Kniffen.

When an open-ended assignment such as this is given, one can expect excellence and creativity.

Self-Appraisal

In order to develop confidence in art making, students must feel comfortable taking risks. When you talk with a student about his or her work, find a balance between praising the work too highly (unless it deserves it) and appearing to hate it. Art is personal, and criticism has to be tactful. Rather than saying, "This needs improvement" (in which the student hears "My, what an ugly face you have"), encourage the student to appraise the work with questions such as "What do you think might happen if you moved this line?" or "What is the next thing you might do on this?" Let them know that yours is only one opinion, and that ultimately they must make the final decisions. I have found that when students ask a couple of fellow students for suggestions, it is helpful to both parties.

Grades in the Art Class

Most secondary school art teachers grade work primarily on completed art projects, and there may be only six per semester. Tell the students that these are the "big exams" in your art class. Try to work your evaluation expectations into your grading sheets for each project, allowing students to determine whether they have met the criteria before the artwork is turned in to see if more needs to be done. Some "perfectionist" students may not meet deadlines, and you can issue an in-progress grade that will be raised if the student completes the project shortly. Let them know that the grade will be revised to reflect the complexity of their work.

Grading must be completely objective according to your criteria. Students easily relate a percentage grade in art to those they receive in other classes. Since units can run very long (sometimes weeks), these grades become very important to the semester grade. A written test is usually given less weight in the semester art grade. Although most grades are entered on a school's website, with both students and parents having access to them, you may find that students still need to be reminded of their responsibility to keep track of their progress to avoid being surprised that a missing project will result in a lower semester grade.

Schools and districts handle excessive absenteeism differently, with students usually being allowed to complete all work missed for *excused* absences such as illness, doctor appointments, and religious holidays, but some penalty given for a certain number of unexcused absences.

Portfolio

In general, all art students will keep their work in a portfolio. Independent study students and students in Advanced Placement will maintain an online portfolio that might be used later to apply for admission to an art school.

A journal is particularly useful at this level. Students can paste in works or sketches they drew on a scrap of paper outside of class. Art teacher Cara Deffenbaugh found that her students sometimes left her sticky note observations in their sketchbooks as artifacts. These journals became part of the students' portfolios.

Overcome the "I Can't Draw" Syndrome

Art is so much more than drawing, and while students can be taught to draw, they need to be told that each person is valued for unique experiences and ideas and that you will build on the skills and knowledge they already have. Reassure them that just as they couldn't expect to play the piano or baseball without learning the basics, *anything* new has to be learned and practiced. Students who have been taking art since early elementary years may arrive in secondary school with greater confidence in their abilities to problem-solve and ready to try anything. One art teacher tells students that "talent" is less important for success in art class than the ability to listen to directions and work hard.

The first project should be nonthreatening, one in which all students have the same opportunity to succeed, no matter how well they draw (perhaps a collage). If students get off to a good start, they are usually willing to try different things later.

Never Draw on Students' Work

If you want to show students a way to improve their work, use a piece of tracing paper, place it on the artwork, and draw on the tracing paper, then wad it up and throw it away! Or *draw* it with a fingertip or pencil eraser. Teacher Joan Larson says she is famous for her "air drawings" over student work. Or make a hasty line or two on a sticky note. If you make changes for them, you are essentially telling them that you are a better artist and that their work isn't any good.

Teach Art History Often and Keep Them Moving!

Teacher Helen Moore feels that art history should be part of every project, every medium. She teaches classes in several subjects, introducing students to art history through games. She places posters on tables around the art room, giving students various standards for selecting a poster or portion of a poster. They use sticky notes to place on a poster that they think meets certain stated criteria, and have lively discussions as they look, examine, defend their selections, and learn! When the teacher plays devil's advocate, asking questions that challenge students to consider why they made their selections, everyone stays involved.

Teach Visual Literacy

The purpose of art education is to teach students to see and interpret. Students will become design-literate consumers by becoming aware of beauty, whether it is found in nature or created by designers. Good taste is not necessarily instinctive. Discussion, criticism, and analysis of good and poor design should be part of every art course. Get students to find examples of "kitsch" (good design taken a step beyond its intended use—for example, a reproduction of the *Venus de Milo* with a clock on her stomach). Explain that every time they select something to wear or decorate a room, they are making choices about design. Seeking to develop creativity, imagination, and originality is basic to the teaching of art.

Keep the Room Clean

All students should be expected to do their share in keeping the art room respectable. Most are more than willing to clean up their own mess, but have to be encouraged to share work throughout the room. Assign a small, different group each week to be responsible for the extras: the paper cutter table, the sink, scraps picked up from the floor, and work tables. It certainly isn't fair to expect the last class of the day to clean up after all the previous classes, and that class usually is already responsible for putting chairs or stools on the tables. The evening cleaning crew should never have to clean anything but the floor. One teacher labels the art tables or rows with numbers and rotates the cleanup of the common areas by the numbers. To show the system is fair to all, a large calendar is posted with a number written for each class day.

Closure

Having discussed how you handle the first few minutes of class, the last few minutes are also important. Begin cleaning in time for students to do a good job and not leave it for you to do (five minutes for normal work, ten minutes for 3-D work). After work in progress is stored and work spaces are cleaned, students may remain at their desks or tables to visit. When students line up at a door, some feel they need to get an early start to the next class. Have a moment of closure that might sum up the good work that was accomplished that period or talk about the coming day. If you begin the year with the expectation that they will remain seated, it is relaxing and calming for everyone.

The Art Classroom

Add Visual Excitement

There are always a few days before school begins when you can think about the first impression your classroom will make as students walk in the door. As a visual artist, you have access to an unlimited number of art reproductions, timelines, and instructional placards. Yes, these are wonderful and useful in teaching, but in profusion can become a little too much of a good thing. Change them frequently if you want students to notice them.

Where Is the Color?

Are your walls the same as other walls throughout the school, or might you request the opportunity to paint at least one of them in an up-to-date museum color? Or as teacher Meg Classe did, paint each wall in a *different* museum color: dark purple, Naples yellow, magenta, and cornflower blue (or lime green). Perhaps you can use fabric as inspiration, draping it somewhere just to soften things a bit. If you have a bulletin board, cover it in color before adding pictures to it. If you have collected folk art or souvenirs from your travels, display them. Make your art room an exciting place to be.

Teacher's Desk or Work Table

Arrange your room so you can see every face and the door from your desk. Don't allow students to sit with backs to you or to sit behind you. Make sure you can see students' eyes when you are talking. Try not to sit behind your desk much, as you will be a more effective teacher when you move around—a lot! The desk is a barrier between you and students that can make it difficult for the shy student to ask you a question. You'll never find the "hiders" unless you move around. Be flexible when arranging student desks and tables. What works well for one project may need to be completely moved around for the next one. If you work with students in a computer studio, perhaps your desk should be placed more to the side so you can monitor students' progress. Students will often be seated at a stationary table, but should have freedom to be up and moving as they get materials, observe other students' work, or find a different spot from which to draw.

Equipment and Materials

Where to Put It

There is seldom as much counter space as you need to keep materials out for easy use. Normally materials are brought out as needed and stored in a closet until needed again. Make every effort to find a place for everything, and keep it there until needed. Have locking storage for expensive or specialty equipment. If there is something that you know you might need one day but don't have room for now (clay or paper, for example), perhaps it can be stored in a closet not too far from the art room.

Storing Supplies

Depending on your storage situation, there is nothing more colorful than stacks of paint or paper or yarn arranged on top of cabinets like a spectrum. Think how much you enjoy going into an art supply store—can you create that same atmosphere in your classroom? And, of course, if you have cabinets, *arrange* some of the great things you have collected for a still life on top of them. This could include all kinds of wheeled vehicles, musical instruments, large machine parts, discarded large toys, an antique chair, and so on.

Label materials such as markers, clay, and liquid paint by date, placing the newest materials behind the purchases of the previous year and using the older items first. If you find you have materials that are several years old and you never get to use reasonably fresh items, give the old stuff away to other teachers in your school or send an e-mail to art teachers in your district or state, announcing a grand giveaway.

Student Storage

Ideally you have a drawer or shelf for each class where work in progress can be stored in a "portfolio." Students are expected to bring their own drawing pencils, eraser, black fine-line marker, and sketchbooks to class (and to label all of these with their names, using the marker). A storage place for wet work may be a drying rack or newsprint to protect the floor of the hallway outside the art room.

Loaning Supplies or Equipment

If a student wants to borrow something valuable (even your pencil) during class hour, have them leave a *forfeit* (keys or something small you can keep safely in your pocket) that can be retrieved when they return the equipment. If you loan something that will leave the classroom or overnight, ask people to sign it out. Mark *anything* that might be borrowed in large letters with permanent black marker.

Safety

Yes, secondary school students are physically capable of doing almost anything adults do, but they are not fully experienced, and sometimes they do not think as far in advance as

you would like (I always felt they were 98 percent adult, 2 percent little kid). You owe it to the students to provide safe materials, a safe environment, and instructions on proper use of tools. Never take their safety awareness for granted. Specific safety reminders are also given in the appropriate chapters in this book (ceramic, sculpture, and printmaking).

General Safety Suggestions

• No matter their ages, a few students can be counted on to point a staple gun at someone and see if it "shoots." Allow a staple gun to be used only after you have given instructions and gotten a guarantee from the student that it will be used only as you have agreed.

• Extension cords should not snake across floors. Compliance with local fire codes regarding these is imperative. If they must cross a floor, covers may be placed over them to protect students from tripping.

• Check to make sure that your fire extinguisher has been inspected or replaced each year. Make sure you understand how to use it.

• Have electrical equipment (kiln and electric drill) inspected each year for safe operation.

• Flammable solvents should be properly stored in a metal cabinet.

• A kiln ideally should be in a well-ventilated area. It should be properly vented and have eighteen inches of space between it and any wall. Students should be told never to touch it or anything that is drying on top. If it is adjacent to the art room, firing should be done overnight.

• If students are working with something that might splash or cause a foreign object to get in their eyes, insist that they wear safety goggles.

Safety in Cutting

Students should know how to use a craft (X-acto) knife and a metal ruler to make a straight cut on paper.

- Make the assumption that the edges on precut purchased paper are straight.
- *Always* keep the guard on the paper cutter. When giving instructions on proper paper cutter use, remind students to always check to see where the holding hand is before bringing the blade down.
- If students cut on a paper cutter, point out that they can measure at the top ruler, using the grid on the bed of the paper cutter to perfectly align the paper. Show them how to hold the paper with the left hand so it does not move or slide.
- Whatever the cutting tool (single-edged razor, craft or X-acto knife, or linocut tools), remind the students to always keep the noncutting hand behind the blade in case the knife slips.
- Count craft knives and make sure all are returned at the end of the hour.
- If cutting through thick board, several short cuts may be needed to go through the layers.
- To cut a "window" in paper or cardboard, the cuts extend slightly beyond the corner so the corner will be perfectly square and the center will fall out. Use a metal ruler, preferably one with cork backing, and place the ruler over the *mat* area, not the hole, holding the ruler firmly in place. If the cutter slips, the border will not be damaged.

Recommended Safe Materials for Schools

Manufacturers go to great pains to develop safe materials for students, and if you still have materials that do not have the CP (Certified Product) or AP (Approved Product) manufacturer's seal that is given by the Art and Craft Material Institute, I recommend you discard them. Even university classes have adopted the following nontoxic materials and methods:

- CP or AP pencils, watercolors, tempera, acrylic, oil sticks, crayons, chalks, and colored pencils
- CP or AP water-based inks instead of oil-based inks
- CP or AP pastes for papier-mâché or CP or AP cellulose for papier-mâché
- CP or AP clear acrylic emulsion to fix drawings
- CP or AP lead-free glazes for ceramics
- Mineral spirits instead of turpentine or kerosene
- Water-based markers
- Shellac containing denatured alcohol
- Food or vegetable dyes (onion skins or tea) in place of procion dyes
- Oil paints that end in *hue* (cadmium red hue) instead of toxic cadmium-based paints

Get Support for the Art Program

Keep the Administration Informed

When a student or staff member has done something special, send a memo to the principal and put it in daily announcements and on the school's website. Personally invite all administrators and guidance counselors to the exhibitions or send a handwritten invitation (another use for student power). Discuss student artwork with administrators, pointing out a student's creative approach to problem solving. Discuss different students' approaches to the same project and explain why you encourage those differences.

Ask for Administrative Support for Your Budget

A strong art program costs money! You will never have as much money as you would like, but try to get enough to support a strong curriculum. Keep accurate records of your expenses. Conserve supplies and keep equipment repaired, replacing only as needed. Some districts auction items no longer needed, with the proceeds going back to the department that sold them.

Plan Ahead for Large Expenditures

If you plan a large project such as a mural and it will improve the appearance of the school, you may be able to obtain funding from the administration. If the curriculum is changing, try to get sufficient money to start new courses from some source other than your yearly budget.

Invite Visitors

Encourage administrators, school newspaper and yearbook teachers, and parents to drop in on your class if you have something special going on or even if you don't. Invite visitors to talk with students and to discuss their work with them. The opportunity for an administrator to talk with students during class is rare. Visitors enjoy observing both the bustle and quiet activities of the art department.

Show Off Your Students and Your Program

Visual arts specialists understand the importance of fine arts courses in education and have an opportunity to *show* what is happening in the classroom, whereas many disciplines can only use testing. School administrators, guidance departments, and sometimes state lawmakers play a vital part in decision making about your curriculum. You, the visual arts expert in your school, must be prepared to let others know that art has a *curriculum*, just as any other discipline does.

Your Website

Many districts now encourage or expect each teacher to have a regularly updated website, which is a link inside the school's overall website. This is a place to tell the community about your background, degrees, qualifications, exhibitions, and experience, including photos of your own artwork. Your website will also probably include a page for each of your classes. A course outline (syllabus), special handouts, notices of upcoming art shows, pictures of student artwork, even digital slide shows can be included on each class's page. This can be a great way to communicate with parents and students. An automated signature at the bottom can be a link to contact you by e-mail. Your district may have a "Publication of Student Information" consent form that is signed by the student's parent or guardian and will allow you to photograph your students and their work for the district's websites. Of course, with the ease of getting that information out, you need to keep it updated on a routine basis (preferably monthly).

Get Support from the Staff

Get to Know Staff Members by Name

In a large school it is all too easy for teachers in every department to remain in their offices, getting to know close colleagues well. You can get to know other staff members by becoming involved in school committee work, working as a class sponsor, or becoming a representative for your teacher association. Don't be a stranger! Look at a yearbook to connect faculty and student names with faces.

Act as a Resource Person for Other Teachers

Many non-art teachers realize that student learning can become more interesting when students are asked to add visuals to a project. As your school becomes more "art-oriented," it benefits everyone. Many teachers simply want suggestions or ideas for something that might enhance a project. Send a memo to the teaching staff offering to help them in any way you can. Help when you can with suggestions for posters and bulletin board decoration. Suggest to teachers that they enlist help from any of their students who take art. Offer to help create a literary and visual art magazine showcasing short prose and poetry. Often your students' art works well with the themes in student writing.

Get Support from Students

Display Student Work

Make students proud that they "belong" to the art department. Because constantly changing exhibits is time-consuming, let students help in creating displays. Students become aesthetically discriminating when they see all the different interpretations of one assignment displayed together. Label pieces with easy-to-read student names (in at least fourteen-point font). Put signs near the displays indicating the name of the class in which the works were made and any prerequisites for taking that course.

Ask Students for Suggestions

Students and teacher work together to help make a class successful. It is not the exclusive responsibility of one or the other. If the classes are good, students will support the program. No form of promoting enrollment is as strong as students talking with each other about courses. Examine your classes each year; see which projects were less successful than others or definitely need to be replaced. Try new things. Don't be afraid to "bomb" once in a while. A good saying for art teachers is "It is better to be among the wounded than the watchers." Or, as art teacher Lauren Davis used to say, "No guts, no glory."

Encourage students to ask questions when they don't understand. If there is something they especially want to learn, they should let the teacher know. Don't be afraid to let them know that you are also asking questions of yourself, willing to make changes, and always trying new teaching approaches. Ask the students; they will tell you.

Artist of the Week

Think of the thirty or more students a year to whom you can give the lasting memory that once he or she was an Artist of the Week. It can't always be the person who draws best or who intends to pursue a career in art, but perhaps a student who has just one outstanding work to show that week. Seeing their name on a placard next to a small display can give great satisfaction to students. Awarding a certificate signed by the art teachers and principal is a nice addition.

Make Your School Look Good

Make Your Program Visible

Just as successful sports programs and musical and dramatic events give students opportunities to share their talent, an art program should show what your students are doing. One advantage to displaying artwork is that it needn't be a one-time event, but can be ongoing.

Hang Artwork by *All* the Students Outside the Art Classroom

Although you might prefer to hang only outstanding art, all students benefit from having their work exhibited. If you hang the stronger works at each end and in the middle, every student's artwork looks good. Students should automatically identify their work by using a fine-line black marker to *print* the following information on a preprinted label: name, grade level, title of the work, name of the course, and teacher (the card also serves to inform other students which courses they might like to take next year). Keep labels and a black fine-line pen in a box lid taped to your desk, and students can label work for display (and neatness is appreciated).

Changing Exhibits of Student Artwork

Mount displays on walls throughout the school such the wall outside the main office, inside the library on top of bookshelves, and in glass-fronted cases in the entry hall. These displays should be changed regularly. A general rule of thumb is that the farther the artwork is from the art room, the stronger it should be. Standard-size frames that are affixed to the wall and open easily make frequent changes possible.

Principal's Art Collection

At the end of the year, hold a contest in which the winner will leave a work of art as part of a permanent display in the principal's office, the library, guidance department, or other prominent location. A parents' organization could sponsor this contest, furnish a small prize, and frame the work of art. It costs little more to affix a brass plaque with the student's name and the year to the frame, and the student will never forget the honor. A digital print of the artwork can be made to include in the student's portfolio.

The One-Day School Show

Near the end of each semester, hold a huge one-day show in the school entrance lobby (if your department doesn't have a large enough area) in which *every* student in the department has at least one work on display. At the spring show, feature a few students who are graduating with a grouping of their own work. This display requires a great deal of student power and help from a couple of parents. Send special invitations home with students for all parents and grandparents, and invite district officials. If you can coordinate the visual arts exhibit with a musical or dramatic event that brings in community members, so much the better.

Invite teachers to all-school art shows through written and personal invitations. Ask your students to give their teachers adequate notice, so that those teachers can bring an entire class to see the show for fifteen minutes or so.

The purpose for doing all this work for a *one-day* exhibit is that you often have to move worktables and chairs out of the area to make space for viewers, and you would not want any of the work to be taken or defaced. Schedule a few students each hour to act as hosts throughout the exhibition.

District Art Exhibition

Even if yours is the only high school in a county, you still can have an art department exhibition somewhere outside the school. It may be a community library, recreation center, mall, or bank, but make the effort and give it publicity. A large district may sponsor an all-district, all-grade-level show to which all students and their families in the district are invited. It offers a chance to see what is happening in the other high schools. This event might be held inside a big mall or all-purpose recreation center.

District Gallery Website

Another venue for an ongoing district art display is a district Gallery Website. This is a good place for a district to spotlight artistic growth from kindergarten through twelfth grade. It can be set up so a viewer can look at just ceramics, for example, from grades K–12 or compare photography from each of the district's high schools. It is important that teachers keep the Gallery Website current, so viewers always see new and exciting things.

Monumental Artwork for the School

Think Big   Look for an empty spot crying out to be filled with a large work of art, or see if existing artworks in such a spot are dated and need to be replaced. Get permission and funding first! To get inspiration, look at artwork done for new buildings and hotels. Two possible projects are wall murals or huge bas-relief wall sculptures. If you know that you will be physically unable to hang something large or will need scaffolding, enlist the help of the district's building and grounds staff. Plan ahead: estimate time schedule, costs, dedication ceremony, and publicity. Some schools use tiles made by students to enrich an outdoor seating or garden area.

Public Relations

Publicity Guidelines

Local newspapers, community newspapers, Internet newsletters, and TV stations are always looking for interesting stories. If your students have participated in an art-related service project or have completed a monumental work of art for the school, try to get recognition for their work. First discuss with your principal the possibility of getting publicity for a student or group of students.

Many school districts have public relations departments that specify the policy about publishing students' names with photos. Use permission forms if necessary. If adults are featured in an article with students, identify them by name and title (for example, Principal John Jones and Art Specialist Mary Doe).

If you submit an article about this event, include the 5 Ws and H: who, what, when, where, why, and how. If this is an event to which the public is invited, be specific about the date, time, school name, address, and phone number or e-mail of a contact person for further information.

Principal's Newsletter

Most schools post their news on the school's website once a month. Update the community on what the Art Department is doing—shows, competitions, and the like.

Competitions

Keep your eye open for opportunities throughout the year for local or national art competitions for high school students. Some of these offer financial benefits such as college scholarships or cash prizes. Others may be juried shows or opportunities for students to have their work displayed or published. Local businesses sometimes sponsor a competition for a logo design or artwork to be used in an advertisement. One of these *real* applications might be beneficial to an entire class, but you do have a curriculum to teach and may prefer to offer some of these to a few individuals to enter if it appeals to them.

Read the directions carefully about how and when the work must be presented and how it will be returned. Fortunately, many art competitions can now be juried by sending the work online or by sending a CD. If work must be sent and returned by postal mail or any other method that will cost, make sure you consider it a worthwhile competition. Follow presentation directions to the letter! If the regulations specify framed work with wire attached for hanging, it will likely be rejected if the work isn't ready to hang. Also keep in mind that some students will want to keep their original work or at least color photocopies of it to show at college portfolio reviews.

Type "high school art competitions" into a search engine to bring up competitions sponsored by banks, specific states and counties, colleges and universities, and art supply companies. The Congressional Art Competition is sponsored annually by the House of Representatives. Entry information may be found on the Internet. The art is displayed in Washington, D.C., and the winning student often is invited to attend, expenses paid. Area universities will sometimes host a high school exhibition in a nice gallery setting, with a reception for the opening. This is a great chance for high school artists to feel success.

School-Business-Community Partnerships

Public Art

State and local transit authorities sometimes sponsor a call for entries for public art that will be used to decorate the interior or exterior of their offices or transit stops. Many communities around the country have organized city arts groups that welcome student assistance in producing public art.

Temporary Mural

Construction sites often use temporary plywood fences to protect pedestrians. Get in touch with the local construction company and ask permission for your students to paint a mural on one of these fences. The merchant should be willing to prime the fence and supply the paint. These murals usually remain in place for a year or so and offer an opportunity for students to put their skills to use.

Permanent Murals

Many communities and neighborhoods commission permanent paint-by-number outdoor murals to be painted on the walls of buildings, as in the Grove neighborhood of St. Louis. Through these projects old brick buildings are enlivened with beautifully painted murals. A concrete dike wall near Chesterfield, Missouri, was recently painted under the auspices of Chesterfield Arts by students, community residents, and artists. This mural is intended to remain in place and will presumably be refreshed as needed.

Floodwall Mural

Gumbo (Chesterfield), Missouri, 500 feet long × 8 feet high. The wall was power-washed and primed, then painted with premixed acrylic water-based paint. Outlines and numbers were drawn by a few volunteers at night, using overhead projection, with each number representing a specific color to be used on outlined shapes. This community mural was completed in one hot day, under the supervision of artist Stuart Morse and with the help of the entire student leadership team, which comprised fifty eighth- through twelfth-grade students representing seventeen schools and/or homeschool groups. Chesterfield Arts and their student leadership team facilitated the one-day paint-out, with more than three thousand members of the community helping to paint.

Floodwall mural detail

Floodwall mural detail

A Local Bank

Banks usually have generous lobby space where student work can be displayed, and some welcome the opportunity to attract visitors. If they are open to such an exhibition, ask them if they are willing to give prizes and ribbons to the students. This can become an annual or biennial event.

Businesses

As businesses are upgrading equipment such as computers, copiers, or display boards, they may be willing to donate good used equipment to the school. Even if they cannot help you the first time you ask, they'll keep you in mind for the future. Follow up your request in writing.

Families

Let parent groups know about your need for donations of used equipment. For example, people who have switched to digital cameras are willing to give film cameras if their children's school still has a darkroom program. A tax-deductible donation should be acknowledged on school stationery.

Personal Development

Make Time to Create Art

Teaching students every day the thing you know and love is a grand opportunity. When you remain a practicing artist, you cannot help but identify with the student who is struggling for an idea or unable to make the medium do what he or she has in mind. Remember that you became an art teacher because you were good at art and could always come up with original ideas. For many of us, *teaching art* may be our finest art form, but we can continue to improve on our personal motivation to learn and to create art. Become an "artist who teaches."

Join an Existing Arts Group in your Community or Region

If you live too far from such a group, make arrangements to meet monthly with a few friends who are also artists. Time to just "talk art," not "teach art" is the greatest gift you can give yourself. Visit the museums within your region or whenever traveling. Most of them can display only about 20 percent of their collections, so displays are ever-evolving and -changing. Take advantage of any museum classes offered to art specialists, because you will always come away with something new and useful.

Take Advantage of Internet Resources

A great many resources are available for teaching and learning on such websites as YouTube. If you want to know how to do or teach something, type in the subject, and there will be someone there to demonstrate (some appear to know the subject well; others appear less adept). It is as simple as typing in what you want to know and selecting carefully. Many teachers have joined Pinterest and get frequent updates on what is happening in the art world today. If you find something of interest to you, keep it.

Become an Active Member of the National Art Education Association

You automatically become a member of your state art education organization when you join the National Art Education Association (NAEA). This state group is usually divided into regions that have regular workshops from which you and your students will greatly benefit. Most state art organizations also have a blog that will be helpful. You will find that a solution to a problem also faced by other art teachers is no further away than your computer.

Apply for Grants

Further your experience in art. A number of foundations offer travel opportunities for art educators, many of which occur during the summer. Friends of mine have won grants to go to Washington, D.C., and other places in the United States, as well as Australia, Japan, and China, by planning ahead and filling out grant applications. Consider whether you can offer to pay for some portion of the expenses and how you will follow up with your students and colleagues following such an experience; include that plan in your application.

Keep Abreast of Current Research in Your Field

Don't make changes just for the sake of change, but do enhance your program by teaching more historical background or art appreciation skills. Analyze your curriculum to ensure that you are trying new things and that you have made recent upgrades to some of your tried-and-true projects. Question, question, question colleagues about what has been exciting to *their* students lately.

Continue Master's-Level Studio Classes

Although most art teachers have at least one area of expertise, it is likely that at some point you will be asked to teach something about which you know very little. Great! Good teachers nod . . . and get busy. This gives you an opportunity to learn something new, go back to school and get graduate credit, do a lot of reading, and learn a new skill. This new class may become your favorite subject to teach. Classes at universities or art centers may be taken as quickly as possible, and sometimes you are learning something one day and teaching it the next. There are many good books at the library and tutorials on the web, and as you teach yourself something, writing it down step by step—presto!—you are prepared to share it with your students. Nothing you ever learn is wasted!

Organize a Field Trip by Bus

Get students out of the classroom and into a different environment in which to draw, paint, or take photographs. Decide what you want students to gain from a field trip and prepare them carefully. Let them know in advance what they are expected to achieve as a result of this field trip.

- If drawings or sketches are expected, be specific about how much you expect students to accomplish during the trip.
- If photographs will be taken, tell student the minimum number of shots expected.
- If you are visiting a museum show, you may ask students to write about it or interpret it in a work of art. Perhaps they could mentally "collect" a work of art and write a poem about it.

Planning

- Let students help you make the decision for a destination. This can get a lively conversation going early in the semester as you are becoming acquainted.
- Preview the exhibition so there are no surprises and you are prepared to discuss questionable images.
- Plan far ahead to get the trip onto the school calendar.
- Setting the date between the fifth and twelfth weeks of the semester is ideal—you know the students by then, and enough time is left for students to benefit from sketches or photos they may have made on the field trip.
- Pick a great season of the year unless you are going to a scheduled exhibition out of season.
- If going to a museum, decide if you wish to arrange for a docent-led tour.
- Make a list of materials and equipment needed. Let students assist you in distributing and collecting them to ensure supplies are on the bus.
- If a student does not go on the trip, you must have a substitute in place to supervise him or her. If only one or two students stay behind, perhaps a colleague will take responsibility.
- For weekend field trips by train or plane, work through a travel agent for the best value.

Teacher Notification

Notify teachers by memo or e-mail at least two weeks in advance, explaining the purpose of the trip and the date. Include a list of students, alphabetized and separated by grade level. Students should present a field trip notice to each teacher and let the teacher know they appreciate being allowed to go. Offer to allow the student to make up missed work during your class period. Request that teachers let you know if a student cannot miss his or her class and therefore cannot go on the field trip.

The Permission Slip

This should explain where the student is going, what time the bus will leave and return to school, the cost, and arrangements for lunch. Students may not understand the reasons behind the permission slip, but you must protect yourself and the school district from possible lawsuits in the event something untoward happens on the trip.

Finances

If no money has been budgeted for field trips, students may be willing to pay for it, or you can hold a fundraiser. In calculating the cost, assume that fewer students will actually go than say they will. That way if someone is ill or backs out at the last minute, you should be able to absorb the cost. This also allows you to pay the transportation if a student cannot afford to pay for the trip.

It is best to have the money and permission slips collected by the secretary or bookstore at your school. If there is not a signed permission slip, the money is not accepted.

Transportation

Students should not be allowed to drive on a field trip unless your school has special permission forms to be signed by parents. If students are injured while driving, it is yours and the school's responsibility. It might be possible to let parents drive a group if the school agrees.

- Make sure you have a signed permission slip for all the students before they get on the bus (no slip, no trip!).
- Fill the bus to make the trip most economical. Your district may pay for the bus. If you choose to use a charter bus rather than school bus, your transportation department may recommend a provider.
- Always know where you plan to stop for food (purchased or picnic).

A Few Simple Goals

- Bring back all the students who went with you. They must bring a watch and commit to meet you in time to return home with the rest of the group.
- Keep an accurate list of who actually goes. If cell phones are allowed, get each student's number. Count heads as they get on, have two students count with you,

and make sure everyone is on the bus before it leaves for the next stop. The buddy system and your attendance list let you quickly know the name of anyone is missing. Bring at least one more adult along, if possible.

Expectations for Behavior

Secondary students sometimes resent being asked to stay close to the teacher, and a different set of rules may apply for some locations. School rules apply as always.

You must clearly state what behavior is expected:

- They must not go anywhere without a buddy to keep track of when they need to be back on the bus.
- Define the exact geographic boundaries within which they must stay.
- Let them know that they should use good common sense and that they could destroy all hope for future field trips if they don't abide by the rules. Although it seems excessive, suggest that they think carefully about whether a behavior or act might embarrass their parents, teacher, or school. Clearly state the consequences if your rules are broken.
- Talk about appropriate dress for the location and weather. Some items may be left on the bus if not needed.
- Talk about respect for speakers or presenters at the destination.

The In-School Field Trip

Guest Speaker

This type of trip takes one hour of a school day and is planned when a guest speaker or visiting artist is willing to speak to all the art students for one or two periods. Many states sponsor artists in residence who will speak to schools. You may be asked to pay expenses for a speaker, or the administration or a parent group may agree to pay. It can be a very rewarding experience for students.

The procedure for organizing is to

- Reserve a place where all the students might fit comfortably (such as the auditorium or gym).
- Follow the notification procedure for teachers as previously listed.
- Ask the speaker what equipment will be needed (screen, microphone, or projection system). Arrange for a reliable person to operate such systems.
- Prepare the students as discussed previously.
- Invite parents and other classes if space permits.

The Art of Teaching Art

The Universal Curriculum of Art

The *art* of teaching art is in a state of constant change. Our students can use the Internet to see artwork in museums or easily research the work of a single artist. But let us never get so caught up with gadgetry and the latest in technology that we forget we are *visual artists*. We are doing our students a disservice if we do not offer a balanced curriculum that includes studio experience, art history, and aesthetics.

Students are introduced to the elements and principles of art at an early age, and the concepts are reviewed and reinforced as they progress through art classes. These continue to be seen as the *bones,* the structure. They offer us an ordered way of examining both student and historic artwork. As students become accustomed to looking at and talking about art and using *art* terms, they instinctively become more sophisticated in applying this structure to their own artwork.

The History of Art

Art history falls naturally within the teaching of art as you discuss discoveries in the field. Use reproductions found in art books and on the Internet, and show short film excerpts to open discussions. Make a conscious effort to incorporate art history throughout the year, along with each technique you are teaching.

Cross-Curriculum and Cultural Connections

Students need to be taken beyond recognizing a few famous works of art, to be able to identify the general time frame when something was created or to perceive the culture from which an artwork came. The timelines in this chapter may help your students understand that art was not created independently, but reflects what was going on in other fields such as music, literature, science, politics, and social change. Styles in art are related to the culture of the time, whether there was famine, prosperity, deep religious fervor, or repression. As you teach, make connections with current world events and what students are learning in their other studies throughout the day. Help them to see the connections on their own.

Figure 2.1 This graphic view of the National Visual Arts Standards is reproduced with the permission of the National Art Education Association, 1806 Robert Fulton Drive, Reston, Virginia, 20191.

Art Appreciation

Learning to appreciate art is also a skill to be acquired. We are teaching students to see and to interpret what they see, whether the technique is traditional, as with architecture, sculpture, drawing, or painting, or it uses modern technology such as video, social media, and other Internet connections. Combinations of media are commonplace today, with the lines being crossed between sculpture and painting, photography and digital compositions.

Core Arts Standards

The purpose of Core Arts Standards, written by fine arts specialists in every state, is to ensure that students in all schools and all districts throughout the United States will receive a comparable education in the arts. The Core Arts Standards include five fine arts disciplines: dance, drama, media arts, music, and visual arts. The standards are intended to close the gap between high school and college or career. The National Coalition for Core Arts Standards, a web-based set of standards (http://nccas.wikispaces.com), January 2014, assists arts teachers in keeping abreast of developments. Dennis Inhulsen, National

Art Education Association (NAEA) president and visual arts team writing chair, describes the process:

> The dynamic Web-based grade-level standards will be structured by using the tenets of *Understanding by Design* (UbD). Well known by educators and authored by Grant Wiggins and Jay McTighe, UbD structures will support high-quality lesson and unit design by placing a high priority on **Enduring Understandings** or the **Big Ideas**, supporting inquiry-based instruction with **Essential Questions**, laying out a scope and sequence of Standards, and providing **Cornerstone Assessment Examples** within the Framework.
>
> —*NAEA News*, December 2012, p. 24

Dr. Jennifer Allen, at a Missouri Art Education Association workshop in May 2013, said, "When teaching shifts from teaching by memorization, it will instead be teaching by performance and measuring performance." She added, "One reason art is important in a balanced curriculum with multiple subject areas is that it teaches students many things. It is already literacy and numeracy based in that many of the words common to both of those subjects are also part of the art curriculum."

The standards will put more emphasis on real-life problem solving. This is not new to visual art teachers, as art involves little memorization, and most art projects are *about* problem solving. A finished project in art is the equivalent of a major test in another subject such as English or math. Most art teachers create a rubric to encourage students to take responsibility for their own learning and assessment.

One key component of Common Core Standards is to give students more group learning opportunities. As a peer group, with all working toward the same goal, students offer differing opinions and ideas, and all work harder and challenge each other. Students learn to appreciate and work with someone whose thinking patterns are different from theirs.

Help students make connections between what they already know from other disciplines and their own knowledge and experiences. Allow them time to become patient problem solvers, but become aware when it is time to intervene. You may have to remind them that they need to persevere—to do the hard thing.

District Curriculum

If you are in a large district, you may be working within a district-wide curriculum. This curriculum plan should be general enough to allow each individual art specialist to work within his or her own strengths as a teacher, yet ensure that all students within a district are being offered a comparable education in the arts. Or you might be the only art teacher in your county, teaching art to all the students from kindergarten through high school. You *know* what these students have learned through their presecondary school years and what they yet need to learn. You know the other staff well and have learned how great it is to teach cooperatively, occasionally incorporating other disciplines within the art curriculum. And the staff is aware that art knowledge can be used occasionally to give a change of pace to academic courses.

Assessment

Assessment has always been an integral part of teaching art, but will be of more importance as the effort is made to standardize teaching throughout the United States through adoption of Common Core State Standards across the curriculum.

Teachers in most districts write goals and objectives for a lesson plan, teaching basic skills before introducing students to complex projects. The goals are what you expect all students to learn in the lesson. Objectives are more specific and include measurable expectations. Students have more involvement in their own learning by understanding what is expected of them. Teachers develop scoring guides in advance, making sure the students are aware of expectations. In lengthy art projects (ceramics or a large painting, for example), teachers often grade at intervals toward a final grade.

Learning Styles

Some experts feel that each lesson plan should be presented orally, written on the board, and visually demonstrated to accommodate students' various learning styles. At times teachers post a step-by-step "recipe" for a technique on poster board or give handouts so more time can be spent working with the students' creative efforts, rather than repeatedly answering the same "what do I do next" questions. One teacher laminates the directions for film processing for students to read while standing at the sink developing film. Although the Common Core Standards in other disciplines encourage students to analyze how to approach a solution, some art projects almost require a step-by-step approach when the project is introduced.

Creative Problem Solving

Art teachers have traditionally posed problems for students to explore. This, after all, is what art is all about. When we are "in the zone," we tend to lose all track of time and our surroundings. The same general creative problem-solving (CPS) process has been used by businesses and think tanks. You may find that if you check the Osborn-Parnes Creative Problem Solving Process on the Internet you will find something to enhance the way you present a project. The *process* is to define the problem, gather the information that will be needed to accomplish the task, come up with potential solutions, and move into action.

Try It Yourself First

Keep in mind that even if you are teaching a medium with which you have little experience, you know the basics of art or can learn them! Take a class at night or in the summer! Read books and search the Internet to teach yourself and get tips on teaching that medium from experienced pros in that field. Internet tutorials are great. *Always* try something yourself first to figure out the pitfalls before introducing it to a class.

Assignments with Options

Introductory exercises often are quite simple in appearance, but these will not be *portfolio* pieces—or the ones you will display at an end-of-semester art exhibition. Many of them can be pasted into a student's sketchbook for reference. Each medium offers a challenge just to learn to use it, but you need to further challenge students to be creative by giving options.

Coming Up with Original Ideas

The Internet may also help students as they try to come up with original ideas. One teacher allows students to search the Internet for ideas, and students may take a sheet of paper to the computer lab, bringing back several small rough thumbnail drawings that may be used as reference for their own artwork. It is a fine line between inspiration and plagiarism. Picasso, Andy Warhol, and many other artists have "interpreted" another artist's work in their own unique styles. A discussion about the difference between copying and plagiarism might cover the idea that using other people's art is the same as using their words.

Using the Internet for Inspiration

The Internet is such an integral part of students' lives that taking advantage of its potential as an aid to creativity is a necessity. Students have almost unlimited ability to research and see work by artists from all cultures and times. They may choose to join an online art community like Pinterest to keep track of artists whose work they admire. Teachers find it a useful tool as well.

Appropriate Topics for Secondary School Students

For some students, an introductory course might be the only art class that will fit in their schedules, and this is when a teacher hopes to foster a lifelong appreciation of the visual arts. Whatever course you are teaching, give students a way to select their own subject matter.

Themes for Today's Artists

Time spent in class discussion about any of the topics listed here may open new vistas for your students. You might pick a single topic and post it on the board, asking them to define it, perhaps remembering an incident in their own lives that they will never forget, and considering how they might show it on paper. A few extra minutes will be well spent to involve them in finding a personal solution to an assignment.

Topics that might be of special interest to students today are going green, community involvement, cultural awareness (East meets West), cross-curriculum learning (such as music-art, writing-art, math-art, and geography-art), sustainability in architecture, and "What's next on the Internet?" Let students look at historical and contemporary examples to identify a few basic themes that continue to inspire artists. Following are a few possibilities:

Conflict

Cultural influence

Dream world

Energy

Environment

Family: present

Family: future

Friendship

Fright

Good or evil

Heroes

Honor

Human rights

Humor

Injustice

Loss or sadness

Majesty

Mystery

Myths

Patriotism

Peaceful resolution

Personal identity

Place and time

Politics

Power

Privacy issues today

Shyness

Social justice

Spirituality

Tolerance

Essential Questions

Essential questions are difficult to answer and require thoughtful consideration and research. They often begin with *what, how, which,* or *why,* and can never be answered with a yes or no. They charge your students to go beyond the *how to* of an art lesson to consideration of the greater picture of art in their lives. Arts specialists know that research has shown right-brain development, problem solving, and abstract thinking skills are a direct result of artistic challenge. You might even ask your students to devise a single "class question" for investigation that will benefit their lifelong learning. If you ask an essential question, try to prepare an answer for it to share at the end of the class. Here are a few examples:

What is the point of doing art?

Why is art necessary?

How has art changed through time?

How can art help us know something about people from the past?

When would it be appropriate to censor art?

What are choices a painter must make before beginning to work?

When would an artist find it best to make every decision in advance?

How can art be helpful to society?

How does art change our thinking?

Why might art change the way we look at things?

How is art today different from art a hundred years ago? Fifty years ago? Twenty-five years ago?

How might you analyze a work of art if you read that a critic didn't like it?

How does time change the way critics see art? (Consider the work of artists such as Norman Rockwell or Marcel Duchamp.)

If there isn't anyone to see it, can good art exist?

What do I love most about art?

How does art affect *my* life?

What is different about some art that identifies it as modern?

Should anyone have the right to tell an artist what he or she may want to express?

The Elements of Art and Principles of Design

Artists of cultures and time periods throughout history have produced items for daily or ceremonial use that the modern world perceives as beautifully designed works of art. The artists who created them had no knowledge of formal art terms and concepts, yet instinctively applied pleasing design. It was only about one hundred years ago that Arthur Wesley Dow, a pioneer in the field of art education, proposed the formalization of composition and structure in art based on the elements of art and principles of design. The elements of art are line, color, shape, form, value, texture, and space. The principles of design are applications of the elements of art. These terms are often also used when discussing art: unity, balance, proportion, contrast and variety, emphasis, movement, and rhythm and repetition.

Bloom's Revised Taxonomy

Bloom's Revised Taxonomy, familiar to most classroom teachers, has been updated as Bloom's Revised Taxonomy of Learning. The major change is that Creating is now seen as the premier force behind other changes in teaching in general.

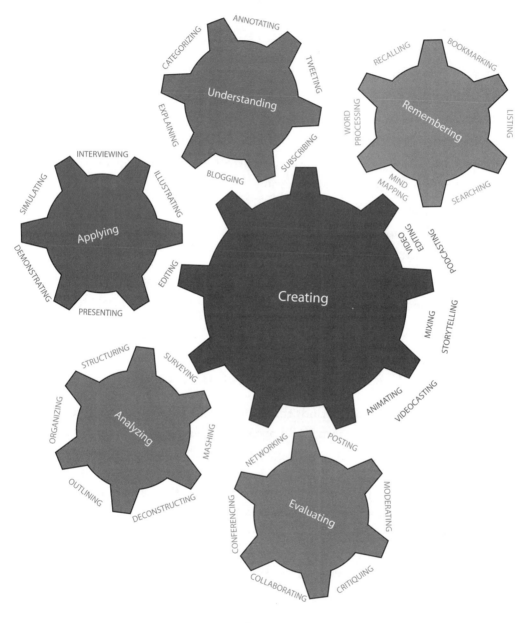

Bloom's Revised Taxonomy
The interlocking of cognitive processes
©2012. Kathy Schrock. All rights reserved.

Figure 2.2 Kathy Schrock has adapted a new way of looking at the use of Bloom's Revised Taxonomy (www .schrockguide.net/bloomin-apps.html) that shows Creating at the heart of everything else. This is especially useful in relating the fine arts to Common Core Standards.

LINE

We see line as we look at the branches of a tree, a plowed field, a road going off into the distance, or on the horizon. Movement and direction, energy, and restfulness can be depicted through the use of line, which is often used to lead the eye to the main subject in a work of art.

Line styles: angular, bent, bold, blurred, broken, continuous, converging, criss-cross, coiled, curving, delicate, dynamic, expressive, flowing, heavy, implied, interrupted, long, meandering, parallel, radiating, rhythmic, scribble, short, solid, spiral, static, straight, thick, thin, wavy, zigzag

Emotional Qualities of Line

Diagonal lines produce tension, suggest movement and action, and dominate attention

Horizontal lines are restful and calm, used to represent horizons

Vertical lines are formal and suggest poise, balance, or support

Wavy	Straight	Thick	Thin	Spiral	Curved	Zigzag

Hatching	Hatching	Wood grain	Combination	Parallel	Meander (Greek key)	Interrupted

Perpendicular	Scribble	Combination	Overlapping	Spirals	Thick, thin, dots	Line pattern

How to Use Line Styles

Calligraphic: add grace to a composition with gently curving lines

Character: make variations in thin or thick, emphasized or delicate lines

Contour: outline a subject with a single line

Cross-hatch: make sets of hatched lines set at different angles over the first for density

Density: control the darkness of an area by spacing lines more or less closely

Expression: communicate ideas by emphasizing some line qualities

Gesture: quickly draw lines to define the subject

Hatch lines: draw parallel lines closely or farther apart to control value

Implied: create an interrupted line that is implied as complete

Perpendicular: use to add stability or to frame a subject

Stipple: make dots closer or farther apart to control value

Weighted contour: make differences in the thickness of a single line for emphasis

COLOR

Every time you choose something to wear, decorate a room, or select a car to drive, you are using a color scheme—colors that you think look beautiful. We see subtle variations of bright hues, neutral color schemes, and even colors that we associate with certain emotions. Artists often consciously plan their artwork through knowledge of specific color schemes.

Color has three properties: hue, value, and intensity. The color wheel is a means of organizing colors in the spectrum. The only colors not on a color wheel are the neutrals: black, white, tan, and gray.

Color Schemes

Triadic: primary or secondary colors or variations, such as red-yellow-blue or orange-green-violet; these are an equal distance apart on the color wheel

Monochromatic: one color with variations in value achieved by adding white, black, or other colors

Analogous: colors that are next to each other on the color wheel

Complementary: colors that are opposite each other on the color wheel such as red/green, yellow/violet

Split complement: colors opposite each other and on either side of the true complement, such as red–blue green or red–yellow green.

Symbolic Colors

Black: evil or mourning
Blue: sadness or melancholy
Red: anger
White: purity
Yellow: cowardice or hazard
Pink: love and romance
Violet: royalty
Green: nature and fertility

Terms Used in Color

Arbitrary color: an artist's choice of nonrealistic color to communicate an idea
Cool colors: those on either side of blue on the color wheel
Hue: an actual color, such as red, in its purest intensity
Intensity: brightness or dullness (grayness) of a color
Intermediate (tertiary) colors: those between secondary colors, such as blue-green or red-orange
Local color: natural color seen in normal daylight
Neutrals: white, black, tan, or gray; complementary colors neutralize each other also
Primary colors in light: cyan (blue), magenta, and yellow
Primary colors in pigment: red, blue, and yellow
Secondary colors: achieved by mixing primary colors, such as violet, green, or orange
Shade: a hue with black added
Tint: a hue with white added
Tone: a grayed hue
Warm colors: colors around orange on the color wheel

Drawn from *Against the Enamel of a Background Rhythmic with Beats and Angles, Tones, and Colors, Portrait of M. Felix Feneon in 1890,* by Paul Signac, 1863–1935.

32

HANDOUT

SHAPE

Two-dimensional shape has height and width. The area may be enclosed by line, but some shapes with indistinct edges are defined by their inner structure (such as a cloud). A tree or an elephant can be identified by shape, even if the color is strange. Two-dimensional form achieves the illusion of form through the use of shading and perspective.

Drawn after poster design, 1974, by Jacob Lawrence, 1917–2000.

Shape and Form Definitions

Abstract: shapes that may be based on reality
Amorphous: lacking definite form (such as clouds)
Complex shapes: a combination of one or more shapes
Cone: circular form that comes to a point at top
Cube: six-sided boxlike form
Cylinder: circular form open at the top and bottom
Free-form: irregular and asymmetrical shapes (such as oil spills)
Geometric shapes: triangles, rectangles, squares, parallelograms, circles, ovals, and pyramids
Implied shapes: defined by space, line, value, and color
Natural shapes or forms: rocks, clouds, and water
Negative shape: the area surrounding the main form
Organic or biomorphic shapes: living organisms such as animals, fish, or flowers
Positive shape: the main form of a composition
Sphere: a perfectly round or circular shape

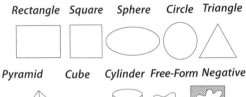

Using Shapes

Overlap shapes to create a feeling of depth
Shape appears to be a complete form, even when surrounded by an interrupted line
Shapes parallel to the sides of a composition create a feeling of tranquility
Shapes at angles to the sides of the paper appear to be pulling the sides inward
Large shapes at the bottom of a composition give it stability
Large shapes at the top of a composition give the feeling it may topple at any moment
Modeling of shape (shading on rounded surfaces) gives a sense of volume

FORM

Three-dimensional form has height, width, and depth. An example is sculpture, which has three dimensions. Sculptors are aware of the importance of the openings and space around the outside of the sculpture, referred to as negative space.

High relief (French: haut-relief): attached form that has significant depth
Low relief (French: bas-relief): attached form that has shallow depth, height, and width
Mass: shape in three dimensions, such as sculpture
Negative shape in three-dimensional art can be the air that surrounds a form or a hole that lets air through the shape
Texture in a form can call attention to an area the artist wishes to emphasize

Drawn after, *UNESCO Reclining Figure,* 1957–1958, Henry Moore, 1898–1986.

33

VALUE

Value describes variations of a hue, ranging from the lightest to the darkest. Any artwork utilizes value to lend emphasis, contrast, or balance to the composition. Value can even be shown in a one-color object such as sculpture through differences in depth and texture. Any artwork utilizes value to lend emphasis, contrast, or balance to the composition, and it may be used to expressively communicate ideas.

Terms Used

Aerial perspective: change in value indicating distance (more distant objects are lighter)
Chiaroscuro: light and dark areas in a composition
Contrasting values: differences in dark and light
Gray scale: tones ranging from lightest to darkest
Monochromatic: different values and variations of one hue
Shade: black added to a pure hue
Tint: white added to a pure hue
Tonal gradient: subtle changes in value
Value scale: a means of showing differences in value

Ways to Use Differences in Value

Blend: make soft transitions from light to dark
Hatch: draw parallel lines close together or far apart
Cross-hatch: create intersecting sets of parallel lines
Exaggerate: exaggerate reality by emphasizing darker values to strengthen a composition
Gradation: show a gradual darkening from light to dark
Highlights and cast shadows serve to direct the viewer's attention
A range of values gives the illusion of form in transparency and reflection
Shade (modeling): show roundness by darkening edges
Stipple: make dots to create light and dark areas
Volume: show volume by darkening outer edges
Weight: give weight to a composition by using darker values near the bottom, lighter at top

Drawn after *The Great Wave off Kanagawa, c. 1830–31,* Katsushika Hokusai, 1760–1849.

Drawn after *Delusions of Grandeur, 1967,* René Magritte, 1898–1967.

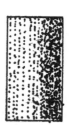
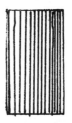

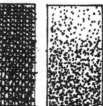

TEXTURE

Texture in an artwork may be actual (it can be felt) or implied (it looks real but isn't; it's an illusion). A collage or assemblage may have actual texture applied to the surface. The paintings of Vincent van Gogh that were rich in texture featured thickly applied paint. Sculptors use texture effectively by varying smooth and rough areas to call attention to one surface or another. Viewers often are tempted to touch both paintings and sculpture to sense the texture. Sometimes the texture is repellent—one can tell by looking it will not feel pleasant.

Pattern and texture are sometimes confused, but pattern is deliberately repetitive, used for decorative purposes. Pablo Picasso often used pattern to imply texture.

Pattern

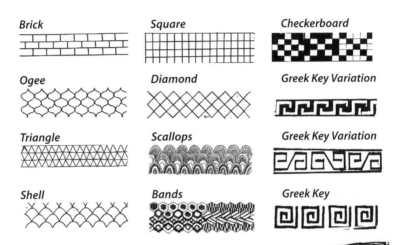

Brick	Square	Checkerboard
Ogee	Diamond	Greek Key Variation
Triangle	Scallops	Greek Key Variation
Shell	Bands	Greek Key

Actual Texture

Smooth   Velvety

Rough   Prickly

Bumpy   Sandy

Horses, drawn after Deborah Butterfield, 1949.

Apply texture to

Fill a broad, open one-color expanse with pattern to create interest

Make a realistic simulation of a texture such as bark

Create texture differences with changes in light and dark areas

Enliven a composition, create relief, or change value

Deliberately abstract real texture with invented pattern in a painting

Emphasize differences within the same work of art to communicate idea

Apply pattern to

Make a border that corresponds with the artwork

Give interest to an area that is broad and uninteresting

Call attention to an area

Head, 1966, drawn after Roy Lichtenstein, 1923–1997.

SPACE

Space is the area that a subject occupies in two-dimensional or three-dimensional artworks. It is the area around objects and between them. Drama is often added to a composition through the use of open space that calls attention to the actual subject. Renaissance artists used geometric forms such as rectangles, triangles, and circles or formal perspective to create the illusion of space. Sculptors feel that the negative space created by holes or around the outside of a form are as important as the form itself.

Terms Used

Actual space: the space that can be measured

Implied space: two-dimensional illusion of space

Shallow: no actual depth or illusion of depth

Negative space: the area surrounding a form

Positive shapes: forms that are drawn or constructed

Foreground: the area closest to the viewer

Middle ground: the area between the foreground and background

Background: the area farthest away

Picture plane: the flat space defined by height and width

Drawn after *Reclining Woman,* 1957–58, Henry Moore, 1898–1986.

Ways to Use Space

Aerial perspective: making areas farther away lighter and less sharp

Linear perspective: organizing space using geometry

Vanishing point: lines meet on the horizon at this point

Figure-ground relationship: the figure (or form) is distinct from the ground

Foreshortening: the illusion that the form projects outward

Projecting form: an object that actually projects outward

Gradients: showing distance through a gradual change in value

Drawn after *Snow in New York,* 1902, Robert Henri, 1865–1929.

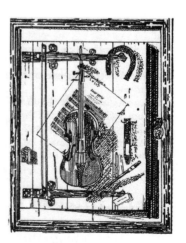

Drawn after *Still-Life: Violin and Music,* 1888, William Harnett, 1848–1892.

UNITY

Unity is how the elements of art and principles of design are used in a piece of artwork to produce a unified and interesting end result. It is the consideration of the complete composition, adding color here, simplifying an area there, and considering balance, variety, and emphasis. As artists work, they sort through options, making changes that create an overall harmony. They can create an exaggeration, a push-pull, or visual tension that creates a bond between forms. Placing a form near an edge of the picture plane is one way to create such tension. The use of symmetry is another way to achieve unity or stability. Repetition of form or the regular placement of motifs can create stillness. Asymmetry leads to a livelier organization that can still be harmonious as the eye is led through the composition.

Terms Used to Describe Unity

Symmetry: balancing elements equally

Asymmetry: unequal balance of form

Coherence: all parts coming together in harmony

Dissonance: abrupt changes and apparent disunity

Dominance or subordination: one main element dominates, with others complementary to it

Harmony: combining elements of art to create a restful composition

Proportion: can be normal or exaggerated

Detail drawn after *Achelous and Hercules,* 1947, Thomas Hart Benton, 1889–1975.

How to Achieve Unity through Use of the Elements and Principles of Art

Balance the weight of objects

Cluster small objects together

Create a variety of forms

Design a circular or triangular composition

Focus the eye on one major center of interest

Isolate important details to emphasize the dominant form

Limit the variety of shapes, colors, or lines

Make everything radiate from a central point

Organize elements through geometry

Overlap objects or figures

Simplify the color scheme

Surround the dominant form with space

Use convergent lines to direct attention

BALANCE

Balance is achieved by giving equal weight to two halves of a composition. The upper and lower halves of a composition should also be considered when thinking of balance, with weight somewhat heavier on the lower half of an artwork to keep it from appearing to fall forward.

Terms Used to Define Balance

Symmetrical (formal) balance often results in a static composition

Exact symmetry: mirror images on two halves

Asymmetrical (informal) balance is somewhat livelier

Radial balance: all elements radiate from a central point

Overall balance: there is no specific focus or emphasis, yet balance is achieved with the use of design elements and principles such as color, line, shape, value, and repetition

Apply balance to

Express the idea of rest or disquiet by using symmetrical or asymmetrical balance

Create a radial design that contains several objects

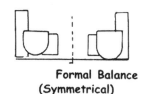

Formal Balance (Symmetrical)   Informal Balance (Asymmetrical)

PROPORTION

Proportion is the relative size and scale of one object to another within an artwork. It can also refer to realistic facial or figure proportions. The hands and head of Michelangelo's David were not in proportion to the rest of the figure, but expressed Michelangelo's vision of strength. Ideal proportions may look more pleasant, but stressing features that deviate from the norm yields more dynamic portraits.

Definitions

Facial proportions: all faces have features that are relatively proportionate in everyone

Foreshortening: the portion of a human figure that is closest to the artist will be shown as much larger to create a three-dimensional object on a two-dimensional page

Scale: the relative size of objects and their relationship to everything within a composition

Cutout of Animals, Artist Unknown.

CONTRAST AND VARIETY

The design principle of contrast is used to bring a work of art to life. Contrast and variety in composition refer to differences that separate one form from another. This is usually accomplished by contrasts in intensity of hue, the use of complementary colors, or changes in value. "Op" (optical) artists such as Josef Albers, Bridget Riley, and Victor Vasarely used the principle of simultaneous contrast in their compositions. They took advantage of the tendency for the eye to see forms as darker or lighter, or larger or smaller, depending upon the background used.

Definition

Simultaneous contrast: optical illusions caused by size, intensity, and placement of colors

Types of Contrast

Drawn from Seated *Odalisque*, 1928, Henri Matisse, 1869–1954.

Figure/ground	Subdued/intense
Bright/dark	Abstract/realistic
Large/small	Defined/loose
Rough/smooth	Symmetrical/asymmetrical
Monumental/intimate	Wide/narrow
Patterned/plain	Thick/thin
Warm/cool	Bold/delicate
Soft edges/hard edges	Young/old

EMPHASIS

The principle of emphasis is used to focus attention in a composition. It may be an isolated form or the largest, brightest, or darkest area. Attention can be drawn to the focal point by convergence of lines (as in da Vinci's *Last Supper*), textural interest, or contrast between light and shade. In general, a composition is more interesting if the area of emphasis is not in the center, but instead placed to the left or right.

Definitions

Center of interest: the focal point of a composition; often not in the center

Converging lines: lines may be used to direct attention to the focal point

Contrast: the center of interest is indicated by being lighter or darker

Dominant: describes the major element of a composition

Focal point: the first thing the eye sees when viewing an artwork

Isolation: one form is set apart from others

Rule of thirds: an imaginary ticktacktoe grid, with the main subject placed at an intersection

Subordinate: elements repeat or complement the dominant form

MOVEMENT

Movement in art allows the viewer's eye to move smoothly from one area of design to another. This can be accomplished by creating an invisible pathway of color, shape, lines, and edges that gives flow and order to the design. The viewer's eye is directed by a feeling of movement or rhythm to the point of emphasis.

Movement can be created by

Anticipated movement (a figure in action)

Action (such as people dancing or diving)

An arrow or pointing finger

Invisible pathway: an implied line that leads the eye from one shape to another

Optical illusions created by repetition

Blurry outlines that convey motion such as those seen in photos

Diagonal lines can create movement

Similar shapes can connect and overlap

Flow moves the eye to the focal point, around the composition, and back to the focal point

Drawn after Diego Rivera, 1886–1957.

RHYTHM AND REPETITION

Repetition is the use of color, line, or shape in more than one place in a composition. Repetition such as that seen in a checkerboard or wallpaper pattern can be boring unless relieved by some variation in color or emphasis is given to one area. Pattern is created by the repetition of the elements of design and can be used to give an implied texture to a composition. Rhythm can be established in a composition through the repeated or alternate use of an element or motif in much the same way it exists in music.

Drawn after *Les Demoiselles d'Avignon*, 1907, Pablo Picasso, 1881–1974.

Definitions

Pattern: the systematic use of line or motif

Random pattern: groups of similar motifs arranged randomly

Rhythm: the use of pattern to create movement

Tessellation: the interlocking of shapes in an overall pattern to apply rhythm

Art History

The following timeline handouts can be reprinted to help students generally understand the relationship of art to other important events that were happening within a time period. Art and architecture are enduring records of ancient and modern civilizations.

TIMELINE # 1   35,000 BC - 500 BC

35,000 BC - 5000 BC	5000 BC - 3000 BC	3000 BC - 2000 BC	2000 BC - 1000 BC	1000 BC - 500 BC
VISUAL ARTS FRANCE, *Cave Paintings* Lascaux and Altamira 35,000 -15,000 BC *Venus of Willendorf* *Venus de la Corne* FRANCE, *Venus Figures* c. 25,000 BC	*Narmer's Palette* c. 3000 BC EGYPT, *King Zoser Step Pyramid*, 2630 BC EGYPT, *Great Pyramids*, 2530-2470 BC	EGYPT Old Kingdom, 2940-2134 Middle Kingdom, 2040-1640 BC New Kingdom, 1550-1070 BC EGYPT, Temple at Edfu, c. 230 BC IRAQ, *Ram Caught in Thicket* 3000 BC ENGLAND, Stonehenge, 2300-1600 BC	EGYPT, *Queen Hapshepsut's Funerary Temple* 1480 BC EGYPT, *William* the Hippopotamus, 1900 BC EGYPT, *Tutankhamen* (King Tut). c. 1352 BC	CHINA, Painting 1028 BC *Scythian Stag* 7th-6th century BC IRAQ (Babylon) *Ishtar Gate*, 575 BC Etruscan 750-200 BC iTALY, *Apollo from Veii*, 510 BC GREECE, *Dipylon Vase* 800-700 BC GREECE, *Charioteer of Delphi*, 500 BC
MUSIC	EGYPT, harps & flutes 4000 BC CHINA, bamboo pipes c. 3000 BC	CHINA, 5 tone scale c. 2500 BC Denmark - trumpets c. 2000 BC	TURKEY, Hittites, guitar, lyre, trumpet c. 1500 BC SYRIA, musical notations c. 1300 BC	BABYLON, seven tone scale, c. 800 BC GREECE, Pthagoras introduces the octave c. 600 BC SUMERIA, earliest recorded music 800 BC
CULTURES JORDAN, Wall of Jericho 8000 BC CHINA, Yang Shan Long Shan culture 7000-4000 BC	EGYPT, Egyptian Kingdoms 3500-100 BC JAPAN, Jomon Culture, 5000 BC EUROPE, wooden plow, c. 4000 BC	IRAQ, Sumerians 3500- 2000 BC Cotton produced in India, Peru, Egypt c. 2500-2000 BC Mycenae 2300-1100 BC	CHINA, Shang Dynasty, 1766-1122 BC CHINA, Chou Dynasty 1122-256 BC EGYPT, Ramses the Great 1304 BC	ITALY, Rome founded, 753 BC *She Wolf*, 500 BC CHINA, Confucius, 551-475 BC MEXICO, Olmec Culture 850-150 BC
LANGUAGE ARTS	IRAQ, Sumerian Cunieform writing, c. 3500 BC	EGYPT, Hieroglyphic writing 3000 BC	First Chinese Dictionary, 1100 BC AFRICA, Oldest Sanskrit Literature, 1500 BC	GREECE, Homer's *Iliad and Odyssey*, 750 BC INDIA, *Diamond Sutra* Scroll, 868 BC GREECE, Greek alphabet, c. 400 BC GREECE, Sappho, Greek Poet, c. 612-570 BC
MATHEMATICS Egyptian Calendar c. 5000 BC	EGYPT and Babylonia develop number systems 3000 BC	EGYPT, 365 day calendar, 2772 BC		Pythagoras develops scientific mathematic foundation, 530 BC
SCIENCE Use of Fire c. 12,000 BC EASTERN EUROPE, horses domesticated 6000 BC Potters Wheel 3200 BC	MIDDLE EAST, Sundial c. 3500 BC EUROPE, bronze weapons, 2300-1800 Bc CHINA, EGYPT, Irrigation, c. 3150 BC	Chinese observed eclipse of the sun, 2155 BC	CHINA, Silk Production, 1500 BC EGYPT, Papyrus, 1500 BC Iron Age 1400 BC	GREECE, Hippocrates born, 469 BC CHINA, woodblock printing, 618 BC ITALY, False teeth developed 700 BC
SOCIAL STUDIES Woven Cloth c. 5000 BC	EGYPT, Upper and Lower Egypt united, 3100 BC	EUROPE, Scythians, 8000-700 BC	IRAN, BABYLON, *Hammurabi's Code of Law* 1290 BC	TURKEY, Trojan War, 1185 BC MIDDLE EAST, Israelites leave Egypt, 1250 BC EGYPT, Alexander the Great conquers Egypt, 332 BC

TIMELINE # 2 500 BC - AD 500				
500 - 300 BC	**300 - 100 BC**	**100 BC - AD 100**	**AD 100 - AD 300**	**AD 300 - 500**
VISUAL ARTS GREECE, *Parthenon*, 448-432 BC GREECE, Sculptors Phydias, c. 500 - 432 BC Praxiles, c. 350-330 BC *Calf Bearer*, c. 600 BC GREECE, *Temple of Athena Nike*, 427-424 BC	GREECE, *Nike of Samothrace* 190 BC GREECE, *Venus de Milo*, c. 140 BC GREECE, *Laocoon*, by Polydorus, 200 BC	ROME, *Pantheon*, c. 118 BC -AD 25 ITALY, *Villa of the Mysteries*, Pompeii, 100 BC ITALY, Pont du Gard, 1st century ITALY, *Colosseum*, AD 72-80	ITALY, *Trajan's Column*, Rome AD 114 Roman *Baths of Caracalla* AD 212-216 ITALY. *Marcus Aurelius*, AD 100	ITALY, *Arch of Constantine* AD 312-315 ITALY *Emperor Constantine* AD 306-337 CROATIA, Diocletian's *Palace*, AD 300,
MUSIC GREECE, Choral Music, c. 500 BC Musician, Pindar, 520-447 BC	GREECE, Aristotle's *Musical Theory*, c. 340 BC			GREECE Memodos' hymns, AD 500 PERU, Flutes, horns, tubas, drums, AD 450
CULTURES TURKEY, Greek Theater Epidaurus, 400 BC AFRICA, Nok culture 500 BC-AD 200	USA, mound builders, Ohio Valley, 100 BC - AD 40 PERU, Nazca peoples, 300 BC - AD 700	MEXICO, Zapotec and Monte Alban cultures, 200 BC -AD 208 CHINA, Han Dynasty 206 BC - AD 220	USA, Serpent burial mound Ohio, AD 10-400	MEXICO, Colima culture, 200 BC - AD 300 BYZANTINE EMPIRE, Justinian, AD 483-565 USA, Mississippi Valley culture AD 450-500 MEXICO, MAYA civilization, AD 470
LANGUAGE ARTS GREECE Euripides, 484-406 BC Aritstotle, 384-322 BC Socrates, 470-399 BC Plato, 428-348 BC	INDIA, *Bhagavad Gita*, c. 200 BC ITALY, Roman poet, Horace 65-8 BC TURKEY, *Theatre of Epidaurus* 350 BC	MIDDLE EAST, First four books of *Bible's New Testament* c. AD 70-100	CHINA, Calligraphy, AD 175 GREECE, Plutarch, Greek historian, AD 47-120	
MATHEMATICS	GREECE, Hipparchus, trigonometry, c. 140 BC GREECE, Euclid, deductive mathematics, c. 300 BC			INDIA, Algebra used, AD 500 Decimal system, AD 500
SCIENCE GREECE, Hippocrates c. 469 BC NIGERIA, Nok culture forges and smelts metal for tools 500 BC		CHINA, paper making, AD 105 CHINA, discovery of magnetism, c. AD 80 GREECE, *Pedanius Dioscorides* llisted 600 drugs and 1000 herbs c. AD 45	USA, Native American production of potato, corn, tobacco, chocolate, and tomatoes, AD 100-500	
SOCIAL STUDIES INDIA, Buddha, 552-480 BC IRAN, *Prince*, Persepolis, c. 500 BC	EGYPT, *Rosetta Stone* created (translation of Hieroglyphics to Greek), 195 BC CHINA, *Great Wall*, c. 214 BC ITALY, *Republic of Rome*, 207-27 BC	ISRAEL, Christianity, Life of Jesus, AD 1-30 INDIA, Kushan Dynasty AD 78-250	ITALY, Mt. Vesuvius erupts at Pompeii, AD 79 UK, London founded, AD 43 TURKEY, Constantinople founded, AD 330	ITALY, End of Western Roman Empire, AD 476

TIMELINE # 3   500 - 1000

	AD 500 - 600	600 - 700	700 - 800	800 - 900	900 - 1000
VISUAL ARTS	TURKEY, *Hagia Sophia* 532-537 JAPAN, *Horiju Temple,* AD 535 CHINA, scroll landscape, AD 535	ENGLAND, *Purse from Sutton Hoo treasure* AD 655 CHINA, *Horse,* Tang Dynasty, c. 618-907 ISRAEL, *Dome of the Rock,* Jerusalem, 691	INDIA, *Cave Temple at Ellora* AD 700 INDIA, *Mamallapuram* early 8th Century MEXICO, Classic Maya Art 300-900 MIDDLE EAST, Islamic art calligraphy, mosaics, 650-1200	SWEDEN, *Animal Head* SWEDEN, *Oseberg Burial Ship,* 825 - 1000 SPAIN, *Mosque of Cordoba,* 900 MALI, Kingdom, 800-1500	USA, 2nd Pueblo Period, Southwest, 900 CHINA, Sung Dynasty 960-1280
MUSIC		CHINA, orchestras formed AD 619	Gregorian Church Music: Germany, France, England 750		England, *Winchester Cathedral Organ,* 980
CULTURES	Byzantine Empire, 500-1453 PERU, Paracas culture, AD 500 JAPAN, Asuka Period, 552-645	CHINA, Tang Dynasty 618-907 MEXICO, Mayan culture, 600 JAPAN, Nara Period, 645-745		JAPAN, Early Heian period AD 784-897 USA, Native American 2nd Pueblo Period, 900	MEXICO, Olmec Classic Period 1000 PERU, Chimu culture, 900-1465
LANGUAGE ARTS	GREECE. *Hero and Leander,* Epic Poem, AD 550	EGYPT, library at Alexandria, 640 CHINA, book printing, AD 600	MEXICO, *Chinkultic Disk,* 590 IRELAND, *Book of Kells,* 760-820	*Utrecht Psalter* (Psalm Book), 832	
MATHEMATICS	INDIA, decimal system, AD 595	INDIA, Concept of 0, AD 600		Alfred the Great, 24 hour measurement system 886	
SCIENCE		CHINA, cast iron, AD 618	EGYPT, sugar grown, AD 710	FRANCE, crossbow used, 851	CHINA, Canal Locks invented 980
SOCIAL STUDIES	MIDDLE EAST, Life of Mohammed, AD 570-632		GREECE, first Olympics, AD 776 IRAQ, Baghdad founded by Muslims, 762	GERMANY, Charlemagne, First Holy Roman Emperor 742-814	Ottonian Rule, 900-1150 Leif Ericson arrived on American continent, 1000

TIMELINE # 4   1000 - 1500

1000 - 1100	1100 - 1200	1200 - 1300	1300 - 1400	1400 - 1500
VISUAL ARTS ROMANESQUE, 1000-1150 FRANCE, *Bayeux Tapestry* 1067-1083 USA Native American *Deer Mask*, 800-1400 Viking Art 1050-1100 FRANCE, *Mont St. Michel*, 1060-1500	GOTHIC, 1100-1400 FRANCE *Chartres Cathetral* 1140-1175 FRANCE, *Abbot Suger's Chalice*, 1147 TURKEY, *Blue Mosque* c. 1150	PRE- RENAISSANCE 1250-1470 ITALY, Cimabue, 1240-1302 ITALY, Giotto di Bondone, c. 1266-1337 SPAIN, *Lion Court, Alhambra Palace*, 14th century FRANCE, *Notre Dame,* Paris, c. 1250	NORTHERN RENAISSANCE 1350-1600 *Madonna and Child,* 14th century BELGIUM, Jan van Eyck refines oil painting, 1390-1441 BELGIUM-FRANCE, Rogier Van Der Weyden, 1399-1464 ITALY, Raphael, 1483-1520 ITALY, Botticelli's *The Birth of Venus*, 1480	EARLY RENAISSANCE 1400-1450 FRANCE, *Tres Riches Heures* Limburg Brothers 1400-1430 ITALY, *The Last Supper,* Leonardo da Vinci, 1495-1498 iTALY, Castagno's *David*, 1450 ITALY, Ghiberti's *Gates of Paradise* c. 1404-1424
MUSIC Berno Books on musical theory, 1008 Music written down as notes by monks, 1026	Secular music begins, 1100 FRANCE, troubador musicians, 1125	GERMANY, Dresden boys' choir, 1220	FRANCE, Paris Musician's Guild, 1330-1773 ITALY, Pope forbids use of counterpoint in church music 1322	First printed music, 1465
CULTURES NIGERIA, Yoruba Kingdoms founded, 1000 USA Native Americans, *Anasazi Pot* 700-1750	JAPAN, Kamakura Period 1185-1333 EGYPT, Saladin commander of Egypt, 1138-1193 USA, Utah, *Rock engravings,* c. 1150	PERU, Inca, 1200-1530 CHINA, Yuan Dynasty (Mongol) 1271-1368 USA. *Mesa Verde Cliff Palace* 1150	*JAPAN, Muromachi Period, 1333-1573* *CHINA, Tomb Elephant* Ming Dynasty 1368-1644	PERU, Inca, *Macchu Picchu,* 1450-1500 NETHERLANDS, Erasmus, 1454 humanist scholar-philosopher EUROPE/MIDDLE EAST, end of Byzantine Empire, 323tt-1453
LANGUAGE ARTS Duncan of Scotland killed by Macbeth, 1040 FRANCE, *Reynard the Fox* fable, 1176		FRANCE, *Roman de la Rose,* 1225- 1270	ITALY, Boccacio's *Decameron*, 1348-1353 ITALY, Petrarch, Italian Poet 1304-1374 ENGLAND, Geoffrey Chaucer, 1343-1400 *CanterburyTales,*	GERMANY, Gutenberg's *Bible*, 1454
MATHEMATICS				MEXICO, *Sun Stone*, Aztec Calendar, 1450-1500 GERMANY, Johannes Muller develops application of decimal, 1460
SCIENCE	CHINA, invention of gunpowder, c. 700 CHINA, rocket, 1100 ITALY, magnetic needle compass in use, 1150	Magnifying glass invented by Roger Bacon, 1250 Eye glasses invented, 1285		GERMANY, Printing press, movable type, 1450 lunar nautical navigation, 1474 Leonardo da Vinci draws a flying machine, c. 1490
SOCIAL STUDIES ENGLAND, William the Conqueror, 1028-1087 MIDDLE EAST, First Christian Crusade, 1096-1099		ENGLAND, *Magna Carta*, 1215	EUROPE, Black Death 3/5 of population killed by plague, 1348-1361	FRANCE, Joan of Arc, 1412-1431 Columbus sails to West Indies, 1492 GERMANY, Martin Luther, 1483-1546

1500 - 1550	1550 - 1600	1600 - 1650	1650 - 1700	1700 - 1750
VISUAL ARTS **ITALY, HIGH RENAISSANCE 1450-1520** ITALY, Leonardo da Vinci's *Mona Lisa,* 1503-1506 ITALY, Michelangelo's *David,* 1504 ITALY, Bramante's *Tempietto,* 1502 ITALY, Raphael, 1483-1520	MANNERISM, 1525-1600 BAROQUE, 1590-1750 ITALY, *Villa Rotunda,* begun 1566, architect Andrea Palladio, 1508-1580 MEXICO, *Cathedral,* Mexico City, 1563 TURKEY, *Blue Mosque,* Constantinopole, 1557	NETHERLANDS, Judith Leyster 1609-1660, *The Jester* NETHERLANDS *The Jolly Toper* by Frans Hals 1627 INDIA, *Taj Mahal,* c. 1635 CHINA, Ming Dynasty, 1368-1644 *Temple of Heaven*	EUROPE, ROCOCO ART 1700-1800 NETHERLANDS, Rembrandt's *Polish Rider,* 1655 NIGERIA, Benin culture 1650-1900 ITALY, Borromini's *San Carlo alla Quatro Fontana,* 1665-1667	ENGLAND, *St. Paul's Cathedral* Christopher Wren *1675-1710* FRANCE, Houdon's *Voltaire Seated,* 1778 USA, *Independence Hall,* Philadelphia, c. 1751
MUSIC	Bartolome Spolone, madrigal composer, 1529-1586 ITALY, Violin invented by Andrea Amati, 1553	ITALY, Antonio Stradavari's violins,1644-1737	Antonio Vivaldi, 1678-1741 George Frideric Handel 1685-1759 Johann Sebastian Bach 1685-1750	ITALY, Piano invented by Bartolommeo, 1710 Baroque Music, c. 1700
CULTURES ENGLAND, Anglican church 1534 PERU, Pissarro conquers Peru, 1533	Kingdom of Asante, 1600	CHINA, Qing Dynasty, 1644-1911 USA, Jamestown, Virginia, 1607 Santa Fe, New Mexico, 1610 Plymouth Rock, 1620 Harvard founded, 1636	USA, Witches hanged in Massachusetts, 1692 USA, Quakers settled, 1668	
LANGUAGE ARTS FRANCE, François Rabelais 1494-1553 NETHERLANDS, Erasmus' *Colloquia,* 1519	ENGLAND, William Shakespeare, 1564-1616 SPAIN, Cervantes' *Don Quixote,* 1605-1615	ENGLAND, King James version of the *Bible,* 1611		ENGLAND, Jonathan Swift *Gulliver's Travels,* 1726 USA, Benjamin Franklin's *Poor Richard's Almanac,* 1732 ,
MATHEMATICS MEXICO, *Sun Stone Calendar,* 1450-1500	Modern calendar, 1582	SCOTLAND, Logarithms, John Napier, 1614, Geometry, 1637 FRANCE, Pascal invents calculator, 1642 ENGLAND, Slide rule invented, William Oughtred, 1620	Isaac Newton's *Theory of Gravity,* 1684	
SCIENCE FRANCE, Nostradamus, Astrologer, 1503-1566 Pistol invented, 1540 Halley's Comet sighted, 1531	BELGIUM, Mercator's Map, 1569	ITALY, Galileo, 1564-1642 astronomical telescope, 1609 Thermometer, 1616, ITALY, Barometer, 1643, Evangelista Torricelli	NETHERLANDS, Bacteria identified, Antony van Leeuwenhoek, 1683	
SOCIAL STUDIES USA, Cortez brings horses to America, 1519 ARGENTINA, CHILE Ferdinand Magellan explores Tierra del Fuego, 1520	USA, Hernando de Soto discovers Mississippi River, 1541 ENGLAND, defeat of the Spanish Armada, 1588 ENGLAND, Henry VIII 1491-1547	Dutch East India Company, 1602 USA, First Thanksgiving shared, Native Americans and Pilgrims, 1621 JAPAN, Tokugawa Shoguns, 1603-1868	USA, Marquette and Joliet explore Mississippi River, 1673 USA, Pennsylvania founded by William Penn, 1681	ITALY, Pompeii and Herculaneum discovered, 1745

TIMELINE # 6   1750 - 1875

1750 - 1775	1775 - 1800	1800 - 1825	1825 - 1850	1850 - 1875
VISUAL ARTS USA, COLONIAL PAINTERS 1564-1750 USA, *Monticello,* Thomas Jefferson, 1772	USA, George Catlin 1796-1872 *Native American Portrait,* USA, John J. Audubon 1785-1851 *Birds of America,* 1827	ROMANTICISM, 1800-1825 USA, ROCKY MOUNTAIN SCHOOL, 1800-1890 USA, HUDSON RIVER SCHOOL 1825-1875 USA, *Raven Clan Hat,* Chilkat/Tlingit early 19th century *George Washington Crossing the Delaware,* 1851, Emanuel Leutz, 1816-1868	USA, Mary Cassatt 1845-1926 USA, William Harnett, 1848-1892. FRANCE, *Little Dancer of Fourteen years,* Edgar Degas 1834-1917 *"Whistler's Mother"* USA, James Abbott McNeill Whistler, 1834-1903	REALISM, 1850-1880 FRANCE, *Paris Opera House,* 1861-1874 FRANCE, Edouard Manet's *Fifer,* 1866 FRANCE, Henri Matisse, 1869-1964 USA, Henry Ossawa Tanner, 1859-1937
MUSIC AUSTRIA, Wolfgang Amadeus Mozart, 1756-1791 GERMANY, Ludwig van Beethoven, 1770-1827 Premier of *Beggar's Opera* 1750	AUSTRIA, Frans Schubert 1797-1828 ENGLAND, pianoforte developed by John Broadwood, 1783	GERMANY, Felix Mendelssohn, 1809-1847	USA, New York Philharmonic established 1839	FRANCE, Claude Debussy 1862-1918 GERMANY, Richard Strauss 1864-1949 USA, Scott Joplin, 1868-1917 RUSSIA, Sergei Rachmaninoff 1873-1943
CULTURES		SOUTH AMERICA, the "Liberator" Simon Bolivar, 1783-1830		JAPAN, Meiji Restoration, 1868 Women's Suffrage Movement 1869 USA, Barnum's Circus, 1871
LANGUAGE ARTS ENGLAND, William Wordsworth, 1770-1850 ENGLAND, *Encyclopedia Brittanica,* 1770	ENGLAND, Thomas Paine's *Common Sense,* 1776, and *The Rights of Man,* 1890	SCOTLAND, Sir Walter Scott's *Ivanhoe,* 1820s ENGLAND, Jane Austen's *Pride and Preudice,* 1813 ENGLAND, Charles Dickens, 1812-1870, *A Tale of Two Cities,* 1859	RUSSIA, Tolstoy, 1828-1910 *War and Peace,* 1865-1869	Harriet Beecher Stowe's *Uncle Tom's Cabin,* 1851/1852 Robert Frost, 1874-1963
MATHEMATICS				
SCIENCE USA, Ben Franklin's lightning rod, 1752 ENGLAND, Joseph Priestly and Rutherford discover Nitrogen, 1772	ENGLAND, James Watts' steam engine, 1769 USA, Eli Whitney's cotton gin 1793 Smallpox vaccine, Jenna, 1797	FRANCE, stethoscope invented by René Laennec, 1816 ITALY, Alessandro Volta invented electric battery, 1800	FRANCE, Daguerrotype, 1839 USA, Telegraph, 1844, Samuel F.B. Morse ENGLAND, Darwin's *Origin of the Species* (Theory of Evolution), 1859	FRANCE, Louis Pasteur's *Theory of Germ Fermentation,* 1861 RUSSIA, *Periodic Law of Elements,* Dimitri Mendeleev, 1869
SOCIAL STUDIES USA, Boston Massacre, 1770 Boston Tea Party, 1773 USA, American Revolutionary War, 1775-1783	USA, *Declaration of Independence,* July 4, 1776 Hawaii discovered by Cook, 1778 FRANCE, French Revolution begins, 1789	USA, War of 1812 BELGIUM, Napoleon's loses Battle of Waterloo, 1815	ENGLAND, Queen Victoria crowned, 1837	USA buys Alaska from Russia 1867 USA, War between the States (Civil War), 1861-1865

Copyright © John Wiley & Sons, Inc.

TIMELINE # 7		1875 - 1950		
1875 - 1900	**1900 - 1920**	**1920 - 1930**	**1930 - 1940**	**1940 - 1950**
VISUAL ARTS IMPRESSIONISM, 1870-1905 ART NOUVEAU, 1880-1910 POST-IMPRESSIONISM 1886-1920 FRANCE, van Gogh's *Sunflowers*, 1888 FRANCE, Paul Gauguin's *Tahitian Women on Beach*, 1891,	FAUVISM, 1905-1907 CUBISM, 1907-1920 FUTURISM, 1908-1915 FRANCE, Picasso's *Old Blind Guitar Player*, 1903 ITALY, Boccioni's *Unique Forms of Continuity in Space*, 1913 FRANCE, Aristide Maillol's *Seated Woman*, 1901 FRANCE, Rodin's *The Thinker*, 1880-1900	GERMANY, BAUHAUS, 1919-1933 DADA, 1916-1922 SURREALISM, 1914-1940s SPAIN, Salvador Dali 1904-1988 SPAIN, Joan Miro, 1893-1983 ENGLAND, Henry Moore 1898-1986 *Reclining Figure*, 1926 USA, Harlem Renaissance 1916-1940 Romare Bearden, 1911-1988, *She-Ba* c. 1935	USA, Art Deco, *Chrysler Building* 1930, William van Alen FRANCE, George Rouault's *The Old King*, 1937 GERMANY, Self Portrait, Max Beckmann, 1884-1950 USA, *The Midnight Ride of Paul Revere*, Grant Wood, 1931	ABSTRACT EXPRESSIONISM 1945-1960 POP CULTURE, 1945-1965 USA, *Love*, Robert Indiana, 1928 USA, Andy Warhol, *Self Portrait* 1927-1987 USA, Jacob Lawrence, *The Great Migration Series #58*, 1941 ITALY, Marino Marini's *Horse and Rider*, 1949
MUSIC USA, Louis Armstrong 1890-1971 Irving Berlin, 1888-1989 USA, Boston Symphony Orchestra founded, 1881 USA, Carnegie Hall opens, 1891	USA, RAGTIME, 1901 USA, Leonard Bernstein, 1918-1990 USA, Los Angeles Symphony founded, 1919 USA, Ella Fitzgerald 1917-1996	USA, Grand Old Opry, Nashville, 1924 USA, Nat King Cole, 1919-1965 USA, Musical *Showboat* by Jerome Kern and Oscar Hammerstein, 1927	USA, Swing era, Duke Ellington, 1930s and 1940s Electric guitars introduced 1936 USA, *White Christmas*, Bing Crosby, 1942	USA, *Chattanooga Choo Choo* is first Gold Record, 1942 USA, LP (long playing) record introduced, 1948
CULTURES INDIA, Mahatma Ghandi 1869-1948	USA, San Francisco earthquake, 1906 USA, NAACP is founded 1909 USA, First time for income tax 1913 Women's Suffrage movement, 1910-1928	USA, Prohibition (no liquor sales), 1920		CHINA, Peoples' Republic, 1949
LANGUAGE ARTS USA, Mark Twain's *Tom Sawyer* 1876	ENGLAND, *Hound of the Baskervilles*, 1902 Arthur Conan Doyle	ENGLAND, *The Mystery Affair at Styles*, Agatha Christie, 1920 F. Scott Fitzgerald, 1896-1940 *The Great Gatsby*, 1925	John Steinbeck, 1902-1968 *Of Mice and Men*, 1937	USA, *Watch on the Rhine*, Lillian Hellman, 1940 ENGLAND, *Blood, Sweat and Tears*, Winston Churchill, 1941
MATHEMATICS	USA, Albert Einstein's *Theory of Relativity*, 1905			
SCIENCE USA, telephone, 1876 USA, lightbult, 1879 contact lens,1887 Roentgen discovers X-rays, 1895	GERMANY, Aspirin, 1897, Felix Hoffman USA, 1903, Wright brothers make first flight Gene theory, 1910 FRANCE, Radium, Marie and Pierre Currie, 1902	USA, Discovery of Nylon and Neoprene, 1931-1934 Wallace Carothers ENGLAND, Alexander Fleming discovers Penicillin, 1926 PANAMA, Panama Canal, 1904 GERMANY, Leica Camera,1914	Jet engine, 1936 Photocopier, Chester Carlson, 1938	USA, Fermi splits the atom, 1942 Computer, 1944
SOCIAL STUDIES MEXICO, Pancho Villa, 1878-1923 Cause of Malaria found, Ronald Ross, 1897 GERMANY, first Zeppelin flies, 1900	CHINA, Boxer Rebellion, 1900 RUSSIA, Revolution, 1917 AUSTRIA, Archduke Ferdinand asassinated, beginning of World War I, 1914 Model T, Henry Ford, 1908 Titanic sinks, 1912	USA, 1929, Stock Market Crash USA, Lindbergh flies solo across Atlantic, 1927 League of Nations, 1920 Death of Lenin, 1924		USA, Atomic Bomb dropped on Hiroshima, end of World War II, 1945 INDIA, British rule ends, 1947 MIDDLE EAST, Israel established 1948

TIMELINE # 8   1950 - PRESENT

1950 - 1965	1965 - 1980	1980 - 1990	1990 - 2000	2000 - PRESENT
VISUAL ARTS POP ART, 1950s and 1960s USA, Robert Rauschenberg, b. 1925 ABTRACT EXPRESSIONISM 1945-1960 USA, COLOR FIELD PAINTING, 1950s and 60s USA, *Geodesic Dome*, Buckminster Fuller, c. 1960	USA, SUPER REALISM 1967-1977 FEMINIST ART 1960s to present USA, Roy Lichtenstein's *Head*, 1966 USA, *Giant Hamburger*, 1969, Claes Oldenburg AUSTRALIA, *Sydney Opera House*, 1959-1973 USA, *Tourists* Duane Hanson 1970	USA, ENVIRONMENTAL ART 1964-Present USA, Georgia O'Keeffe, 1887-1986 USA, Deborah Butterfield's *Reclining Horse*, c. 1980 *Goldfish Bowl*, Roy Lichtenstein, 1981 Jeff Koons' *Michael Jackson and Bubbles*, 1988	NEO-EXPRESSIONISN 1978-1986 Guggenheim Bilbao, Spain Frank Gehry, 1997 Humana Building, Michael Graves, 1988 Keith Haring, 1958-1990	Benjamin Edwards, b. 1970 Computer Graphics, *Maman*, Louise Bourgeois 1999 USA, Christo and Jeanne Claude *The Gates*, Central Park, NY 2005 2012 ENGLAND, *Shard, Renzo Piano*
MUSIC RUSSIA, Sergey Prokofiev, 1891-1953 ENGLAND, The Beatles, 1962 USA, Elvis Presley records *Blue Suede Shoes*, 1956	USA, Elvis Presley, 1935-1977 USA, Woodstock Festival and Concert, 1969 USA, Louis Armstrong 1772-1971 NETHERLANDS, Video Disk, 1972 USA, musical *Jesus Christ, Superstar*, 1971	USA, Beatle John Lennon is killed, 1980 USA, Compact Disk Player invented, 1984 USA, Chuck Berry, 1926-*rock and roll* music , 50s-present	CDs outsell cassette tapes for recorded music, 1992 onward USA, Rock and Roll Hall of Fame Museum opens, 1995 Frank Sinatra, 1915-1998	USA, Hip-hop USA, Rap Music, 1970s-present Michael Jackson, 1958-2009
CULTURES USA, Alaska and Hawaii achieve statehood, 1959 USA, Brown vs. Board of Education, end of segregation 1954	CHINA, Cultural Revolution 1965-1973 EGYPT, Aswan Dam, 1970 USA, Roe vs. Wade, abortion legalized, 1973		World Wide Web, 1993 USA, O.J. Simpson acquitted of murder, 1995	You Tube invented, Steve Chen, Chad Hurley, and Jawed Karim, 2005
LANGUAGE ARTS J.D. Salinger's *Catcher in the Rye*, 1951 William Vaulkner's *The Reivers*, 1962	USA, Harper Lee's *To Kill a Mockingbird*, 1961	Alice Walker's *The Color Purple*, 1983 Larry McMurtry's *Lonesome Dove*, 1986 *Bonfire of the Vanities*, Thomas Wolfe, 1988	Frank McCourt's *Angela's Ashes*, 1997 CANADA, *The Life of Pi*, 2001. Yann Martel	ENGLAND, J.K. Rowlings *Harry Potter Series*, 2000-2009
MATHEMATICS Mathematicians work on computers, 1945-present ENGLAND, Fiber Optics, 1955	USA, Bar code (computer scanned), 1970			
SCIENCE USSR, Sputnik, first space rocket, 1957 USA, Hydrogen Bomb developed, 1954 USA, Polio vaccine, 1955 Dr. Jonas Salk	USA, First human heart transplant, 1967 ENGLAND, first test tube baby born, 1978 USA, Hybrid car, 1974, Victor Wouk USA, Digital camera prototype, Steven Sasson, 1975	AIDS is diagnosed, 1982 USA, Artificial heart is developed, 1982, Dr. Robert Jarvik USA, Gene transfer, 1989, Rosenberg, Blaese, Anderson Doppler radar invented, Christian Andreas Doppler, 1988	Dolly the Sheep is cloned 1997 First kidney transplants, 1995 USA, Hubble space telescope, 1990 1998. Google launched	Octuplets born through embryo implantation, 2009 Pluto downgraded from planet status, 2006 Human Genome Project, 2003 Toyota's Hybrid car, 1997-2003 "Curiosity" Rover lands on Mars, 2012
SOCIAL STUDIES ENGLAND, Queen Elizabeth crowned, 1952 EUROPE, Common Market, 1957 OPEC formed with 13 nations 1960 KOREA, war, 1950 - 1953	ISRAEL, Seven Day war, 1967 USA, John F. Kennedy assassinated, 1968 USA, Martin Luther King assassinated, 1968 USA, Astronauts land on the moon, 1969	CHINA, Tianamen Square incident, 1989 USA, First woman Supreme Court Judge appointed, 1981 ARGENTINA, Falkland Invasion, 1982	GERMANY, Berlin Wall comes down, 1961-1989 MIDDLE EAST, Gulf War, 1991 USSR dissolved, 1991	**Arab Spring, 2011** USA, Twin Towers destroyed 9-11-2001, War in Iraq begun 2003 JAPAN. Tsunami hits nuclear reactor, 2011

A Few Basic Skills

Old Skills Perfected, New Skills Learned

We know that artists must learn certain basic skills before they are able to produce quality works of art. Students can understand the concept that they must learn to walk before they can fly. As you present a project, you will find that if they have spent some time on simple exercises beforehand, they will have learned a few basic skills and they can "fly" when offered open-ended personal expression assignments.

The Thumbnail Sketch

Students should be shown how to work out ideas. They need to understand that a thumbnail sketch is a small quick rough sketch in proportion to the paper on which it will be finished, not a finished product. Tell them these will not be graded, but are simply a way to come up with original ideas. It is good to demonstrate how quickly and roughly a sketch is made.

Students should try out several ideas quickly to come up with one sketch that is worth turning into a more finished sketch. Generally the first idea isn't great, but as it evolves or as students combine ideas, it becomes more personal. To challenge them, let them know that you would expect to see a minimum of three sketches finished within a ten-minute period. This is normally a nontalking time. The act of drawing almost seems to make good ideas come.

Measuring

One of our math teachers told me that when she had her students creating a work of art that required students to measure, the only students who really knew how to use a ruler as a drawing guide were the *art* students. Let's hope they leave art classes with that skill at a minimum. Because most of the rest of the world is on the metric system, students should also have an understanding of the approximate metric equivalents to inches. Most art classes have rulers that feature both inches and metric measurements.

Enlarging with a Grid

This method is used to transfer a small drawing to a larger surface, using a ratio such as one inch equals ten inches. Mark at one-inch intervals along the top and bottom of the drawing starting on the same side. Use the ruler to make parallel lines all the way across. Do the same procedure along the sides of the drawing. The surface onto which the design is transferred must be in exact proportion to the small drawing. Lightly make a grid on the larger paper, making exactly the same number of squares, but larger. It may be necessary to use a yardstick for the larger paper. If the student is working on canvas or wood, charcoal might work better than pencil. The lines should be light enough that they can be erased later. Grid lines made on the original can be done on tracing paper or clear acetate. You can also buy heavy see-through grids to set up in front of your still life (one standing model with adjustable strings is called the Dürer grid).

Gluing

Attaching one piece of paper to another (as in a collage) can be messy unless proper technique is taught. Students have probably worked with white liquid glue and library paste. When students are pasting something where glue *must* be applied clear to the edge, have them place the piece to be glued on a catalog page or slick magazine page, applying glue evenly with a finger, a hard plastic credit card, or brush. The page of the catalog is then turned to avoid getting paste on the front of the next item. When YES! glue is applied to the edges in this manner, the paper lies flat and dries quickly. I do not recommend using rubber cement, as it tends to yellow and dry out on the paper after a year or so.

Cutting a Mat

A mat shows off the artwork and is normally used for work that will be displayed anywhere outside the art department foyer. Invest in a good mat cutter if you teach in a high school. It will be your best friend! Teach your advanced students how to mat their own work using the mat cutter. A mat cutter simplifies cutting ordinary poster board or fourteen-ply mat board. In general, photographs (even colored ones) and black-and-white drawings look best mounted in black, gray, or white mats. If cutting by hand with a craft (X-acto) knife, a metal yardstick should be used to ensure straight edges. Lightweight poster board mats may be purchased precut in some of the sizes listed here.

Measure Twice, Cut Once!

- Cut the outside dimensions of a mat in a standard size so standard frames may be purchased (8×10, 11×14, 12×16, 16×20, 18×24, or 24×30 inches).
- Mat borders should be two to three inches larger than the artwork.
- Use a yardstick to line up diagonally from corner to corner, both directions, making a small X on the exact center *back* of the mat board.
- On the back, measure half the size of the opening in each direction from the X.
- Use a T square to line up on one edge of the mat board, drawing a straight line on all four sides.
- Confirm with a ruler or yardstick that the opening that will be cut is the correct size.

When Cutting with a Knife

- Place a metal ruler, preferably one with cork backing, over the *mat* area, not the hole, holding the ruler firmly in place. Use a small mat cutter or craft (X-acto) knife to draw the cut along the metal ruler. If working with fourteen-ply mat board, make shorter cuts until you have gone through all the layers. Cut slightly beyond each corner so the mat will drop out. This way, if the cutter slips, the border will not be damaged.

Drawing

Everyone Can Learn to Draw!

If you believe that everyone can learn to draw, you can convince your students. While some of the students in your classes love drawing, and do it at every opportunity, many others will quietly sidle up and inform you, "I can't draw." What an opportunity for you to teach them that they can indeed learn to draw!

Sketchbooks

Students can begin a small sketchbook in your class that will be invaluable to them throughout the course. In the first five minutes of class, while you are taking attendance, write or put something on the board for them to draw or respond to in writing. They can draw something from imagination, a detail from a poster, or a twig with a leaf that you brought in. Suggest they write the date in a corner of a page, perhaps jotting a random thought or something they noticed on the way to school. Many artworks today incorporate handwriting as well as color and design, and students may come up with something to use in a later composition.

What's Going On?
Hue Lam, charcoal, 12 × 15 inches. This drawing is so lifelike one can almost hear the noises this monkey makes. Mehlville High School, St. Louis County, Missouri, teacher Julie Webber.

If you require students to maintain a sketchbook, particularly as part of their assessment, you also have an obligation to look at these on a regular basis. Encourage students to draw in their sketchbook both in and outside of class. A spiral-bound sketchbook that will lie flat is ideal, but it can also be a three-ring binder with unlined, hole-punched pages. It can have sketches made on separate paper, glued in later, along with found ephemera (paper items like postcards, ticket stubs, receipts, or cards). Further instructions for art and nature journals appear near the end of this chapter.

Some students will discard paper after paper if allowed because of overly high expectations of themselves. One sheet of paper per student is adequate for most projects. Remind students not to worry about making "mistakes," and in most cases ask them not to use the eraser, but rather to begin by drawing lightly, adding firmer strokes when they are confident they have the "right" line.

Because many drawing assignments may become portfolio pieces, or serve as the basis for them, a good drawing program should include at least one fully shaded pencil drawing and one color drawing. Students should have a project that requires enlarging in correct proportions, and other projects that give them experience drawing organic and geometric forms. Life drawing generally refers to drawing the human figure from observation. Artists also create observational drawings of scenery, animals, flowers, or a still life. In working from a photograph, compositional choices have already been made, and are not as challenging.

Class Critique   Throughout the year take time as a class to assess drawings by hanging them around the room. One teacher distributes sticky notes on which students are asked to write something positive that they see in each picture. After these have been posted, students may be willing to talk about their own work in a class discussion and hopefully can find something positive they can say about a classmate's artwork. Inform students that "I like it" is too vague to be an effective criticism, and their comments need to be more specific.

History of Drawing   So many artists, so many techniques! For an extra credit assignment, encourage students to search the Internet for examples of an artist famous for

Catharsis
Matt Barr, charcoal, 24 × 19 inches. This drawing is not just a self-portrait, but a strong personal reflection. Parkway Central High School, St. Louis County, Missouri, teacher Cara Deffenbaugh.

his or her drawing. A medium-size poster, small booklet, or brief digital presentation based on their research may be shared with the class. Keep a list of students' choices to avoid having more than one student select a specific artist. Students might experiment using an artist's technique such as that of Vincent van Gogh (1853–1890), José Clemente Orozco (1883–1949), André Derain (1880–1954), Edvard Munch (1863–1944), Fernand Léger (1881–1955), Käthe Kollwitz (1867–1945), Rembrandt van Rijn (1606–1669), or John Marin (1870–1953).

INTRODUCTORY EXERCISES

Time Needed: 3 to 5 fifty-minute class periods

Materials: drawing paper, pencils, fine-line black markers, colored pencil, charcoal, pastels, ink, erasers

Goal: Students explore a variety of ways of making marks, being open to trying materials they might never have used before.

Objective: Students demonstrate through drawings that they have learned to effectively use at least four different media: pencil, ink, charcoal, colored pencil, marker, pastel, or oil pastel.

Begin skill building with nonthreatening drawing exercises such as the ones listed here. You wouldn't have students do these all at once because the boredom factor is easily reached by secondary school students. Exercises might be given on an as-needed basis for practice on a separate piece of paper before introducing a project where the skill is needed. They can be done in the students' sketchbooks. Have students label the tools or techniques for future reference. Suggest that students work in random small patches on a single piece of drawing paper or organize into a grid, using a ruler. Teacher Marilyn Palmer requires her students to do a *value strip* in each drawing medium they use, just before beginning the actual project. The value strip is a one-inch wide strip divided into ten segments, with white on one end, black on the other, and eight shades in-between.

Pencil

Make even strokes with several different types of pencils, comparing the darkness you can achieve using the same amount of pressure. Write the pencil numbers next to the patches.

Use a number 2B drawing pencil to make a smooth, continuous value.

Make different values with very small, even strokes, seamlessly blending to the next line until you have ten different

Catskills

Tim Smith, pencil and eraser, 11 × 14 inches. This pencil drawing emphasizes certain areas with the side and tip of pencil and the use of an eraser as a *drawing* tool to make broad strokes cutting across foreground and background.

St. Louis Cathedral
George Schweser, charcoal, 18 × 24 inches. The artist enriched this charcoal drawing by also using a rag, eraser, and white chalk as drawing instruments

values (almost white to the darkest gray or black).

Vary the thickness of a line by applying pressure softly or firmly. Try using the same technique to make an undulating line of varying widths.

Ink

Dip a brush in ink to make variations. Make straight, parallel, wavy, zigzag, curved, and converging lines.

Make a value strip using water to lighten the ink to make gradations.

Drawing Pen

Make *value* differences with a drawing pen (like a roller ball pen).

Hatching. Make parallel lines increasingly closely spaced together to eventually become almost completely black (no scribbling).

Crosshatching. Turn the paper and intersect lines at different angles.

Stippling. Use the tip of the pen to make dots, close together or farther apart.

Combination. Use stippling and hatching together to give texture to a background.

Charcoal

Use several different kinds of charcoal: hard, soft, charcoal pencil.

Draw white chalk accents on charcoal or use charcoal and eraser to get variations.

Dry Pastel

Experiment with pastel strokes.

Combine three variations of one hue.

Use a hue with its analogous colors from the color wheel.

Make slanted lines in a single color, close together and farther apart.

Combine the slanted lines with similar colors that might work in a sky.

Draw with the side of the pastel.

Draw with a sharp point or corner.

Do crosshatching with complementary colors.

Oil Pastel

Begin with a dark hue, add a middle color, then finish with the lightest color.

Firmly fill in an area. Go over it with a lighter color.

Use a sharp instrument to make a design through two layers to reveal the underlying layer.

Dip oil pastel in a solvent such as mineral spirits to draw with as if it were a painting material.

Marker

Carefully apply marker in even, parallel strokes. This is a difficult technique to do well, but can be done effectively to fill an area.

Draw with black water-based fine-line marker in combination with watercolor, which allows the marker to bleed, giving a somewhat *loose* look to the drawing.

Colored Pencil

Experiment with variations in pressure and evenness of drawing.

Combine colors in dots as the pointillists did, allowing the eye to mix the colors.

Textures

Draw real texture such as tree bark or the fur on an animal.

Invent textures that might be used to show variations in the background such as sky.

Show variations in grass by making it longer, shorter, thicker, thinner, or gone to seed.

Negative Space

Lightly outline an object and fill in the area around it with shading to show the negative shape.

Fruits and Vegetables
Scott Boyd, pencil, 10 × 12 inches. Preliminary realistic pencil drawings require the student to draw exactly what is seen. Oakville High School, St. Louis County, Missouri, teacher Joan Larson.

Abstract Fruits and Vegetables
Scott Boyd, pencil and marker, 10 × 12 inches. The abstract drawings of apples (l), and cucumbers (r) show what a student can do when challenged to create a number of abstract drawings. Teacher Joan Larson, Oakville High School, St. Louis County, Missouri.

PROJECT 3-2
CONTOUR HAND DRAWING

Time Needed: 3 to 5 fifty-minute classes

Materials: drawing paper, 6B and 4B pencils, scissors, glue stick, masking tape, black fine-line marker

Goals: Students show sensitivity in making simple contour drawings of their hands by combining a variety of poses on one page, unifying them with line or an object.

Objective: Students choose a personal symbol or favorite song, using more than one medium to unify a composition of similar objects.

FOR THE TEACHER

For some beginning students, an almost immediate reaction to being asked to do a drawing of their own hand is to lay it flat on the paper and trace around it. Whatever the result of this first drawing, ask them to sign the drawing and put a date on it. Although students may have done blind contour drawing at an earlier stage in their development, there is always room for improvement as they mature.

Vocabulary: blind contour, modified contour, contour

Art History Connection

Introduce students to the work of artists who excelled in drawing. Not all were smooth and beautiful—let them see the outline "graffiti" drawings of Keith Haring (1958–1990) or contour drawings by Henri Matisse (1869–1954) or Andy Warhol (1928–1987).

Alternative Project
Figure Drawing

A student volunteer can pose for everyone in the class to draw. Blind contour drawings with marker or pencil are rapid and fun. A later twenty-minute pose enables students to apply what they have learned about drawing from observation using charcoal or graphite.

FOR THE STUDENT

In a blind contour drawing of your hand, you will look only at the object you are drawing, keeping the pencil point on the paper, not lifting it. A true blind contour drawing will not be very good, yet anyone would know when seeing it that it is a hand.

Draw What You See, Not What You Know

Look at different ways to *pose* your non-drawing hand before you begin: open, closed, arched, holding a pencil, and so on. Because you know in advance that you will be expected to fill a large sheet of paper with your drawings, you will make many variations. Start by using a blind contour drawing, just to get yourself into the habit of *looking* as you draw.

1. Blind contour hand drawing (your back is turned when you look at the hand). Use masking tape to hold a sheet of paper on your table at an angle that is comfortable for drawing, even though you are not going to peek at it. Draw slowly and let it seem as though the pencil is actually going around and into each fold of skin of the knuckles or around the fingernails; don't be concerned with the end result.

2. Modified contour drawing. As you draw, it is fine to peek from time to time, but work slowly. You *know* that a fingernail is oval in shape, but as you draw the hand, draw only the portion of the nail that is visible.

3. Draw five or more variations of the hand on this piece of paper. Here are two solutions to completing this drawing.

Option 1

When the drawings are complete, cut them out and arrange them carefully, gluing them on the paper with glue stick. If you feel you have too much room, add another hand or two before completing the drawing.

Lightly draw a curving line to tie the hands together, almost as if the line were a piece of string. In pencil lightly write the words of a favorite song to follow the contours of the line. Go over the pencil-drawn lettering with black fine-line marker. Let it dry, then carefully erase the pencil marks.

Option 2

If you prefer, you can trace the drawings to a fresh sheet of paper. Plan in advance to have one or more of the hands holding a favorite personal symbol or object.

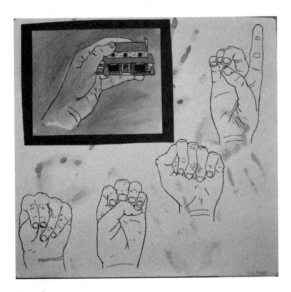

Hands
Dean Randolph, mixed media, 18 × 18 inches.
Parkway Central High School, St. Louis County,
Missouri, teacher Cara Deffenbaugh.

ONE- AND TWO-POINT PERSPECTIVE DRAWING

Time Needed: 5 fifty-minute classes

Materials: 12 × 18-inch drawing paper, pencil, ruler, kneaded eraser, colored pencil

Goal: Students use a ruler to create parallel and converging lines in the development of a cityscape composition that uses one- and two-point perspective.

Objective: Students apply colored pencil by blending and combining two colors to make a third color.

Objective: Students demonstrate the ability to use imagination in transforming this one- or two-point perspective drawing into a personal statement.

Downtown Gateway City
Alex Horstmann, colored pencil, 17 × 24 inches. This student bent and distorted the buildings, yet the buildings were believable because of multiple vanishing points. Pattonville High School, Maryland Heights, Missouri, teacher Beth Kathriner.

FOR THE TEACHER

Many students were taught perspective earlier in school, but it is useful to review methods used by artists through the centuries to show distance and depth. Students may use a ruler to draw parallel and converging lines. This is a good opportunity to get students out of their seats and making perspective drawings around the school in hallways or locker bays.

Art History Connection

By the 1400s Italian painters and architects had found that formal linear perspective could be used to show distance within a painting. Italian architect Filippo Brunelleschi (1377–1446) formalized the "rules" of linear perspective.

Red Grooms (1937–) chose cityscapes as his subject, making humorous drawings, paintings, and three-dimensional collage to interpret New York City and Chicago. His mixed-media collage, *Looking Along Broadway Towards Grace Church* (1981), is a humorous look at New York City using one-point perspective.

Vocabulary and Definitions

Foreground, middle ground, and **background** signify the location of each on paper or canvas.

Linear perspective is a geometric method of showing distance. A horizon line represents the level of the viewer's eye. A *worm's-eye view* would have a low horizon line, and a *bird's-eye view* would have one near the top of the picture plane.

The **vanishing point** is an imaginary point on the horizon at which parallel lines seemingly converge. A common example is a drawing of a railroad or a fence becoming smaller as the lines lead off to a vanishing point on the horizon.

Aerial perspective is the principle that objects farther away appear softer and fainter in color. The closer to the viewer, the brighter colors become. Patterns are also more distinct.

Diminution is the gradual reduction in size seen in objects farther away.

Foreshortening is most often applied to figure drawing. The portions of the body closest to the artist will appear larger. An example is the size of the feet of the form being examined in Rembrandt's *The Anatomy Lesson of Dr. Joan Deyman* (1656).

Overlapping shows which objects are in front and indicates depth.

Preparation

Students should review making cubes according to perspective. This lesson will be valuable as they later do artwork such as landscape or cityscapes. These can be drawn freehand, but rulers might make the task easier. In drawing, each set of parallel lines has a vanishing point, and verticals and horizontals should be straight and parallel to the sides of the paper or canvas.

One-Point Perspective

On a large sheet of drawing paper, draw a line about one-third of the way from the top (the horizon line). Make a dot midway on the line (the vanishing point). Draw

a rectangle of any shape about one-third from the bottom and slightly off to the side. To make a cube in perspective, lightly draw from the four corners of the rectangle to a vanishing point. Keeping horizontal and vertical lines parallel to the edges of the page, draw a horizontal line across the top two diagonals. Then draw a vertical line to the lower diagonal. Erase the pencil diagonals to make a box.

One-Point Perspective

Two-Point Perspective

To draw a building seen from a corner, make the lines diminish in two directions. The same would be true of a car, a refrigerator, or a chair. The vanishing points might not even be on the picture plane itself, but exist in space out to the sides of the drawing. Lightly draw a horizontal line across the middle of the page. Place a vanishing point near each end of the horizon line. Draw a vertical line somewhere near the middle of the horizontal line to be the side of a building. Draw from the top and bottom of the line to each vanishing point. Now draw a vertical line between the diagonals to create a building of any size you wish.

Alternative Project

Perspective Hallway View

Students may draw something like a hallway full of lockers creatively decorated or with an unlikely collection of things inside. Several cars in a parking lot can be drawn using perspective drawing. Adding people, again using perspective, makes the image more interesting.

FOR THE STUDENT

Draw lightly when starting perspective drawings, making heavier lines when you are certain of placement. When you look at a building from the front, you see a simple rectangle. But when you view it from the side, you see a cube. Do a few small perspective *cube* exercises before attempting to make buildings, cars, buses, or other city sights.

1. When you are comfortable doing one- and two-point perspective drawings, draw three one-inch cubes on a piece of typing paper, making one above a line with vanishing points, one centered, and one below the vanishing points. This enables you to adapt perspective to your purposes.

2. Cityscapes have been a favorite subject of artists since at least the fourteenth century, when Italians painted their surroundings. They faithfully painted what they saw. In this project you will *invent* your cityscape, though you may want to use familiar store names.

3. The streets in your cityscape can be as busy or empty as you wish, though real city streets are usually bustling. You can add anything you want: cars, buses, bicycles, people, streetlights, or trees.

4. Take time and care as you use colored pencil to complete your composition. If you have taken the time to draw detail, color just as carefully. As with painting, work throughout the composition as you select colors—repeat a bright color in another area. This will be semiabstract, so you're the decision maker.

TWIG TO TREE LANDSCAPE

Time Needed: 2 to 4 fifty-minute classes

Materials: branches, twigs, ink, small palette, watercolor or drawing paper, watercolors, paper towels, and drawing instruments (pencils, sticks, pens and pen points, and two water containers, for clean and dirty water)

Goal: Students use media with control to draw what they see, yet make it a personal interpretation demonstrating sensitivity to nuances in value.

Objective: Students participate in a class discussion, reflecting on how effectively some techniques were explored—applying texture, using a wash to indicate depth, or combining another material (gouache, colored pencil, or watercolor).

Objective: Students write a reflection of how their own work might be improved if they had the opportunity to redo it.

FOR THE TEACHER

Sometimes teachers are lucky enough to have a whole forest outside the window, or at least a tree or two nearby, but sometimes in the classroom you just have to make do by substituting a twig or a branch for an entire tree. Show students examples of trees as drawn by masters such as Rembrandt, van Gogh, or Wolf Kahn. In this project students will benefit by making a value strip to learn control of lights and darks.

Vocabulary: wash, hatching, crosshatching, stippling, invented texture

Preparation

Gather small branches and twigs that have character—a few offshoots and small twigs. These should be small enough to hold in the hand or place on a desk as a drawing reference. Larger twigs may be stood upright in a sand-filled container.

Introduce students to building an ink wash from light to dark. If they are unfamiliar with these techniques, demonstrate how to show edges and value differences through hatching, crosshatching, or stippling.

Growth
Jessica Boxx, ink and acrylic, 10 × 15 inches. Jessica drew her hands and used her imagination to transform the fingers into the roots of tree branches. Pattonville High School, Maryland Heights, Missouri, teacher Beth Kathriner.

Alternative Project
Metamorphosis

The twig project can be combined with drawing hands as the tree branches become extensions of the fingers, as shown by a student in Beth Kathriner's class.

Alternative Project

Color Pastel Landscape with Trees

The famous painter Wolf Kahn (1927–) became known for the stands of trees he chose as his basic subject. Whether his trees were interpreted in pastels or paint, his artworks often use contrasting, brilliant colors such as magenta, vivid purple, bright yellow, or lime green to show light filtering through the trees. Students might indicate a time of day and luminosity (bright light) coming through trees using foreground, middle ground, and background as they draw trunks.

Alternative Project

It's Out of My Control

Ink on gessoed paper. Students apply gesso roughly on a piece of paper one day in advance. The ink drawing will be somewhat out of control because of ridges, and these "mistakes" may open students to experimentation.

FOR THE STUDENT

Ink is a permanent medium that will almost surely stain your clothing if you spill it. Take care! Ink can be diluted with water to achieve lighter values. Keep a paper towel next to your painting for testing value first. It is not difficult to make an area darker, but much harder to lighten it after you have made it too dark. A wash is often built up in successive layers until the desired degree of darkness is attained.

1. Plan ahead for which areas will remain white and which you want to be very dark. Use pencil to *lightly* and quickly draw the composition, which will include a horizon line and at least one large tree, with other trees farther in the distance. For a single tall tree, you may prefer to orient the paper vertically.

2. Another option is to think of the edges of a forest, with the front trees mostly the same size, getting higher, smaller, and thinner the farther back they are.

3. For the sky, make a *wash* by loading your brush with diluted ink, starting at the top and painting across the page. Further dilute the ink and make the next broad horizontal stroke. Continue with consecutively lighter strokes until you have reached the horizon line, remembering to leave the tree trunks unpainted.

4. Decide which is the shadowed side on the trees and which the one that is in at least partial sun. You can make *real* or *implied texture*, which means you may draw bark as you see it, or you can use closely placed curved parallel strokes to make *hatching*. If you want an area to be quite dark, you can use parallel strokes at an angle to the first group to do *crosshatching*. Another option is to use *stippling* (small dots), placing dots closer or farther apart, depending on how dark you want an area to be.

5. Keep in mind that trees farther away will have less detail and be lighter in color than the biggest (and therefore closest) tree.

6. Complete your drawing by finishing the bottom part of the composition with an ink wash and line drawing combination. White highlights can be added if necessary by using opaque white watercolor (gouache).

7. Place your drawing on the floor and stand off from a distance to look at it. Examine it for value differences. Is your closest tree the darkest? Do you see depth when you look at the horizon line?

DRAWING BONES

Time Needed: 5 to 15 fifty-minute classes

Materials: 12 × 18- or 18 × 24-inch drawing or colored pastel paper

Content Connection: Science

Goal: Students research and discuss the importance of bones in some cultures and time periods: reliquaries (bone containers), skull preservation in some cultures, and skeletons used in religious references today such as Day of the Dead celebrations.

Goal: Students select drawing media to create a range of values or color that show the beauty of this subject.

Objective: Students create a finished drawing that demonstrates understanding of the elements of color, value, and space.

FOR THE TEACHER

Bones have been a favorite subject for artists from Leonardo da Vinci and Michelangelo to today's art students. There is so much to be learned from drawing them, whether they are human, animal, or plastic. Georgia O'Keeffe (1887–1986) often incorporated human and animal bones in her paintings.

As with learning to draw the human figure, learning to draw bones is infinitely interesting and personal. If this is done before students are introduced to figure drawing, the students are more likely to incorporate the underlying structure in their drawings. Not all high school art departments are going to have a skeleton, but perhaps you can borrow one from the science department. Or students can draw from animal bones or small plastic models.

Vocabulary: anatomy, Conté crayon, foreshortening, proportion, artistic license

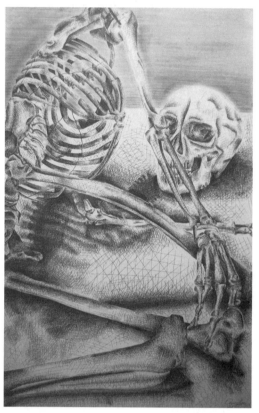

Skeleton

Angelou Song, mixed media, 24 × 15 inches. This carefully composed drawing is from Parkway Central High School, St. Louis, Missouri, teacher Cara Deffenbaugh.

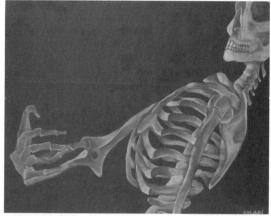

Figure/Portrait

Shannon Adlabi, pastel, 18 × 24 inches. The pastel drawing on black paper uses analogous and complementary colors. Parkway West High School, St. Louis County, Missouri, teacher Marilyn Palmer.

Proportions of the Human Figure

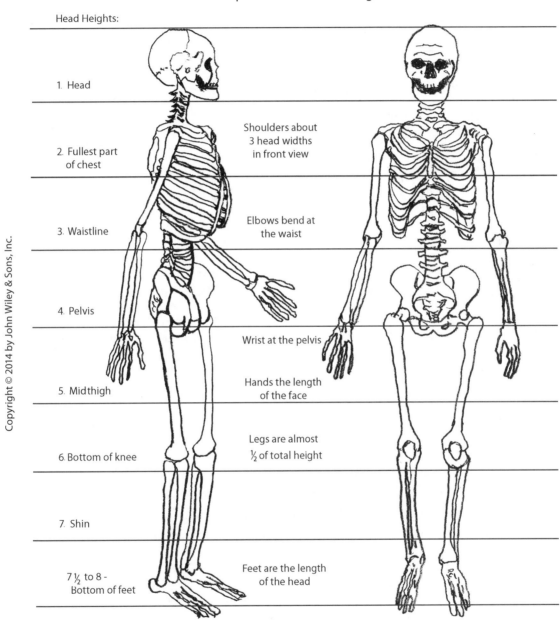

Head Heights:

1. Head

2. Fullest part of chest

3. Waistline

4. Pelvis

5. Midthigh

6. Bottom of knee

7. Shin

7 ½ to 8 - Bottom of feet

Shoulders about 3 head widths in front view

Elbows bend at the waist

Wrist at the pelvis

Hands the length of the face

Legs are almost ½ of total height

Feet are the length of the head

Fully grown adults average 7 ½ to 8 head heights tall
Children's heads are proportionally much larger

Developed by Joan Larson

To introduce students to human proportions, copies of these handouts are distributed to students in introductory classes to be placed under drawing paper as they select appropriate clothing to make an interesting composition. Oakville High School, St. Louis County, Missouri, teacher Joan Larson.

Indian and Johnny Reb
Ross Mohesky, pencil, 10 × 12 inches. Oakville High School,
St. Louis County, Missouri, teacher Joan Larson.

Bard-King and His Knight
Taylor Clark, pencil, 10 × 13 inches. Oakville High School,
St. Louis County, Missouri, teacher Joan Larson.

Alternative Project
Build a Body

Art teacher Joan Larson introduces beginning students to human proportions by distributing an 8½ × 11-inch handout with side and front views of a human skeleton. The students tape a piece of copy paper over the handout and use colored pencil, adding faces, features, flesh, and fabric to "build a body." She uses standing front and profile views to help them learn the proportions.

Preparation

Discuss the principle of the head as a unit of measure (a figure is about eight heads high). One drawing teacher has students fold an 18 × 24-inch drawing paper into eighths. They draw lines on the folds with heavy black marker, then label what portion of the human form should hit that spot. They use this as a guide under their actual drawing paper to help with proportions. Point out that students may need to invent value differences and show depth by using artistic license. The addition of color to an all-white subject can also make it more interesting.

FOR THE STUDENT

If you are lucky enough to have a real (or plastic) skeleton to observe as you draw, it isn't necessary to include the entire form. Perhaps you will choose to draw only a portion. Here are some of drawing media from which you may choose to draw bones.

1. **Ink or ballpoint pen.** If you choose to draw with a fine-line marker or pen, *lightly* draw an outline in pencil. Show edges, not by outlining, but by using hatching (closely drawn lines) and crosshatching (lines at an angle to the first set of lines) to show differences in value. You can crosshatch in many different directions to make almost pure blacks.

2. **Pastels.** To draw the skeleton with pastels, work on dark paper. To make the skeleton more interesting than pure white, select a single hue (red, green, violet, blue, yellow, or orange). Use what you have learned from the color wheel and make subtle changes with analogous colors (that surround the hue on the color wheel) and slight touches of the complementary color.

3. **Charcoal.** Charcoal works well on white paper, but also looks very nice on gray. A combination of two varieties of charcoal (one hard, one soft) enhanced with white chalk gives a sophisticated rendition of bones, singly or in combination.

4. **Conté crayon.** These hard pastels have been used for centuries for observational drawings. The old drawings are as beautiful today as when freshly made by the Old Masters. Conté comes in a limited number of colors: sanguine (blood red), bistre (brown), white, and black. They cannot be easily erased or covered, but still give a wonderful result.

5. **Mixed media.** You may find that the use of only one form of drawing material does not give the effect you want. Sometimes several materials such as ink and pastel can be combined on the same surface. Or several different drawings can be cut or torn and glued on a new surface as a collage.

PROJECT 3-6
FIGURE DRAWING

Time Needed: 3 to 5 fifty-minute classes

Materials: 18 × 24-inch paper, charcoal, kneaded eraser, white chalk, blending stumps, fixative

Goal: Students will demonstrate sensitivity by taking an observational drawing beyond realistic art to personal interpretation, inviting the viewer to learn more about the artist.

Objective: Students will explore the use of more than one variety of charcoal, transforming its appearance through the use of a kneaded eraser and enhancing it with another material.

Maddy
Alec Wehmeier, charcoal, 18 × 24 inches. A relaxed pose such as this allows the model to remain almost motionless for longer than a standing pose. Parkway South High School, St. Louis County, Missouri, teacher Eric Ludlow.

Emphasis on a Subject
Christopher Davis, charcoal, 18 × 24 inches. The same subject drawn at the same time as *Maddy*, by Alec Wehmeier (left), but from a different vantage point. Parkway South High School, St. Louis County, Missouri, teacher Eric Ludlow.

FOR THE TEACHER

In prehistoric times the first drawing medium may have been charcoal, when primitive people realized it could be used to make marks on rock. It has always been a forgiving medium for students because of the ability to easily make changes, while working loosely and in a large format.

Preparation

Before introducing students to them, familiarize yourself with the varieties of charcoal and related materials to find out how they can affect a composition. Charcoal comes in many forms: vine charcoal (charred willow), compressed charcoal (charcoal mixed with a gum binder that makes darker marks), and charcoal pencil. Charcoal drawings can be altered by using compressed rolls of paper (blending *stumps* and *tortillons*) or a mat board strip ¾ × 3 inches long. Kneaded erasers, white chalk, or white pencil may be used to lighten or accent. Workable fixative protects works in progress and allows pictures to be further changed.

Drawing a Figure

The head (from top to chin) is generally considered to be about one-eighth of a human's total height and is the common unit of measure when deciding how to place a figure on the page. Introduce students to measuring the human figure by holding up a pencil to view the model with the arm fully extended, closing one eye, and measuring by placing the top of the pencil at the top of the head and placing the thumbnail on the pencil at the chin. The thumb is placed on the pencil where the chin is seen. Seven to eight of these head lengths assist in determining proportion.

An introduction to drawing the figure could be quick sketches in which the model tries to hold several action poses for one minute as fellow students draw several small poses on a single sheet of paper. Suggest the students lightly draw one line that gives the general direction of the back or angle of the shoulder. These warm-ups may save time when students are ready to draw the entire figure.

Vocabulary: even tones, blending stumps, highlights, proportion, rough in, gesture drawing

FOR THE STUDENT

The beauty of charcoal is that it is *forgiving*. If you make a mistake, don't erase, but just draw over the line until you get it right, then confidently make it darker when you know it is right.

1. Loosely rough in the drawing with the side of a one-inch piece of vine charcoal. Your drawing will *not* be clean and will probably become smudged, but will be more interesting when the structure of your drawing becomes apparent.

2. If you are drawing a person, the straight lines you make may eventually become part of the background. The proportions of the human form are about eight head lengths. If the entire figure won't fit on the page, it is better to draw what will fit than to worry about getting it all on the paper. Begin with an underlying structure of ovals, or use lines that depict the angle of the shoulder or the curvature of the back.

3. Don't attempt to fully complete just one portion of the drawing, but instead work all over the picture. You will find that making important lines darker will make the drawing more interesting.

4. The range of darks and lights are challenging, but are the basis of working with one color. You have many tools that can help, such as the kneaded eraser used as a drawing tool to change areas of dark and create highlights (lightest areas).

5. In the drawing process, the work can be sprayed with workable fixative, which allows you to continue to darken or lighten areas. Ultimately you might wish to highlight with white pencil or chalk.

6. When you have finished, the entire artwork can be sprayed again with fixative.

SELF-PORTRAIT, BLACK AND WHITE

Time Needed: 4 to 5 fifty-minute classes

Materials: 12 × 18-inch drawing paper, pencil or charcoal

Goal: Students examine self-portraits of artists through generations, interpreting what qualities have caused them to endure.

Objective: Students demonstrate sensitivity and subtlety in use of media, incorporating personal symbolism in a portrait.

FOR THE TEACHER

Students may draw this self-portrait in any medium or combination of media that they prefer.

Hundreds of examples of self-portraits by artists exist, as most artists reached a point in their lives when they happened to be the only subject around. Rembrandt's earliest self-portrait was a drawing done when he was about fifteen years old.

The Mechanics of Baseball
Jack Luth, pencil, 14 × 17 inches.
DeSmet High School, St. Louis County, Missouri, teacher Emily Dames.

Preparation

Lead students through these measurement systems to help them understand how to draw what they see. Encourage them to do these drawings at home also. Although each person's face is different, there are several things we tend to have in common. Have students look at themselves in a mirror as you go through this process, each person holding a ruler or pencil to confirm that these observations apply to their own faces as they face forward. This is what they will observe:

- The head is basically an egg-shaped oval, larger at the top than the bottom.
- If a vertical line is drawn down the middle to line up features, a horizontal line across the eyes will be at a right angle.
- When the head is tilted, the horizontal line will always intersect the center line at a right angle.
- The eyes are *halfway* between the chin and the top of the head.
- If the space between the eyes and the chin is divided roughly in thirds, the nose will be a little more than one-third, and the mouth about a third between the nose and the chin.
- The space between the eyes is the width of an eye.
- The eye is in line with the place where the ear is attached (which is convenient for sunglasses).

- The bottom of the nose is in line with the place where the bottom of the ear is attached (lesson: the ear is big)!

- The corners of the mouth are directly below the centers of the eyes.

- The edges of the nose are directly below the inner corners of the eyes.

When the head is tilted, students can still lightly draw curved lines that will assist in placing features where they belong.

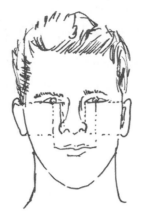

Facial Characteristics

FOR THE STUDENT

Do these preliminary drawing exercises on a small piece of paper, as they are not intended to be finished works of art (though some may end up being that beautiful).

Draw your eyes as carefully as possible. Look for a long time to observe areas that have visible lines and areas with no apparent lines. Notice differences in value—where the paper should be left white and where it should be dark. Even though you don't see much black, an effective drawing has value differences.

Draw a nose. Look carefully and discern where you actually see line and where there is a difference in value. Draw the shape of the nostril by drawing the value you see. If there is no line visible, don't draw one. Look at drawings by great artists to see how they have shown the form of the nose by gently shading the sides.

Draw the mouth. Don't outline the lips or the result will disappoint you. Instead, look in the mirror and draw the darkest part of the mouth, which is the line in the middle. The lower lip often is shown by the shadow underneath it, rather than a line on the lip itself.

Try other features. Practice by drawing ears, hair, chin, and so on. The more you practice, the easier it will become.

Drawing the Face

- Do a drawing of your face. It may take several days, so there's no need to hurry. Look carefully at yourself and the shape of your face. Don't attempt to depict all the details in color or clothing, but draw only a portion. Don't try to smile, as it is difficult to hold the pose and often looks artificial.

- Apply what you have already learned about the placement of your features on your face and how to draw them.

- To draw hair, look at the direction your hair grows. Some areas of the hair are darker than others. Don't try to draw every hair, and especially don't scribble it in, but try to draw some strands of hair in the direction it goes. You will have areas that reflect light in your hair and in your eyes (highlights). Let those differences show.

- Look for shadows that make shapes, rather than using uninterrupted lines to draw the outside of the face.
- Walk away from your picture and squint through your eyelashes to see differences in value. There should be blacks in the picture, even if the only place you actually see black is in the pupil of your eye. Hold the picture up to a mirror and look at it to see if any improvements can be made.

Reflection
Kevin Foster, graphite and color, 20 × 22 inches. Parkway South High School, St. Louis County, Missouri, teacher Eric Ludlow.

PASTEL SELF-PORTRAIT

Time Needed: 10 fifty-minute classes

Materials: large, high-quality drawing paper, pencil, soft pastels

Goal: Students demonstrate an understanding of real or simulated texture in a self-portrait.

Objective: Students show proficiency in pastel, demonstrating an understanding of building up layers and blending two complementary colors to make a third color.

FOR THE TEACHER

Some artists prefer to begin on toned paper ranging from black to lighter tones. The paper might have *tooth* (texture) or even a light sand finish that holds pastels. Pastels may be used as drawing or painting tools. The difference is that in drawing with pastels, line is allowed to show more often. Dry pastels are pure pigment mixed in a chalk-like binder, compressed into sticks. They come in various degrees of hardness, leaving more or less pigment on textured or sanded paper. Soft pastels contain more pigment and less binder and consequently the colors are more intense. Pastel pencils allow greater detail than sticklike pastels. Pastels of all degrees of hardness are freely combined, with the exception of oil pastels.

I'm Cold
Jennifer Juang, pastel, 28 × 40 inches. Parkway North High School, St. Louis County, Missouri, teacher Grant Kniffen.

Art History

The use of pastels originated in northern Italy in the sixteenth century. During this period, painters blended pastel to resemble oil painting, and at times it was difficult to distinguish the difference. In the late nineteenth century, Edgar Degas (1834–1917) and other French impressionists changed the traditional method of pastel application by emphasizing individual strokes and by placing colors side by side with little or no blending. Degas and his protégé Mary Cassatt (1845–1926) were great masters of pastel. Show students Degas's work to illustrate the many ways pastel may be applied within one work of art. He achieved luminosity in his paintings by working from dark to light and using a variety of strokes.

Other famous painters who used pastel are Paul Klee (1879–1940), Willem de Kooning (1904–1997), Leonardo da Vinci (1452–1590), Jean-François Millet (1814–1875), Joan Miró (1893–1935), Claude Monet (1840–1926), Edvard Munch (1863–1944), Odilon Redon (1840–1916), Henri de Toulouse-Lautrec (1864–1901), and James McNeil Whistler (1834–1903).

Vocabulary: artistic license, double-mat, fixative

FOR THE STUDENT

Historically, portrait artists included clues about what a sitter did for a living. When Rembrandt painted his many self-portraits, he chose to wear a hat or costume from his collection. Children were often shown holding a favorite toy. A woman might be dressed in finery, certainly in her best dress and jewelry, and she might have a dog at her feet to symbolize faithfulness. Sometimes a view out a window in the background might show a church steeple or a boat in a harbor. What clues can you include that describe you? Can you think of a symbol or an item that might represent you at this point in your life?

1. Try to envision what the finished picture will look like. What will go in the background? Might it be a place you love to go to on vacation?

2. You may choose to lightly outline with charcoal because you can use a paper towel to erase as needed.

3. *Artistic license* allows the artist to use colors that appeal and allow the illusion of roundness, shadow, and depth. You may not see yellow or violet or rosy tones in your skin, but sometimes you use those colors simply because they look good.

4. Apply the darkest tones to the darkest areas of your face, neck, and hair before adding midtones for lighter areas. The lightest colors (highlights) are put in last. When you have a pastel in your hand, see where you can apply that color throughout the painting before you set it down.

5. When the pastel painting is finished, you may choose to spray it with fixative for protection. Pastel artists sometimes *double-mat* a painting so it does not touch the glass and damage it.

SOAP RESIST CITYSCAPE MURAL: GROUP PROJECT

Time needed: 3 to 4 fifty-minute classes

Materials: black roofing paper, slivers of soap, white chalk, woodless colored pencils, soft pastel, or oil pastels, paper towels (or black construction paper for the alternative project)

Goal: This artwork might communicate contemporary concerns about the built environment.

Goal: Students work together cooperatively to select subject matter and a method of working that all includes all the students.

Objective: Students blend colors by building up from dark to light, allowing the colors underneath to show through at times.

Old Baltimore
Soap resist and woodless colored pencil on roofing paper, 12 × 18 inches. A drawing was done on black paper using a small soap bar. Areas were filled in with woodless colored pencils, and the paper immersed in warm water to melt the soap.

FOR THE TEACHER

Woodless colored pencils or soft oil pastels may be drawn on pieces of roofing paper (roofing paper is sold by the foot at home improvement stores), and you can cut it into smaller pieces. Each student may use an 11 × 14-inch sheet of roofing paper (get the smoothest available). A sliver of soap (the size provided at hotels) is used to draw all the details on the black paper. After that is done, soft pastel, oil pastel, or woodless colored pencil is used to fill in details, without concern if color covers some of the soap lines. The color on top of lines will vanish when the paper is briefly immersed in a large container of warm water until black lines appear around the colored areas. I used a large grease tray from the automotive department of a hardware store for the warm water. Take the paper out and blot it with paper towels, allowing it to dry completely before going back over it with color to make necessary repairs.

Vocabulary: scale, value, texture, proportion

Preparation

This can be an opportunity to discuss city planning and architecture, historic and vernacular structures, landscaping, preservation, neighborhoods, and the place of people and animals in cities.

Each student can work individually on a desktop, cutting out and later arranging individual artworks for display on a long sheet of roll paper.

FOR THE STUDENT

Consider what your part in a group project might be. You might choose to draw tall buildings or a specific house that you like. Talk with your colleagues about *scale* (the general size of the buildings and their relationship to each other).

1. On a small separate sheet of black paper
   - Practice applying the pastels in short diagonal parallel lines
   - Lift the pastel and make closely spaced parallel lines rather than scribbling randomly
   - Try hatching and crosshatching
   - Experiment with a small patch of the darkest color you have, put a medium color on top, and the lightest color on top of that
   - Use a sharp object to lightly scratch a line though a layer, revealing colors underneath.

2. Make a small sketch of what the entire mural might look like and decide who will work on what portion of it.

3. Use chalk to loosely draw a building before you start to fill it in. You may decide to color solidly, or you can use techniques such as hatching and crosshatching that mostly cover the area, but allow some of the black paper to show through.

4. When the mural is complete, decide as a group whether you want to make cutouts of people, cars, signs, and items that might humanize this mural and make it more appealing.

Alternative Project
Oil Pastels on Black Construction Paper

Oil pastels have a waxy base and resemble crayons, and are sometimes used to embellish paintings in other painting media such as acrylic. They have limited colors, but may be built up from dark to light to achieve rich textures and are especially effective on dark paper. They can be applied thickly to resemble oil paintings and may be dipped in a solvent for paint-like effects (odor-free mineral spirits are now available). The soap-resist project works on good black construction paper, but there may be some bleeding of the paper when it is immersed in warm water.

PROJECT 3-10
THE ART JOURNAL

Time Needed: ongoing

Materials: 6 × 8-inch spiral-bound sketch pad or 8½ × 11-inch hole-punched unlined paper and ½-inch thick three-ring binder, fine-line markers, pencil, colored pencil, glue stick, watercolor pencils, roller ball pen

Content Connection: Literary arts

Objective: Students will maintain an ongoing notebook that contains drawings made over time combined with written observations, notes about the weather, and drawings from observation.

FOR THE TEACHER

You might be establishing a lifelong habit when you introduce students to artistic journaling. It may have little writing in it, or it may be a combination of drawing and writing. Look at journals with the students to help guide them in their approach to drawing. Tell them that if they draw with a roller ball pen, their excuses are premade, and suggest they approach an unplanned line with the credo *Use your mistakes.*

Invite students to look on the Internet at the many different approaches developed by artists to maintaining a sketchbook (type *Famous artists' sketchbooks* into a search engine). Some artists fill every inch with colored pencil, watercolor, or collage. Others do simple sketches in pen or pencil and write descriptions of the place they are, the sounds they hear, the fragrances they smell, and their reactions to everything. The combination of writing and drawing excitingly fills a page.

Content Connection: Literary Arts

Students may develop a journal that reflects sensitivity to the ways literature can be enhanced with art as they recall enjoyment from a favorite children's book. They can write ideas and observations in the same book in which they make sketches of things around them or perhaps try to illustrate a drawing with a poem. Suggest that if they have written something for an English class they can write it in longhand and illustrate it.

Preparation

When all the students have a sketchbook of some kind and a firm surface such as a piece of cardboard or a drawing board, take them outside for a nature walk. They can make a map of the path they took, or you can suggest they draw exactly what they see in six square inches of grass or draw the appearance of bark or a small tree. They might choose to sit silently and listen for a few moments, identifying and writing about the sounds they hear.

FOR THE STUDENT

Before you begin, decide on your personal rules for your own art sketchbook or nature journal. For example, you might decide that you are not going to erase, scribble over, or tear out and wad up a page. It is a waste of time trying for perfection. Instead, go over what you consider to be a mistake with darker color or crosshatching or add color to it or paste a "correction" on top of the error.

1. Record the date and your name somewhere on a corner of the page (not too close to the edge in case you ever become famous and your work has to be framed). You might note the time of day and temperature or even draw the appearance of the clouds that day.

2. You might draw a plant or tree on this page, or perhaps you might draw a friend sitting nearby drawing.

3. Try to draw in your journal every day. It may be something very simple, or you may have entire pages filled with odds and ends such as eyes, or birds, signs, buildings. Record information about birds you see that might help you identify them, such as general size, a forked tail, the shape of the head or beak, or how their wings look in flight.

4. If you draw a weed or flower, take the time to find out its Latin name. When you learn a fact about something you have drawn, write about it on the same page (for example, identify the parts of the eye).

5. Continue to develop some pages. You can go back and doodle on them or write something. Artist Brian Zampier has what he calls a five-year sketchbook. Every year he goes back to the date when he first started a page and adds something to it.

6. When you think your sketchbook is done, it isn't! You can always tweak a page or scan and enter it into a computer and do something more exciting with it. You can add color, surround it with every word to your favorite album, or write the name of some of the eight thousand bird species or hundreds of varieties of purebred dogs.

NATURE JOURNALING WITH CLARE WALKER LESLIE

Time Needed: ongoing

Materials: felt markers, pencil, ball-point pen

Content Connection

Science

FOR THE TEACHER

Clare Walker Leslie, artist and naturalist, has generously provided one of her nature drawings and shared the following techniques for teachers to introduce students to drawing from nature.

This is a sample page I do with students of all ages, and in many varieties of habitats. Indoors, we first write down *Date, Place, Weather, Time,* to place the science of where we are in context. Outdoors, in quiet observation, we note the sky condition and compass direction (wind direction and angle of the sun). We also note the natural (and human) sounds we are hearing, as well as major seasonal colors.

Then, as Nature Detectives, we begin exploring, drawing, and recording what we see in the Place Where We Are. (This is very much in the tradition of the early explorers as well as scientists today—an important topic to discuss with students.) While I am an experienced artist and naturalist, it is important that I draw simply with the students so that they can see how I might draw a spider or bird or deer track. Curiosity motivates our observations. Teachers also must participate as models for students' learning. We are drawing standing up, moving about, with pencils, ball-point pens, or felt-tipped pens. (Students can use a range of types of paper. Often, it is 8 × 11 computer paper clipped to a firm backing, which can then be transferred into a Science Notebook, redrawn indoors, or put into folders for additional Outdoor Journal opportunities.)

I often will use a larger marking pen—and the same form of paper—so all students can easily see my drawings, crude as they may be—but accurate!

We are careful to note size and color when we can. *Students need to understand that this is not drawing as art alone, but drawing as observation and science.* (Further discussion can be continued indoors about scientific illustration, showing how drawing is used in the study of science through the early illustrated journals of such explorers as Lewis and Clark, the scientific studies of Leonardo da Vinci, and the like.)

Usually, we have just one hour in students' busy class day. But it always encourages me that, given just this short time of observation outdoors, students everywhere are amazed

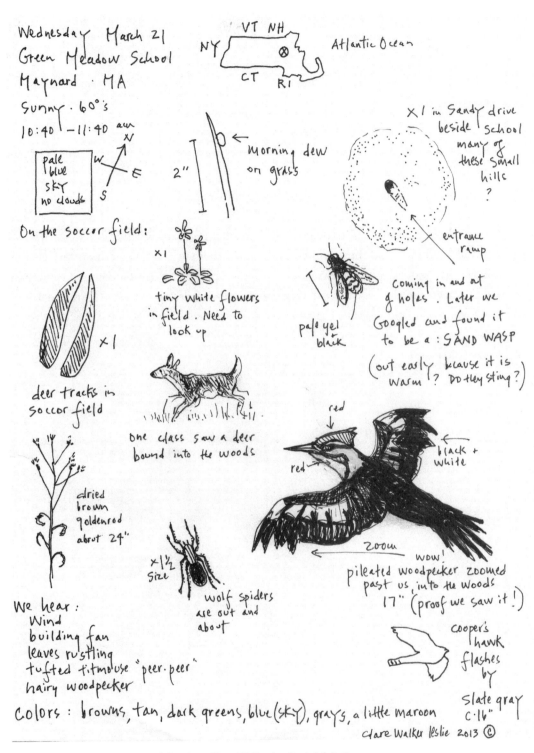

Wednesday March 21
Green Meadow School
Maynard · MA
Sunny · 60°'s
10:40 — 11:40 am

VT NH
NY
CT RI
Atlantic Ocean
⊗

pale
blue
SKY
no clouds

N
W E
S

2"

Morning dew
on grass

X1 in Sandy drive
beside school
many of
these small
hills
?

entrance
ramp

coming in and out
of holes. Later we
Googled and found it
to be a: SAND WASP

(out early because it is
warm? Do they sting?)

On the soccer field:

X1

tiny white flowers
in field. Need to
look up

pale yel
+ black

X1

deer tracks in
soccer field

One class saw a deer
bound into the woods

dried
brown
goldenrod
about 24"

X1½
size

wolf spiders
are out and
about

red

red

black +
white

zoom

wow!
pileated woodpecker zoomed
past us into the woods
17" (proof we saw it!)

cooper's
hawk
flashes
by
slate gray
c·16"

We hear:
Wind
building fan
leaves rustling
tufted titmouse "peer·peer"
hairy woodpecker

Colors: browns, tan, dark greens, blue (sky), grays, a little maroon

Clare Walker Leslie 2013 ©

Outdoor journal observational drawing, Clare Walker Leslie, ink felt-tip pen.

by how much nature does exist just outside their classroom door. My intention as a visiting educator is to show them that

1. Anyone can do this.
2. It's great fun.
3. Curiosity is the basis for learning.
4. Further drawing and nature study skills can be developed with longer time segments and field guides for resources.
5. Nature can be found everywhere, in any season and habitat.

As a teacher and mentor with over forty years of experience in this field, it is critical for me to model students in all these habits and to show them my own excitement for learning.

For further information, please refer to www.clarewalkerleslie.com and the book *Keeping a Nature Journal: Discover a Whole New Way of Seeing the World Around You*, by Clare Walker Leslie and Charles E. Roth.

—Clare Walker Leslie

PROJECT 3-12
HUNDRED NEEDIEST CASES

Time Needed: 10 days of 50-minute class periods

Materials: drawing pencils (available in 4B, 3B, 2B, B, HB, F, H, 2H, 3H, 4H, 5H, and 6H), drawing paper, ink, brushes, charcoal

Objective: Students will apply design elements and principles and sensitivity in a drawing that illustrates the plight of individuals in times of stress and joblessness and the human condition.

Hundred Neediest Cases
Logan Mueller, pen and ink, 9 × 12 inches. This entry in the *St. Louis Post Dispatch* annual high school competition conveys despair. DeSmet High School, St. Louis County, Missouri, teacher Laurie Kohler.

Hundred Neediest Cases
Mason Bracken, pen and ink, 9 × 12 inches. DeSmet High School, St. Louis County, Missouri, teacher Laurie Kohler.

FOR THE TEACHER

An invitation to St. Louis area high school students to enter drawings or paintings that depict a needy person or family has been issued each year since 1954 by the *St. Louis Post Dispatch* in cooperation with the United Way. Articles about those in financial need and area high school art students' illustrations for *One Hundred Neediest Cases* are run frequently in November and December, with the resulting financial contributions helping hundreds of families each year. The student's name and school are always published, and generous art supply gift certificates from a local art supply store are awarded to the top winners of the competition.

Although your students may not have an opportunity such as the one just described for actual publication, you can still assign them to create an illustration that communicates desperation, sadness, hopelessness, sorrow, homelessness, illness, or the loneliness of old age—emotions that one hopes are the opposite of what most young people experience.

The drawings that are featured in the *St. Louis Post Dispatch* communicate these feelings, even though they are staged, and are drawn from a model who was a fellow student, teacher, grandparent, baby sister, or friend.

Art History Connection

The black-and-white drawings, prints, and sculptures of German artist Käthe Kollwitz (1867–1945) portrayed laborers, women and children, peasants, and poor people she saw in the neighborhood where her husband practiced medicine. She found middle-class people "without appeal or interest." She also did many self-portraits throughout her life.

Through examining Kollwitz's work in a book or on the Internet, students may learn how to depict sadness and compassion. She did a series of "death" paintings, and having lost a son in World War I, was strongly antiwar. By the time she was in her fifties, the Nazis were considering sending her and her husband to a camp for her "degenerate art," but she had become too well known as an artist for them to risk such an unpopular action.

FOR THE STUDENT

For this project you are asked to do a black-and-white portrait of a "needy person" or family as if it might be used to illustrate a story for the United Way's annual fund appeal. Although your drawing may not actually be printed in a newspaper, it might be used in a school literary magazine or all-school display. Perhaps you need to look around your family or among your friends for someone who is willing to pose for a drawing or at least for a photograph.

You may draw from photos that you or a family member took, but never use one that has been published! You may have taken or seen a photo of a homeless person with belongings in a cart or someone who lives in a park that gives you an idea for a drawing, but these printed resources may not be used directly. Be aware that you *might* need written permission from anyone whose portrait will be used for actual publication.

1. Look at drawings by Käthe Kollwitz and notice that in addition to the somberness of her subjects, she fills the space almost completely.

2. Because she began drawing only in black and white when she was in her teens, Kollwitz was keenly aware of *value* in her drawings. You might have as many as ten different values, some achieved by using one pencil and increasing pressure. You will find that using several differently numbered pencils will allow you greater range.

3. Remember that the whitest white you can get is the drawing paper. Leaving portions of it showing is standard practice. You may choose to fully develop a portion of the portrait, while leaving other portions apparently unfinished.

4. If you work in ink, a variety of line styles can be used, though in this case it is more effective to use the same kind of line throughout the drawing. One student illustration shown here uses scribble lines, and another uses short, straight lines. Other students in the same class used *pointillism* (dots) to build up values.

Painting

Introductory exercises in different media may help students later select one medium that they particularly love. Or they may enjoy combining media once they understand the essentials.

Tempera

Most students are familiar with tempera by the time they enter secondary schools. It is relatively inexpensive, water-soluble, and available in liquid or cake form. It is ideal for helping students understand color mixing by combining complementary and analogous colors on the color wheel or creating values and tones. It may be used as a wash by diluting with water, but it resembles oil paint when applied without diluting. Mistakes can be covered because of its opacity, though it cracks if applied too thickly. A luster can be added by mixing in a little polymer medium, and an entire painting can be enhanced (when dry) by "varnishing" with polymer medium.

Acrylic

Acrylic paint is relatively new to the market (only sixty-five-plus years old), having been popularized in the 1950s. It gives much the same effect as oil paint and has advantages and disadvantages. It is water-soluble, so cleanup is easier than solvent-based pigments. Unlike oil paint, it does not crack or change color. It comes in tube or liquid form in bright, premixed colors. It can be used for an

Claire Staring out the Window
Amy Dai, acrylic, 20 × 16 inches. Ladue Horton Watkins High School, St. Louis, Missouri, teacher Daniel Raedeke.

Illumination
Erin Cox, acrylic, 16 × 20 inches. Parkway South High School, St. Louis County, Missouri, teacher Carrie Finnestead.

undercoat to be painted over later with oil paints. It adheres to surfaces such as wood or glass. Some artists use diluted acrylic as if it were watercolor, building up thin layers of transparent color.

Beginners are advised to put out small amounts of color as needed. There are "retardants" available to slow the drying. Many different additives such as gel medium, sand, stucco, glass beads, and fibers may be added to give textural interest to the surface.

Artists are warned to keep brushes in water until needed, as the paint dries quickly and can ruin a brush. When a brush isn't being used, it should be in water. There are many solutions for cleaning dried brushes such as Dow Bathroom Cleaner, acetone (nail polish remover), hand sanitizer or alcohol for soaking, or acrylic paint brush cleaners. It is far simpler to keep them in water until you have a chance to clean them with soap and water.

Oils

Oil paintings from the fourteenth century retain their beauty today, though at times they have needed conservation. Fortunately, artists such as Jan Vermeer (1632–1675), Rembrandt van Rijn (1606–1669), Jan van Eyck (1390–1441), and Leonardo da Vinci (1452–1519) understood their craft and passed down their discoveries through the centuries. Paintings on wood panels have endured well, and paintings on prepared canvas almost as well. They understood that oils are applied from *lean* to *fat* (lean: thinned with mineral spirits or Turpenoid; fat: either straight out of the tube or mixed with an additive such as linseed oil or painting medium to provide greater flexibility and to retard drying). If a thin (lean) layer is put on top of a thick (fat) layer, the top layer dries too quickly and cracks develop over time. One reason van Gogh's work has endured so well is that he worked *alla prima* (all at once), rarely working on a painting more than a day or two.

Oil paint dries slowly, allowing the artist to blend, remove (with a paper towel dipped in solvent), or paint over mistakes. Rich colors can be developed by glazing, a process that allows the underpainting to show through. Textures develop naturally as oil paint builds up. Some artists prefer to use a painting medium that makes blending easier; others prefer to work straight from the tube. Brushes must be cleaned with solvent, soap, and water.

Ponder the Future
Sean Badock, oil, 11 × 14 inches. DeSmet High School, St. Louis County, Missouri, teacher Laurie Kohler.

Water-Based Oil Paint

This new development in paints is applied in the same manner as traditional oil paints, except that the artist will thin the paint with water rather than solvent. In my experience, it dries more slowly than regular oil paints. Brushes are easily cleaned with soap and water.

Pastel

Pastels are considered drawing or painting mediums. A pastel painting may have a combination of drawing *and* underpainting (in watercolor). Some areas are carefully finished (such as a face in a portrait), and other areas deliberately sketchy. Much of the charm of some pastels is their casual, unfinished quality.

Pastel pigment is combined with a binder and compressed into sticks with varying degrees of hardness. Softer pastels leave more of the pigment on the paper. Included in the *dry pastel* family are Conté crayon, chalk, and charcoal. Pan pastels are relatively new on the market and are applied with soft, spongelike applicators. Pastels may be used for emphasizing detail in a watercolor underpainting.

Pastel artists generally put dark masses in first, working from dark to light. Some artists apply spray fixative between layers or on the finished painting, but others prefer not to. Paintings are normally double-matted before putting them under glass, as the painting surface is fragile and should not touch the glass.

Oil Pastel

Oil pastels have a waxy base and resemble ordinary crayons, but do not require the pressure that crayons need to yield rich, vibrant colors. Sets come with limited colors, but may be built up from dark to light to achieve color variations and rich textures. They are especially effective on dark paper. They are sometimes used to embellish paintings created in acrylic paint or similar media. They may be dipped in a solvent such as odorless mineral spirits or Turpenoid to give intense color.

Watercolor

Watercolors in cake form such as Prang or Crayola are most commonly used in secondary schools, though most professionals prefer to use watercolor bought in tubes. Because an effect made with watercolor is difficult to change, artists often draw lightly in pencil and *plan* before applying paint. Discuss a few watercolor basics, giving students an opportunity to experiment with a variety of watercolor techniques, before giving them a painting assignment.

There is no white in transparent watercolor, so white areas must be planned for by leaving areas unpainted or by applying a watercolor resist (frisket). If an area has been painted too darkly, it can quickly be diluted with water and blotted. It is much easier to paint by working from light to dark, building up color. To prevent paint from soaking unevenly into the paper, inexpensive paper should never be erased. An investment in watercolor paper will give students better results. Remind students to look for the unexpected "happy accident," the bit of luck when water puddles and dries unevenly or runs to make something beautiful.

Demonstrate how to mix colors in the lid of the paint box and test colors on a piece of paper before applying to the actual painting. Each workspace should have two containers, one for clean water and one for dirty. Encourage good work habits by asking students to check that individual color pans in the box of watercolors are not dirty and the lid of the box is clean and dry before closing.

Gouache

This water-based pigment, to which white has been added to increase opacity, has long been the choice of graphic designers for their illustrations. It is sometimes used in combination with transparent watercolor. Although it is normally sold in tubes, opaque watercolors, similar to gouache, are now available in pan sets.

Ink

Long favored by Asian painters, black or colored inks are used for sumi-e painting.

Spray Paint

Spray paint has become a major art tool in recent years and for some young artists is the medium of choice. One local art supply store owner says it is their hottest item at the moment. Some "street artists" are also serious studio painters and may be found in cultures all over the world. Some graffiti artwork is actually done on commission, and work by street artists Keith Haring (1958–1990) and Jean-Michel Basquiat (1960–1988) is avidly collected. Shepard Fairey (1970–), a "street artist" for twenty years, is now a mainstream artist with the *Hope* poster he created of President Barack Obama.

Target with Four Faces
Jasper Johns (1930–), 1955. Encaustic on newspaper and cloth over canvas surmounted by four tinted-plaster faces in wood box with hinged front. Overall, with box open, 33 ⅝ × 26 × 3 inches; canvas 26 × 26 inches; box (closed) 3¾ × 26 × 3 ½ inches. Gift of Mr. and Mrs. Robert C. Scull. © The Museum of Modern Art/VAGA, NY.

Encaustic

Although not a new medium (the ancient Greeks and Egyptians used it), molten beeswax mixed with colored pigments gives an entirely different surface effect and richness to painting. Although specialized materials such as solvent-free paints may be purchased through art suppliers, many supplies may already be in the average classroom, ready to be adapted for use in encaustic paintings.

Fresco

The technique of painting fresco murals dates back at least three thousand years. It is the method of painting into freshly laid plaster used in Michelangelo's *Sistine Chapel*, Pompeiian interiors, Mexican murals, Ajanta caves in India, and Marc Chagall's chapel paintings in Nice, France, done in the twentieth century. This method can be adapted to art classes by using premixed spackling compound spread onto a hard surface. Tempera paint works well and gives traditional colors found in fresco paintings. Project 4-1 uses this technique as an alternative project.

PROJECT 4-1
BOWL OF EGGS

Time needed: 2 to 3 fifty-minute classes

Materials: boiled eggs in white bowl, white tablecloth, tempera or acrylic paint, spotlights, palettes (Styrofoam egg carton palettes or magazine pages), watercolor brushes (#11, #7, and #2), 12 × 18-inch white drawing paper, permanent black marker, polymer medium

Goal: Students select and apply elements and principles of art with sensitivity and subtlety, using value differences and shapes, soft edges, and hard edges.

Objective: Students use paint expressively, focusing on dominance and subordination and mixing colors to make a unique interpretation.

FOR THE TEACHER

The still life is found in most periods of art. This is an excellent opportunity to discuss the fascination that Dutch baroque painters had with the "breakfast piece," a painting of a beautifully set table with glassware and silver that appeared to picture an interrupted meal, with broken bread, crumbs on the table, a partially peeled lemon, scattered nuts, and perhaps a butterfly or tiny mouse on the table, eating the leftovers. These "vanitas" paintings symbolized how fleeting life is. Genre paintings of this time period were filled with symbolism that most people of the time understood clearly.

A brief conversation about personal symbols meaningful to this generation of students may be a bit off the track for this project, but perhaps useful in future discussions about subject matter.

Vocabulary: still life, artistic license, analogous, values, complementary color, Dutch "vanitas" paintings, high key, highlights, reflection

Preparation

This introductory project reintroduces many principles of painting that will be of later use, such as mixing and blending colors, selecting appropriate brushes, and care of materials. A disposable "palette" such as two pages from a slick magazine or finger paint paper eliminates daily cleanup. Students use less paint this way and throw away the palette at the end of the hour. Colors are placed around the outside perimeter and are mixed in the center of the palette. This introduces students to the concept of keeping the hue pure, but mixing it with other colors in a different place, just as they will do when working with acrylic or oil paint. Or students can use Styrofoam egg cartons, mixing colors in the lid, and closing the carton overnight. Have students identify their own cartons with permanent marker. Some teachers find it easier to assign brushes to each student at the start of the semester, making them responsible for returning them in perfect condition at the end of the course. Whatever your system, no teacher should end up at the end of a period of painting with a sink full of dirty palettes and brushes.

Set up the still life, lighting it carefully and making sure everyone has a good view from which they will work until the painting is completed. Discuss the fact that when there is no color, it is obvious that some areas are lighter than others. These *highlights* would be left entirely unpainted in watercolor, but here will be painted with undiluted white tempera. To create contrast, students will have to learn to squint to discern differences in value, find the darkest areas in the painting, and paint these as shapes. Suggest to them that there are as many as ten different values in these white eggs.

Alternative Project
Monochromatic Painting

This type of painting can be done with a bowl of lemons on a yellow ground. Look at the way the Dutch Masters painted lemons by peeling one back slightly to reveal the inside of the peel. Green or red peppers, eggplant, cabbage, or other fruits and vegetables are also effective.

Alternative Project
Beans

Art teacher Sue Trent, when at Parkway West High School, St. Louis, Missouri, offered each student a handful of mixed dry beans for an introductory painting subject. The painting can be small or large, but it challenges students to mix paints to match what they see.

Alternative Project
Baroque Still Life

Each student can bring food items and utensils for a gigantic baroque still life. Loaves of uncut bread, grapes, cheese, and fruit can make an interesting painting.

Alternative Project
Abstraction

The bowl of eggs may still look like a bowl of eggs, if a student chooses not to use only realistic color. After all, a pink elephant still looks like an elephant. An abstraction might show the intersections between the eggs, with each egg a different color.

Still Life
Pieter Claesz, Dutch (ca. 1597–1661), 1638, oil on wood panel, 25 ¼ × 20 3/16 inches. The Nelson-Atkins Museum of Art, Kansas City, Missouri. Purchase: William Rockhill Nelson Trust, 31-114. Photo: Jamison Miller.

Alternative Project

Tempera Fresco

Mexican muralists Diego Rivera (1886–1957), Jose Clemente Orozco (1883–1949), and David Siqueiros (1896–1974) created wonderful, vibrant murals in Mexican government buildings and elsewhere. Although they probably used ground pigments for their medium, tempera is an acceptable, inexpensive substitute.

Select a nonflexible surface such as Masonite, medium-density fiberboard (MDF), plywood, or canvas board and apply premixed spackling or joint compound purchased from a hardware store (especially nice when you use a broad applicator such as those used by plasterers).

Before beginning, students should have made a *cartoon* (kraft paper outline drawing) and used a pin or dressmaker's tracing wheel to make closely spaced holes on the outline. When this is placed on the damp plaster and soft charcoal is used to lightly draw on the paper following the outline, the charcoal goes through the openings to give a guide for painting. I devised a "pounce," as used by the old masters, by taking an 8-inch square of cloth and centering several small charcoal pieces, pulverizing them by hammering. A rubber band pulls it all together to make a traditional "pounce." Paints should be prepared while the plaster is drying slightly (damp to the touch, but does not stick to a hand placed on it). If the plaster dries because you do not have enough time to finish painting the buon (good) fresco (fresh) in one day, it can be finished the next day as fresco secco (dry).

 FOR THE STUDENT

A white bowl of eggs on a white surface has no color. If the background is also white, you will have to use *artistic license* to make an interesting painting, inventing color where there is none.

1. Your bowl of eggs composition can fill the entire page, spilling off the edges or showing only a portion of it. True size is unimportant. Lightly sketch the still life first with pencil.

2. This is an exercise in working with a limited palette of colors. Decide whether you want to have a warm palette or a cool palette and select analogous colors in the range.

3. To "gray" or darken colors, mix your chosen color with a touch of complementary color and lighten it by adding white. Darkening by adding black tends to deaden colors.

4. Squint through almost closed eyes to discern differences in value (dark areas between the eggs, under the bowl, and in the folds of the cloth). Paint those shapes in the darkest value. If you paint the *negative* shapes first—the shadows—the outline of the eggs will quickly emerge. *Paint what you see, not what you know!*

5. Work over the entire picture plane as you go. Don't attempt to complete one egg before starting on the next one; while your paintbrush is loaded with a certain color, paint it wherever you see exactly the same value on the still life. Tempera paint dries and cracks if it is built up thickly, so plan ahead before you apply paint.

6. It may be necessary to *invent* a background. A subject such as a bowl of eggs can't just float in the middle of a picture, but needs to rest on something with some interesting detail in the background. Sometimes you may *break up* the background by drawing a line or two and painting different colors where there is a division or making a subtle pattern in a plain background.

7. You have been *graying* colors by mixing small amounts of a complementary color as you paint. It may enhance the painting to add a small amount of pure (bright) hue somewhere in the painting.

8. When the painting is complete, it can be "varnished" with polymer medium or laminated to protect the surface.

ACRYLIC SELF-PORTRAIT

Time needed: 3 to 5 fifty-minute classes

Materials: acrylic paint, pencil, paper, charcoal, fixative, photograph or mirror, canvas or hardboard panels cut to size, acrylic gesso, brushes, disposable palettes, or heavy clear plastic palettes

Content Connection: History or social studies

Goal: Students analyze influences of culture, time, available materials, and location in portraiture.

Goal: Students demonstrate knowledge of color mixing and use of a variety of brush sizes.

Objective: Students engage in experimentation and risk taking to produce an imaginative self-portrait.

FOR THE TEACHER

Artists have always painted self-portraits. Where else will they find a model who is always available or has more patience? Although working from a photograph might be easiest, using photos is a crutch and can become a hard habit for a student to break.

Introduce students to self-portraits by famous artists such as Rembrandt van Rijn (1606–1669), Chuck Close (1940–), John Kane (1860–1934), Pablo Picasso (1881–1973), Paul Gauguin (1848–1903), Judith Leyster (1609–1660), Max Beckmann (1884–1950), Horace Pippin (1888–1946), and Frida Kahlo (1907–1954).

Vocabulary: likeness, contrast, asymmetrical, negative shape, value, artistic style, surrealism, heritage

Preparation

Because this project is especially meaningful to students, it is important that they carefully plan ahead. Brainstorming about what will be in the background is crucial. It is a good idea to have most of the students in the class do paintings of approximately the same size so that they can all move on to the next project at the same time.

Content Connection: History or Social Studies

Suggest that students envision themselves in a painting of an historic figure, wearing the same clothing and in the same type of background.

Alternative Project
Artistic Style

Students might admire the style of a particular artist or time period such as impressionism, expressionism, or the baroque and paint themselves in the costume and attitude of a specific portrait.

Here's Looking at You
Mary Cate O'Brien, 24 × 36 inches. This large acrylic self-portrait shows the artist as a queen. She used doilies as stencils to make the elaborate collar and cuffs. St. Joseph's Academy, St. Louis County, Missouri, teacher Delphine Williams.

Max Abernathy
Taylor Abernathy, acrylic, 30 × 37 inches. This painting pays tribute to Max Beckmann. Parkway North High School, St. Louis County, Missouri, teacher Grant Kniffen.

Alternative Project
Surrealistic Self-Portrait

A surrealistic (above reality) type painting allows students to imagine a background completely unrelated to anything familiar.

Alternative Project
Family Heritage Self-Portrait

This acrylic, mixed-media portrait may be based on a student's heritage, including clues for the viewer such as a costume. Photocopies of old photos, handwritten names, maps, or symbols that represent family ancestry can be transferred to a hard canvas or MDF background by applying art teacher Marilyn Palmer's method, as follows: coat the front of the photocopy (color or black and white) and canvas board with polymer medium, allowing both to dry overnight. The copy paper photo is coated again with polymer medium. While it is wet, place it on the prepared hard canvas or board. Squeegee with a plastic credit card to be sure the paper adheres to the canvas perfectly and there are no bubbles. Allow the canvas and photo to dry overnight. Soak the copy paper with dampened paper towels and rub off the paper backing with a

Escape
Kelly Gruber, graphite and acrylic, 36 × 48 inches. Kelly's self-portrait illustrates her hair flying around her in space. Parkway North High School, St. Louis County, Missouri, teacher Grant Kniffen.

finger, allowing the color photo to adhere to the canvas. Acrylic paint can be used to blend the edges of the photo into the background.

FOR THE STUDENT

This project is going to take time, so plan ahead to make it extra special. Artists who paint their own portraits work by looking in a mirror. You may find it worthwhile to make sketches at home, where you have time to consider your pose.

1. Make several list headings, then write about yourself: your interests, possible careers you envision, information and symbols about your family's history, a surrealistic (beyond reality) dream, or yourself as a famous figure from history.

2. Make several thumbnail sketches in pencil on paper, not concerning yourself about a likeness in this preliminary drawing, but considering what will go in the background.

3. When that decision is made, use charcoal to draw it onto the large board you have selected. Use fixative to keep the charcoal from smearing.

4. When painting with acrylic, remember that it dries quickly. Put out the colors when you need them. If you need a large amount for a background, mix what you need, as it is always difficult to match it exactly. Keep a small amount of a mixed color in a plastic container for touch-up. Keep brushes in water unless they are in actual use and wipe with a paper towel before you paint again.

5. The wonderful advantage to acrylic is that you can cover what has been painted earlier, building up texture.

6. Remember to look at the painting from a distance occasionally to see if you have used lights and darks to make it interesting.

7. When finished, try to frame this painting appropriately, as it is one painting you are likely to keep.

PROJECT 4-3
PAINT TO THE MUSIC

Time needed: 1 to 2 fifty-minute classes

Materials: 12 × 18-inch drawing paper, mixed media, pencil, scratch paper, acrylic, tempera, ink, collage materials

Content connections: Music and literary arts

Goal: Students apply what they have learned about painting to respond to background music as they paint.

Goal: After painting, students should be able to connect painting terms to the musical vocabulary: color, rhythm, pattern, line, and repetition.

Objectives: Students complete a work of art that may or may not be realistic, but that spontaneously demonstrates a reaction to the music. They are able to write a descriptive paragraph or participate in a class discussion about their response to the music.

FOR THE TEACHER

After students have painted something that requires control, such as a self-portrait, a change of pace is welcome. Enhance your studio atmosphere with live or recorded music once in a while. Your school music teacher might allow a few students to bring their instruments and play for your class.

The St. Louis Symphony sponsors a program each year in which students "Picture the Music." Many of the pictures are abstract, but others are quite realistic, depending on images that come to students' minds as they listen. Allow students to suggest what they would like to hear, or select something yourself.

Musical instruments might be part of the composition, or students can visualize a performance they might have attended, trying to interpret the lights, costumes, and general atmosphere.

Author's note: Recently I was invited to arrange for a group of artists to Paint to the Music of a commissioned musical composition for the annual Missouri Chamber Music Festival (*Glisten* by Lansing McLoskey). The composer had written the music while looking at a painting and felt this composition should not be performed unless someone was painting. Twelve artists painted for the duration of the piece (eighteen minutes) at a rehearsal, and all had our artworks on exhibition at the final performance. We started with clean canvases, and paint *out and ready* when the music began, and we stopped the instant the music stopped. It is an exhilarating experience, and I think you will find your students love it.

Art History Connection

Artist Georgia O'Keeffe (1887–1986) was passing by a classroom and heard music, and looked in to see students painting. She decided to try it herself and loved the freedom it gave. She became interested in the idea of *synesthesia* in art—hearing images and seeing

Music, Pink and Blue No. 2
Georgia O'Keeffe, 1918, oil on canvas, 35 × 29 ⅛ inches. Whitney Museum of American Art, New York; gift of Emily Fisher Landau in honor of Tom Armstrong. © 2009 Georgia O'Keeffe Museum/ Artists Rights Society (ARS), New York.

sounds, trying to find relationships between music and art. Her paintings *Music, Pink and Blue No. 2,* 1918, at the Whitney Museum of Art, New York, and *Blue and Green Music,* 1919, at the Art Institute of Chicago, demonstrate her fascination.

Recent interest in art-music relationships have spawned "band art" fundraisers. Artists paint to the music in public, selling the results to attendees.

Content Connection: Music

Perhaps a small group from your school might be invited to play music in the art room as your students paint, or you could paint in the commons during an art show, with music in the background for all students to enjoy.

Content Connection: Literary Arts

The St. Louis Symphony Volunteer Association also sponsors an Express the Music competition for middle and secondary school students who write poetry or essays after listening to a classical music selection. This is so popular as a creative writing motivation that each teacher may send only a few entries, each entry to be read by four separate volunteers to determine finalists for judging by professionals. Some students also illustrate their entries.

FOR THE STUDENT

1. Before you begin, close your eyes and listen. Think of rhythmic lines or shapes you might make that would reflect the rhythm you hear. It might be the staccato beat of percussion instruments or the gentle rolling rhythm of violins or guitars. Some music inspires strident color contrasts or violent, quick movement.

2. Make some quick thumbnail sketches as you listen. You may find that combining more than one of your ideas will give an exciting subject and background.

3. You may find that one musical instrument dominates your mind as you listen to music. You may draw the musician, instrument, sound, strings, or combinations of

these that "interpret" that one single idea.

4. Give thought to the colors you *hear*, considering a color scheme that might unify the composition such as cool, warm, or neutral.

5. You may work in one medium such as tempera, acrylic, or watercolor paint, or a combination, such as crayon-watercolor resist. A photocopy of a musical score could be torn and applied with polymer medium, then mostly obscured with paint.

6. Tape your paper to the drawing board with masking tape. Use your paper horizontally or vertically; either way is fine, and some ideas naturally dictate the orientation you will use.

Show Time
Anthony Randle, foil, paint, cardboard, and glue. This artwork, though not a painting, was inspired by music, and music as subject is always a good motivation. Central Visual and Performing Arts School, St. Louis, Missouri, teacher Alan Kmetz.

7. Because this is not an artwork that will take days to do, just get started once the idea is in your mind. A few light pencil strokes on the large paper will get you under way.

8. When a painting such as this has dried, oil pastel can be used to outline or write words that will give emphasis to some of the shapes and add a bit of emphasis.

THE GREAT OUTDOORS: PLEIN AIR PAINTING

Time needed: 3 to 4 fifty-minute classes

Materials: disposable palette, vine charcoal, oil or acrylic paint, brushes, solvent (mineral spirits for oil paint, water for acrylic or watercolor), medium-density fiberboard (MDF) or Masonite, gesso, grey or black viewfinders, paper towels

Goal: Students relate their own experience to that of other artists in the long tradition of plein air painting.

Goal: Students make and discuss changes they made in their own work after they have created the preliminary composition.

Objective: Students mix and use paint expressively, organizing the composition by applying knowledge of mixing paint to achieve atmospheric differences due to distance.

Olive Orchard
Vincent van Gogh, Dutch (1853–1890), 1889, oil on canvas, 28¾ × 36¼ inches. The Nelson-Atkins
Museum of Art, Kansas City, Missouri. Purchase: William Rockhill Nelson Trust, 32-2. Photo: Jamison Miller.

FOR THE TEACHER

Plein air painting (which means in the open air in French: pronounced *plinn air*) is enjoying new popularity as people who love to paint outdoors leave their studios to get together for community-sponsored paint-outs of regional landscapes. Although outdoor painting may not be quite as easy as remaining in the classroom, it is worth the effort to introduce students to the joy of painting nature from observation. After painting, students will enjoy relating their experience with some of the same problems that impressionists, Hudson River School painters, and contemporary painters faced: moving sun, heat, cold, rain, bugs, wind, or paint drying too fast.

Historical Background

The Barbizon School, French impressionists, and the Hudson River School were composed of groups of artists who painted together. The introduction of special easels and oil paint in tubes (which freed artists from mixing paints by hand in the studio) facilitated painting outside the studio. Artists today have access to a variety of media.

Vocabulary: horizon line, plein air, perspective, aerial perspective, reflection, highlight, artistic license

Preparation

Show examples of the work of various landscape painters, such as Claude Monet (1840–1926), Camille Pissarro (1830–1903), John Constable (1776–1837), Berthe Morisot (1841–1895), Paul Cezanne (1839–1906), Paul Gauguin (1848–1903), Winslow Homer (1836–1910), Childe Hassam (1859–1935), and Joaquin Sorolla (1863–1923). It is interesting that even though these artists painted in the company of friends, each person developed a unique way of seeing colors and depicting the same general scene. As students look at artwork, have them particularly observe differences in value, differences in sky, and water or land color at the horizon line.

Make viewfinders by having students cut a rectangle in gray or black paper in proportion to their painting surface (leaving a two-inch border). An empty slide mount also works. Adjustable viewfinders may be purchased, but are a bit expensive for schoolwork. I have always used a camera as a viewfinder for composing a painting. Suggest students use the viewfinder to isolate a portion of landscape, holding it at arm's length, moving it up and down to decide where they want the horizon to be. Teach them how to place a thumb on the handle of a brush to compare height and width and turn it to determine the angle of an object for transfer to their "canvas." Theoretically, a plein air painting is done in a few hours of the same day, as van Gogh did. Yours will be an ongoing project, but you will spend only a few days on it.

Alternative Project
Pastel Plein Air Landscape

Pastels are good for an introductory project to landscape painting because they do not require brushes, water, solvents, and drying time between layers. Some artists prefer to do a watercolor painting underneath, finishing with pastel. Students can lightly draw with charcoal before beginning their pastel *painting*. Remind students to work from dark to light.

 FOR THE STUDENT

Artist Ken Martin says, "A landscape painting is three things: sky, ground, and what is in between." Plein air painting is fun once you have selected the "in-between" (the focal point).

Use a viewfinder to isolate an area to paint, composing it just as you would compose a photo when taking a picture. You will want some special feature, a "center of interest," which might be a tree or large rock, small shed or corner of a building, a road going off in the distance, a reflection, or a fellow artist seated nearby.

1. In general, consider your canvas divided in a ticktacktoe grid with nine divisions (the rule of thirds). Your composition might be more interesting if the horizon line is on the upper or lower third, not in the middle. A focal point might be best on one of the vertical lines, rather than centered.

2. *Under the paint:* for acrylic or oil painting, lightly draw on the canvas with vine charcoal, then either spray it with fixative or lightly wipe it away with a paper towel. For watercolor, lightly draw shapes with pencil. These will be your guides.

3. Decide how high to make the horizon line, and begin with the sky, so if you later want to paint trees, the sky will have dried, and you don't have to concern yourself with painting "sky holes" on a tree later. Notice as you paint the sky that it is usually lighter at the horizon line unless there is an incoming storm. The lack of sharpness and lighter colors at distances are known as aerial perspective.

4. When painting water, notice that it is darker than the sky, but in the same general tone. The reflections that you show make it actually look like water. Naturally, the reflections are constantly changing, and you will make a decision as to a "moment in time" and stick to it.

5. The wonderful thing about being an artist is your ability to make the rules as to what you put in or omit. It is known as "artistic license."

6. From time to time, stand well back from your work to see if it "carries" well. It is helpful to see if you have enough differences in value to make your painting exciting and keep everything from running together visually. Some artists even keep handy a piece of red plastic through which they can view the painting to discern value differences.

PUBLIC ART: THE WALL MURAL

Time needed: 2 weeks or more of fifty-minute classes, depending on the number of participants

Materials: pencils, paper, acetate transparency, permanent fine-line black ink marker, primer, flat finish acrylic paint (by the gallon), small containers into which paint may be poured, large and small brushes, masking tape, ladder, newspaper, drop cloth, overhead projectors or computer projection system

Goal: Students work collaboratively to develop a concept for a mural to be developed and painted as a class.

Objective: Before beginning the design, a group discussion yields details about which symbols, subject matter, and theme are appropriate for the location and will communicate the mural's meaning and purpose.

Objective: Students complete a mural by cooperatively working to apply the design, color, and finish to a mural.

FOR THE TEACHER

Your job as teacher is to find a blank wall and locate someone to pay for the paint and supplies. You may choose to paint a mural for your school or consider contacting your state or local government to see if they have received a "percent for art" donation from a new business in your community. I have read "calls for art" from regional and state departments of transportation (requests for artists to submit designs to decorate inside a building or public area). Although your students are not yet the professionals these agencies are hoping will apply, high school students *do* have the ability to design and paint artwork of this type.

Work with students as they brainstorm ideas. It may be that much of the painting will have to be done after school, possibly in the evening or on weekends. Much of your work will be done before the painting begins. The location will probably help determine the design of the mural—a senior locker bay might feature senior students and a science department might portray famous scientists or scientific instruments. You, the art teacher, may guide decisions about colors and styles. Encourage student research online and in the library, and encourage every student to come up with a suggestion. The final design might be a combination of many styles, ranging from a spray-painted background to stenciled lettering and outline drawing.

Vocabulary: scale, proportion, muralist, graffitist

Art History

Traces of ancient murals have been found on sheltered rocks and in caves around the world, in Egyptian tombs, and in ancient homes in Pompeii. Many churches and governmental buildings take great pride in their murals. Today's graffiti artists paint "murals" on any flat surface they can find, ranging from boxcars to bridge underpasses.

Mexican muralists such as David Siquieros (1896–1974), Diego Rivera (1886–1957), and José Orozco (1883–1949) painted glorious fresco murals in the 1920s to "unite a mostly illiterate country." During the 1930s murals were painted in government buildings in many regions of the United States. These were supported by the government to give employment to artists during the Great Depression.

Preparation

- Measure the wall and have a fresh neutral background painted with a quality primer. Preparation is much the same for indoor or outdoor murals. Washable acrylic paint is suggested for the entire mural, since custom colors may be mixed and cleanup will be easy. Your local paint store can provide advice as to the amount needed.

- Depending on the height of the mural, you may have to arrange for scaffolding to be erected (safety first!).

- Keep all the finishes the same (for even application, flat is recommended instead of semigloss or gloss). Use satin or semigloss polyurethane for a top coat. If this is an outdoor mural, use outdoor paint, and brush on a clear isolation coat and a final varnish clear coat to protect it.

- The discussion about appropriate subject matter is possibly the most important part of the mural. Students must have involvement in its design, to be *owners* of the mural. Things to discuss are: Location? Why paint a mural in this location? What size? Possible subject matter? Colors? Time constraints? Who is in charge of which tasks? (Be sure to delegate!)

- Digital photos may be incorporated into the mural. Change a color photo in a computer program such as Photoshop to *grayscale* and use *levels* to make the photo into high-contrast black and white. Print the photo onto clear acetate sheets for projecting with an overhead projector. Or, if you have equipment such as a document camera or a computer projection system, a laptop computer can be the source for projecting the image.

- It may be easiest to identify areas of color by number on the master copy, and even on the wall if you have a large number of inexperienced painters.

- When the mural is done, have a suitable "unveiling" ceremony, taking photos and getting publicity into the local newspaper or TV station.

Alternative Project
Paint Panels, Install Them Later

It is possible to paint on panels of reinforced birch plywood, Masonite, or medium-density fiberboard (MDF). Panels may be cut to size at a hardware store and primed with gesso for painting. This approach allows for painting to be done in the classroom.

Alternative Project

Movable Screen

Art teacher Traci Bolda of Columbia, Missouri, has devised a way to paint on movable lightweight birch panels. She used three 3 × 5-foot horizontal birch panels, reinforced with 2 × 2-inch frames and hinged so they would fold like a screen, with wheels on casters for easy movement. The birch panels were attached to the framework with a nail gun. The nailed front edges were covered with wood strips as a frame after it was completed.

Mural. Thirty students in Traci Bolda's class at Hickman High School, Columbia, Missouri, created an acrylic mural on birch plywood that featured sprayed-on graffiti and realistic portraits of the ten "most influential Americans," selected by the school's populace.

Mural on wheels. The back of this mural completed by elementary school students of art teacher Traci Bolda, of Columbia, Missouri, is also painted on movable panels, as described in the movable screen alternative project.

FOR THE STUDENT

A mural is a wonderful undertaking, and you will never forget the time you have spent painting it.

1. Draw a number of possibilities on paper. Consider combining designs from several students to make one final design. If these designs are scanned, then organized by computer, some drawings may be scaled (made smaller or larger) as appropriate. When the final design is selected, make sure it is in proportion to the wall or canvas where it will be painted.

2. Transfer the final drawing to an acetate overhead transparency with fine-line permanent marker (or print it out very dark on the computer). This is the easiest way to project the details and may work best in a darkened area.

3. Tape the acetate in place on an overhead projector or use a document camera or computer projection system to enlarge it to the size you will paint on the wall. Place tape on the floor where you have set the projector to be able to easily continue the next day. Draw the design on the primed surface with pencil or with chalk (colored chalk will work on white primer and can be corrected or wiped with a damp paper towel). On an outdoor surface the chalk will wash away, so pencil is better.

4. If you need straight lines, use a level or weight on a string when making vertical straight lines, and use masking or painter's tape to keep straight painted lines clean. Measure to make sure the tape is straight, pressing it in place with a thumbnail.

5. Remember to always clean your brushes carefully with soap and water, or they will be ruined, as acrylic paint dries rapidly.

6. Remember to sign your names and the date somewhere inconspicuous, and use a slightly lighter or darker color than the background color where you sign.

7. When the mural is complete, brush on at least one coat of clear coat varnish for protection.

WATERCOLOR EXPERIMENTS

Time needed: 1 day

Materials: 12 × 18-inch piece of drawing paper, watercolors, sea salt, brushes, oil pastel or crayon, tissues, plastic wrap, two water containers (one for clean, one for dirty water), black fine-line marker

This exercise introduces a variety of watercolor effects for later reference. Use a sheet of drawing paper and either paint freestyle or fold it neatly into twelve sections. When the painted surface is dry, label each method used in black fine-line marker or printed computer lettering. Remember to have a piece of paper next to your painting on which to test colors.

1. Mixing watercolors (choose two)
   a. Make four values of one color by diluting with water.
   b. Use only primary colors to make secondary colors: red and yellow to make orange; blue and red to make violet; and yellow and blue to make green.
   c. Use secondary colors mixed with primary to make more variation (for example, yellow-green, blue-green, red-orange, or yellow-orange).

2. *Wet-in-wet.* Brush clean water onto a section. Add pigment to the wet areas. Notice how it spreads. While the area is still wet, add another color horizontally; this can be useful for painting skies.

3. *Dry brush.* Remove most of the water from a brush by wiping it on paper. Dip it on a pigment color and paint with the almost-dry brush. Part of the paper will show through the brushstrokes. This technique is useful for creating grasses or leaves on a tree.

4. *Graduated wash.* Paint horizontally at the top with an intense color. Dilute the paint and make the horizontal strokes lighter at the bottom. This is useful for painting skies.

5. *Even wash.* Keep the brush loaded with the same amount of pigment and water to make broad, even areas of color.

6. *Stippling.* Use the brush tip to make little round dots. Try closely related colors and combinations of complementary colors. This "pointillism" method was used by George Seurat to allow the eye to mix the colors.

7. *Blotted.* Load your brush with paint and lay in an area of color on the paper. Wad a tissue and use it to blot into the wet paint. The gradations and lines created by blotting give an interesting texture.

8. *Plastic wrap blot.* A variation of the blotted surface is to place plastic wrap on a wet surface and allow it to dry overnight before removing the plastic. This is especially effective for painting rocks.

9. *Watercolor resist.* Commercial resists such as liquid frisket or white wax crayon are used on the paper before the watercolor is applied. With crayon, pattern or hatching makes the background more interesting.

10. *Kosher salt* sprinkled into wet paint leaves dark areas where the salt attracts the colored water. On a winter landscape it makes a realistic-appearing snow.

11. *Tissue or rice paper collage* glued onto the painting surface before painting gives an exotic textural appeal to a watercolor painting.

WATERCOLOR YOUR WAY

Time Needed: 3 fifty-minute periods

Materials: white paper (sulfite, construction paper, or watercolor paper), watercolor paints, brushes (#12, #7, #1, or #2, Bright #10, and bamboo brush), palette (glass on white paper, white plate, or butcher's tray), water-soluble fine-line marker, water containers, pencil, art gum eraser, resist (frisket, white crayon, rubber cement, masking tape), paper towels

Goal: Students identify contemporary artists whose work plays a role in influencing present-day artwork.

Goal: Students mix watercolors to make different hues and apply several different watercolor techniques to create simulated and invented textures.

Objective: Students create an original watercolor that demonstrates sensitivity and subtlety.

Big Wood Island
John Marin (1870–1953), 1914, opaque and transparent watercolor over graphite on wove paper, 14¼ × 16⅜ inches. The Henry E. Schnakenberg Fund. Wadsworth Atheneum Museum of Art, Hartford, Connecticut. Photo Credit Wadsworth Atheneum Museum of Art / Art Resource, NY.

FOR THE TEACHER

Many painters became famous not because they painted "beautiful" paintings, but because they explored new ways of painting. Some unique twentieth-century painters are Chuck Close (1940–), Jasper Johns (1930–), Helen Frankenthaler (1928–2011), Robert Rauschenberg (1925–2008), Robert Indiana (1928–), Elizabeth Peyton (1965–), and Eric Fischl (1948–).

Walking Factory
Jeffrey Craig, mixed media, 3 × 4 feet. This painting vividly illustrates the possibilities for abstract thinking when students are challenged. Hazelwood Central High School, St. Louis County, Missouri, teacher Tracy Jay.

Carpe Diem
Barbara Aydt, watercolor, 34 × 20 inches. Watercolors are carefully built up by glazing. Courtesy of the artist.

A Chemist
Regine Rosas, watercolor, 18 × 24 inches. Clayton High School, St. Louis County, Missouri, teacher Christine Vodicka.

If you are not familiar with watercolor, read about it in the introduction to this chapter, and if you have time, try some of the techniques listed in the handout on watercolor experiments just before this project. Assure students that their paintings don't have to be realistic interpretations and it is not necessary that other people admire their paintings. A painting should, however, fulfill certain requirements: it should be interesting to look at, make good use of the picture plane, have a center of interest (usually), have a color scheme that expresses the mood of the painting, and be creative and original. Students may have trouble knowing when a painting is finished. If they think that the next thing they do may ruin it, then it is probably time to stop. Suggest that it is better to put the painting aside and look at it for a time than to go ahead and do something that can't be undone (unlike oil or acrylic paint, where "mistakes" can be covered).

FOR THE STUDENT

Decide where the painting's center of interest will be. Although a totally abstract composition may have an overall pattern, generally the viewer first notices one area of the painting. It may be the lightest, brightest, or darkest area, often located on an imaginary intersection of a ticktacktoe division of the picture plane. This "rule of thirds" is often used in compositions.

Every artist sees things differently, and each has something that is fascinating to him or her. Decide what your fascination is.

1. Do at least three or four small thumbnail sketches in proportion to the painting paper. You may find that there is something in each sketch that could be combined to make an overall picture.

2. *Lightly* draw the composition with pencil. If there is an area that you want to keep white, you can either simply not put paint in the area or you can apply a "resist" to it. This painted-on substance (frisket or rubber cement) prevents paint from touching that area and can be removed later by rubbing with a finger.

3. If you work on watercolor paper, you can build up color by "glazing," working from light color to darker. Watercolor sometimes puddles and, when dry, is darker in some areas than others. That is the beauty of watercolor. If you are drawing something from observation, you always have what is called "artistic license." *You* are the artist, and you can make choices that someone else may not have made.

4. Generally, a watercolor painting is "loose" and painted in one sitting. It will look different when dry. You may find that you prefer to work on it over the course of several days, but avoid overworking it. Inexpensive paper will "ball up" if overworked.

5. Unlike oil paintings, which are never matted, watercolor paintings are always matted, usually in white or light neutral colors.

ENCAUSTIC PAINTING

Time needed: 5 fifty-minute class periods

Materials and equipment: heated palette (pancake griddle), hot air gun(s) or embossing heat tools, surface thermometer, two to three folded paper towels per station, natural bristle brushes, encaustic medium (beeswax mixed with gum damar crystals), metal cups for melting wax (muffin tins, shallow tin cans), Popsicle sticks for mixing colors (with pigment sticks, Cray-Pas or oil pastel, oil paint), spring-clip clothespins for handling hot tins, nitrile gloves, fine sandpaper, blue painters' tape, drawing materials (ink, charcoal, soft pencil, pastels), miscellaneous collage materials (cloth, patterned paper, dry flattened leaves, ribbon, fine wire, colored string), nonflexible painting surface (medium-density fiber board, or MDF), ¼-inch birch plywood), scraper (a single-edge razor blade or potters' rib), YES glue

Goal: Students compare and contrast styles and purposes for the use of encaustic from Roman through contemporary pop cultures.

Objective: Students develop an encaustic artwork reflecting a personal outlook after selecting one of the methods shown here.

Rondo Weave: Great Burnet
Lisa Sisley-Blinn, encaustic with oil bar and metal leaf, 18 × 18 inches. This rich, complex surface shows designs created with circular objects and embellished with flowing marks made by incising the surface and the addition of gold oil bar.

Visions: Arroyo Seco
Linda Hertelendy-Wein, 2013, 12 × 12 inches. This image was created in Photoshop by masking and isolating the truck and the sunflowers, then combining them to complete the composition. This was printed several times and applied using direct transfer and an embedded rice paper print. The final layer was direct transfer. The artist, an art educator, says, "This series conveys the enchantment I feel about New Mexico by creating fanciful 'visions' that represent the spiritual essence of being there."

Safety

Make sure you are working in a well-ventilated area. Maintain a safe temperature (200 degrees or so), as wax will spontaneously ignite from 350 to 370 degrees. If it should flame, always have a lid handy to smother the fire. *Do not put water on a wax fire.* However, if hot wax gets on an arm or hand, immediately run cold water over it.

Art History

The technique of encaustic (melted painting with liquid colored wax) goes back well over two thousand years. It was used by Romans in Fayum, Egypt, for portraits of the deceased that were placed on caskets. During the 1950s, Jasper Johns, Robert Indiana, and others painted with encaustic, using banal subjects such as targets, flags, and maps, but enriching the surface with encaustic to produce enduring, fascinating paintings.

Vocabulary: embedding, encaustic medium

FOR THE TEACHER

This popular medium has an almost infinite number of working methods. Basically, you apply melted wax to a nonflexible surface, heat it with hot air, scrape it, and decorate it. Art teachers are often familiar with encaustic painting, having melted wax crayons for batik or for encaustic painting with even young students. Savvy elementary and middle school teachers have students strip paper from the crayons by soaking them in water first. When allowed to dry naturally, they are easily sorted by color and melted in a wax-melter kit (available through art material catalogs). That *is* encaustic painting, but rudimentary!

Preparation

There are fine online video instructions and books on working with encaustic, with many variations on this technique. Instructions given here are based on a class taken with instructor Lisa Sisley-Blinn.

Encaustic materials and equipment (from left, clockwise): natural brushes, Cray-Pas™ crayons, grater, oil bars (for shaving into encaustic medium), metal "rounds" items for making patterns in molten wax.

Brushes rest on heated palette (200 degrees), molten encaustic medium, flat thermometer, soya wax mixed with paraffin (for cleaning brushes), heat guns, surge protector.

Encaustic painting in a classroom setting can mostly use materials and equipment found in a school, but will not necessarily produce archival artwork. You can purchase encaustic startup sets, but I recommend buying inexpensive pancake griddles to use as heated "palettes," flat thermometers (200 degrees is the best painting temperature), and embossing guns. For scrapers you can use potters' ribs or single-edge razor blades (and ask students to return these to you each day).

Set up an encaustic work table with electrical outlets nearby; you might be plugging in more than one heated palette and heat guns. A surge protector to handle these plug-ins is simply a safety consideration. Ideally, students should work on a glass-topped table where spilled wax can be scraped off and reused—or cover the table with kraft paper. For cleanup, students wipe the warm griddle with paper towels. It is best to allow the wax to melt in the brushes before wiping on a paper towel. If this will be an ongoing project, brushes can be dedicated to specific colors and brush cleaning isn't necessary. Provide a few folded paper towels for each student's work station.

To make your own batches of encaustic medium, purchase beeswax and damar crystals (nine parts beeswax to two parts damar crystals; the crystals come in chunks and can be pulverized in a plastic bag with a hammer). You can mix larger amounts by using a slow cooker (such as a Crock-Pot) or metal bread pan. Ideally, you should purchase prepared oil bars, but to make your own colored wax for painting, mix the encaustic medium with oil paint, oil bars, pure powdered pigment, or even acrylic paint (not ideal because it is water-based). Heat the encaustic medium in a shallow metal can or muffin tin and add color, stirring with a Popsicle stick until the paint is dissolved. If you use oil paint, squirt about a three-inch long strip of paint onto a paper towel (to allow it to absorb excess oil), allowing it at least a half hour to drain before mixing it with the encaustic medium. Mix oil paint with encaustic at less than 50 percent oil paint. The setup seen in the preceding figure accommodates up to seven students at a time.

Students should work on a small panel (4 × 4 or 4 × 6 inches) or a piece of high-quality drawing paper taped on a flat, nonflexible surface with painter's blue tape). Any panel larger than 8 × 8 inches should be reinforced with wood strips on the back. To introduce students to encaustic painting, have them work with a limited palette of burnt umber, black, and white. The tips of Cray-Pas or oil sticks may be melted directly on the heated palette and used to add color.

 FOR THE STUDENT

1. To make a very smooth surface, coat the board by applying melted wax with a brush first in one direction, then in the opposite direction. Use a scraper to make the surface flat (a scraper can be a flat object such as a potter's rib or a single-edge razor blade). If the wax that is removed is clean, it can be put back into the melting pot. Colored wax can be saved and recycled into a "mystery color." Allow your brush to rest on the warm palette to keep it ready for instant use.

2. *Embedding a paper design.* If you want to use a computer or paper design, use YES! glue (which doesn't bubble) to attach it to the *untreated* board. The same process applies to drawing on paper with ink, charcoal, and colored pencil. Allow the glue to dry before coating the paper with wax as described in Step 1.

3. *For a white base.* If you want a white base, paint it with encaustic gesso. You can draw directly onto the gesso with soft pastel, charcoal, watercolor, marker, or graphite before adding a layer of wax.

Surface Decoration Possibilities

4. *Photocopy transfer.* Use a smooth flat tool such as a metal spoon, burnishing tool, or bone folder to burnish (rub *very* hard) the back of a photocopy (or print made in a laser printer) onto a smooth prepared wax surface. To burnish evenly, turn the base from time to time, working at different angles.

5. When you are satisfied it has transferred (lift an edge and peek to be sure), spray a little water on the paper photocopy and rub gently with your finger to remove the paper backing, leaving the ink design on the wax surface.

6. *Painting with color.* Apply color in a variety of ways.
   - Use a brush to paint with colored wax.
   - Draw into the wax base with Cray-Pas or oil pastel heated on the palette.

7. *Collage.* Many materials can be embedded in wax: magazine photos, photocopies, cloth, patterned paper, dry flattened leaves, ribbon, fine copper wire, or colored string.

8. *To clean brushes,* warm the brush and wipe with a paper towel. Lightly dip in melted soya wax mixed with canning paraffin and wipe with a towel. If you have different colors of wax in several tins, you can leave the color in the brush, allowing it to harden, as it will melt the next time you use it in that same color.

9. The encaustic painting does not need a top coat of wax. Too many coats obscure the design. You can polish it repeatedly with a soft cloth.

Whaam!

Roy Lichtenstein (1923–1997), Magna acrylic and oil on canvas, 1963. Two canvases, each 68 × 80 inches. Tate Gallery, London, © Copyright. Photo: Tate, London / Art Resource, NY. Permission courtesy Roy Lichtenstein Foundation.

5

Printmaking

A one-color print is a good introduction to printmaking, as it reinforces the concept that most prints are approximately half-dark and half-light. Many secondary school students have already experienced printmaking in earlier classes and understand by now that *printing will produce a reversed image. Preprinting* techniques such as brayer prints and paste paper are successful for all and provide interesting background material for stamping or printing with a linocut. *After-the-print* techniques employ drawing materials, photocopy transfers to enhance the finished print, and collage with print scraps (to make use of less-than-perfect extras).

Relief Printing

In a relief print, a design is carved into the surface of the plate (which is usually made of linoleum or wood). MDF (medium-density fiberboard), a composite plywoodlike material found at building supply stores, can be carved like wood. The uncarved surface of the relief linoleum or wood plate is inked and printed. Soft-Kut®, a rubberlike material, is quite easy to cut and works well for hand transfer, but is unsuitable for printing in a press because the pressure causes it to stretch.

Intaglio Printing

In intaglio (pronounced *intalyo*) printing, the surface of a plastic or metal plate is changed by etching with acid, drypoint scribing, or engraving. After a plate changed in this manner has been inked, the fine lines or dotted areas *below* the plate's surface hold ink after the surface is wiped clean. Dampened paper forced under pressure lifts the ink from the recessed areas.

Monotype

The *monotype* is unique—one of a kind. It can be "inked" on a blank "plate" with water-based marker, ink, or watercolor and transferred to dampened paper that reactivates the dry pigment. A *monoprint* differs in that it is done from a plate that has a permanent design. Depending on how color is added, it can be printed nearly identically many times.

Planographic Printmaking: Lithographs, Stenciling, and Screen Printing

The earliest known planographic prints in which the negative and positive areas are both on the same level of the surface were made thirty thousand years ago, when artists colored their hands with minerals such as manganese and printed them on the walls of caves. Lithographs were enormously popular near the turn of the twentieth century and were made on stone or metal plates that had painted or drawn designs created by artists. Screen prints have a design (usually negative) on a silk or nylon screen. A thin layer of ink is forced through the screen to create a print. T-shirts, specialty wallpaper, and some posters are made with silkscreen (serigraphy).

Materials for Printmaking

Ink or Ink Substitutes

Water-based inks for the secondary school classroom are the choice of most schools because they are nontoxic and cleanup with water is fast and easy. Acrylic ink is another choice of many studios dedicated to nontoxic printmaking.

Watercolor Markers

These are perfect for coloring small plates or making a *proof.* If the marker dries, dampened paper applied under pressure reactivates the color.

Watercolor Marker and Watercolor Paint Combinations

These two coloring media work well together. The combination of the marker's bright colors and softer watercolor paints gives some dramatic effects. The use of dampened paper brings the color to life.

Paper

Papers suitable for printmaking are good drawing paper, hot-press (smooth) watercolor paper, etching paper, or white construction paper. *Fadeless paper* comes in many colors and can be dramatic with a one-color print. Japanese papers, though thin, are well manufactured and accept ink beautifully. Avoid using newsprint or colored construction paper for prints, as newsprint quickly turns yellow, and construction paper fades.

General Instructions

Save Every Print

At the beginning of the printmaking experience, remind students that you expect them to keep every print they make—even the disasters. They may later tear up prints to use for a collage or paste in a book. Or the poor prints might be used as backgrounds for a different form of printmaking. Inked papers are far more beautiful for collage than any papers that can be purchased.

Keep the Paper Clean

Master printmaker and instructor Jeff Sippel says it plainly: "To keep your hands clean, don't touch the ink." That means that it is good to have printing partners who will put fresh paper in place for printing and remove the print to place on the drying rack. Or students can use "pickers" for handling the paper that can be made from folded 1 ½ × 4-inch pieces of mat board. Cotton garden gloves come off easily and may be used by someone who is printing alone.

Applying Ink with a Brayer

Put a small amount of ink on the corner of a glass or plastic surface (to approximately equal a teaspoonful). Roll the brayer in one direction, lifting the brayer with each stroke, distributing the ink evenly until it looks velvety and makes a *shhh* sound. Ink the plate in the same manner, lifting the brayer after each application and spreading it first in one direction, then across the first coat of ink. Second and third prints may look better than the first, as the plate becomes thoroughly inked. *Caution:* If the ink is applied too thickly (in a relief print, for example), it will fill the lines of the design on your plate.

Dampening Individual Sheets of Paper for Printing

To dampen paper, hold a sheet briefly under a faucet or place it in a tray of water, then hold it by a corner to drain before blotting it. Place the paper inside a folded towel or between sheets of blotting paper and gently rub to remove excess water. Inspect the paper before printing to make sure there are no shiny spots. A speedy method of dampening is to spritz water from a spray bottle onto both sides of the paper before blotting it with a towel.

Dampening Quantities of Paper

If many dampened sheets will be needed, cut them to the proper size, then place half of them in a tray of water *one sheet at a time* or they will stick together. When you remove the paper from the water, alternate a wet sheet with a dry one and place the stack of paper in a plastic bag overnight. They will be perfect for printing the next day, and these "stacks" will keep well in a refrigerator for a week or so or in a freezer for up to a year. If not refrigerated, they develop mildew within a week.

Printing without a Press

For hundreds of years artists have made wonderful prints without the benefit of a press. The basic difference between hand-transferred prints and those made with a printing press is that the amount of pressure available with a press might give an embossed (raised) effect.

To Hand-Transfer

Center the plate on top of the paper inked side down, then gently place your hand under the paper, supporting the plate and paper and holding the plate in place while you turn it over. It is more effective to rub on the back of the paper than the plate, because the paper is thinner. Pressure can be applied with the hand, the back of a wooden spoon, a jar lid, a baren (a flat Japanese-style tool), or a clean brayer. To keep the paper from "pilling" as you rub and to protect the back of the paper from ink on your hands, use a piece of copy paper as a cover sheet.

Printing with a Press

For most techniques, a printing press gives excellent results. The press has a metal bed on which the plate rests, with the printing paper on top. With few exceptions, blankets of soft thick felt are used on top of the printing paper and plate to increase the pressure. Test the press adjustment by first running an uninked plate of the same thickness as the one that will be printed with a piece of newsprint on top. If the pressure is firm enough, you will see a slight pattern (the plate mark) on the piece of newsprint. You should *sense* a difference as the print roller encounters the plate.

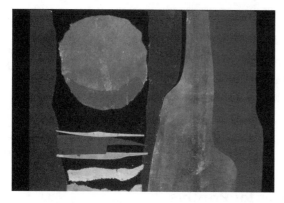

Just Around
Marceline Saphian, monotype collage, 17 × 25 inches. The individual elements in this collage print were individually inked and placed on a preinked dark background. Collection of Brown Shoe Company.

Hand Series #4
Marceline Saphian, monotype, 24 × 32 inches. This is one of a group of prints made by cutting hand shapes from ordinary newspaper. After the ink dries on flimsy elements such as these, they are strengthened and may be set aside for reuse another time.

Water-Based Ink Cleanup

Newspaper used under a cleanup area makes the job easy. Scrape as much ink off the inking plate as possible with a spatula or piece of mat board or wipe off with a paper towel. Run the brayer over newspaper to remove excess ink. Spritz water on the brayer and inking surface and wipe up with paper towels. All cleaning materials may be wadded up within the newspaper and put in a waste container afterwards.

Oil-Based Ink Cleanup

Aim for a *nontoxic atmosphere.* To remove oil-based ink, use ordinary vegetable oil on the brayer and inking plate to soften ink for easy removal with paper towels. Do a final cleanup with an alcohol-based spray (such as window cleaner) and paper towels.

Drying the Prints

Ideally, prints are air-dried on a drying rack where they can be placed flat. They also can be carefully hung on a clothesline with clothespins from the two top corners or on top of clean newsprint placed on the floor. If the dry print is too rippled, it can be flattened by placing it under a stack of books or by quickly ironing on the back after it is dry.

Signing Prints

A traditional method of signing prints has endured for centuries. The artist's signature is in pencil immediately below the print edge, usually on the right side (graphite does not fade, but inks in some pens *will* fade). A title may be included under the print on the left side or the middle, and a number or the initials AP (for Artist's Proof) will be found below the print on the left-hand side or in the center. Beyond the artist's proofs (traditionally up to ten), an edition (identical prints) should be numbered. The number below a print, for example, might be 5/15. The 5 signifies that this was the fifth print made in this edition, and the 15 means that a total of 15 prints were made. If you see a number like 200/2,000, it won't be worth much, as artists rarely do an edition of more than 100 prints.

Archivally mounted etching, free at bottom, hinged mat. The open-cut mat is hinged to the base with archival tape.

Matting Prints

In general, student prints are matted in fourteen-ply mat board in neutral tones such as white, cream, black, or gray. Professionally matted prints use archival mat board with an open mat and a backing of the same size. In archival matting, the print is "hung" by two strips of archival tape on the bottom mat board.

STEM, LEAF, BLOSSOM: A BOTANICAL ILLUSTRATION IN DRYPOINT

Time needed: 4 fifty-minute classes

Materials: drawing paper, 8 × 11 × 1/16-inch plastic "plate," sharp pointed metal tool (scribe, dental pick, or large nail), printing ink, 1 ½ × 3-inch mat board pieces for applying ink, rags (or tarlatan), old telephone book, printing paper, pan for soaking paper, watercolors and brushes, toothbrush, towel, paper towels

Content connection: Science (Botany)

Goal: Students compare and connect the development of printmaking through time periods and cultures.

Objective: Students speculate on how technological advances and research have affected scientific illustration since the time of hand-painted botanical prints.

Objective: Students complete and hand-color a detailed drypoint botanical illustration. They will include lettering that will identify the name and the parts of the flower.

Limon S. Remi
Giovanni Ferrari, 1646, 14 × 9 inches, copper engraving, uncolored, the Netherlands. Courtesy Missouri Botanical Garden, St. Louis, Missouri.

Poppies
Drypoint on plastic, 11 × 14 inches. This design was scribed on 1/16-inch thick hardware store plastic with a sharp instrument such as a nail. When it was inked and wiped, the ink left in the lines was printed.

FOR THE TEACHER

Flowers and plants are excellent subjects for a drypoint print. Line drawings from a real flower (or a silk one) force students to look closely at the value differences. Scientific botanical prints continue to be produced today, as they have been for centuries by artists who enjoy interpreting one subject in detail. Many good examples may be found on the Internet by searching on antique scientific botanical prints.

In drypoint printmaking, ink is forced into marks scratched (scribed) into a metal or plastic surface with a sharp instrument. The actual surface level is wiped almost clean, leaving ink remaining in the recessed areas. When dampened paper is forced into these depressions under pressure, the ink is transferred to the paper.

Vocabulary: scribe, drypoint, hatching, cross-hatching, carding, tarlatan, ghost print, incised

Content Connection: Science (Botany)

Botanical prints show a plant or flower in several different states of development (bud, full flower, the root system). An illustration of a plant such as a fruit tree might show a branch, leaves, the blossom, fully developed fruit, and even a sliced piece of fruit that shows its seeds and inside color.

Alternative Project
Drypoint Portrait

This method also lends itself well to portraiture. Students can work from a drawing of a friend or themselves to make a line drawing that shows value differences.

FOR THE STUDENT

Many botanical illustrations were printed in black ink and later hand-colored. Some botanical illustrators centered a single blossom and stem on a page, while others let the leaves, stems, and blossoms "run off the edges," filling the page. Many used a diagonal or curved design, reflecting that plants rarely grow purely vertically. At times artists included butterflies or worms with the flowers to make their work more lifelike or perhaps to show which insects were attracted to these plants.

1. Do a detailed pencil drawing of one or more flowers on a plant, including the stem and leaves. Develop the light and dark areas by hatching and cross-hatching in pencil. Tape the drawing to the underside of the clear plastic plate. It will print backward from your original drawing.

2. To scratch the plate's surface, press firmly with the point of a scribing tool (or large nail) to make deep lines that will hold ink. The nice thing about drypoint on clear plastic is that you can hold it to the light and see whether you have really developed dark and light areas.

3. *Inking the plate.* Wear gloves to keep your hands clean. When you are satisfied that the plate is finished, *card* (transfer the ink) onto the surface with the narrow end of a 1 ½ × 3-inch mat board strip. With a wadded-up rag, make circular or figure-eight motions that will force ink into the recessed lines from all directions.

4. Place a page from a telephone book *flat* on the inked plate, gently rubbing over the entire back of the paper to remove some of the ink. Although it is possible to wipe the plate almost clean, leave some *tone* on outside edges and corners for artistic effect. Wipe cross-hatched areas carefully to avoid getting darker results than you had planned.

5. *Preparing the paper.* Dampen the printing paper for the best effect. After soaking it for a few minutes, pull it out and let water drip back into the tub before placing it inside a folded towel. Pat the towel with your palms to remove excess water. Make sure there are no shiny spots. The textured side of the paper goes next to the inked side of the plate.

6. *Printing.* To hand-transfer, center the plate in the middle of the printing paper and, holding the paper and plate firmly, turn them over to allow you to apply pressure on the *paper* (which is thinner) rather than the plate. Use a cover sheet of dry copy paper to protect the damp printing paper while you rub it on the back. A wooden spoon can be used to apply pressure evenly.

7. *Cleaning the plate.* If you are using water-based ink, simply clean the plate with water, and dry. A toothbrush helps to loosen the ink from lines.

8. *Coloring or labeling.* After the print has dried, parts of it can be hand-colored with colored ink, watercolor, or colored pencil. Label the plant based on examples you see of antique botanical prints.

WATERCOLOR MONOTYPE

Time needed: 2 to 3 fifty-minute classes

Materials: Yupo synthetic paper or $\frac{1}{16}$-inch clear plastic (from hardware store), watercolor markers, watercolor paint, brushes, paper towels, water, dampened white printing paper, white copy paper (a cover sheet), real or artificial flowers, sponge

Goal: Students learn about contemporary and historic figures in the printmaking field while designing and printing several monotypes (unique prints).

Objective: Students select one monotype technique to create a print that expresses a personal style and advanced proficiency.

FOR THE TEACHER

Art History

In the 1890s, monotype parties became a craze in Paris. American expatriate Maurice Prendergast, known for his scenes crowded with people, created more than a hundred monotypes. Other suggestions are landscapes, seascapes, or still life. Contemporary painter-printmakers such as Jim Dine (1935–), Jonathan Borofsky (1942–), and Janet Fish (1938–) use flowers as primary subject matter, but each one has a unique approach to the subject.

Edgar Degas (1834–1917), a French impressionist known mostly for his action paintings of ballet dancers and horses, used a *subtractive* method that resulted in a white

Theater Rehearsal
Elizabeth Concannon, 2006, watercolor monotype on Stonehenge paper, 11 ¾ × 9 inches, from a Yupo plate. The intensity of this print is achieved by using watercolor almost straight from the tube. The white figures were created by a Soft-Kut block that she had carved to be "people-shaped" and stamping the wet plate on the watercolor background. Because Yupo is plastic, watercolor paint can be removed with a dampened towel or, in this case, a wet handmade stamp.

Roses
Watercolor marker and watercolor monotype prints made by painting on Yupo with brightly colored marker combined with watercolors.

Behind the Fence

Elizabeth Concannon. Watercolors were applied to a plastic (Yupo) plate. White areas were left uncolored. Dampened paper applied under pressure lifted the color from the Yupo, giving a richly colored print.

subject with gradations of white on a dark background (see the dark field monotype alternative project that follows). He often made drawings of the human form.

Preparation

Instructions given here are for three methods of making a monotype. Ideally, paper is prepared in advance by alternating wet and dry sheets and placing in a plastic bag the night before printing. This print may be printed by hand or on a printing press.

Printing with Yupo Synthetic Paper

Yupo synthetic paper doesn't absorb pigment, and it can be easily washed and used repeatedly for years. It is ideal for monotype printmaking because it can be colored with a combination of watercolor marker and watercolors. Although the pigments dry, the printing is done with dampened paper, which reactivates the dried colors. Underlying stains may remain that will not affect a new print. If you wish to remove the stains, place the Yupo in a weak solution of bleach before rinsing and drying. Avoid the use of pencils for making preliminary designs because they may dent the Yupo permanently. If you do not have a printing press, this works very well by rubbing the paper with the hand. Use a cover sheet to avoid tearing or "pilling" the paper.

Alternative Project
Printing with Clear Plastic

This same printmaking project can be done on ordinary $^1\!/_{16}$- or $^1\!/_8$-inch plastic from a hardware store by filing or sanding edges to avoid cutting blankets on a printing press. Some very thin plastics work, and edges would not need to be beveled. When printing by hand, the step to prepare a beveled edge is unnecessary. The surface of the plate should be lightly sanded to accept watercolor more easily.

Alternative Project
Dark Field Monotype

To make a dark field monotype, use a brayer to apply an even coating of ink onto a plate. Make a design directly into the ink with any type of marking instrument, ranging from a rag placed around your finger to a sharp instrument, broken dowel, stiff brush, or a dull pencil. In this process you can place objects such as grasses, string, or cut paper stencils on the ink to produce white images against the dark background.

Alternative Project

Trace Monotype: Black Line Drawing

Start with a lightly drawn sketch on drawing paper the same size as the printing plate. Use a brayer to apply an even layer of ink to the blank plate (plastic or metal). Carefully place the blank side of the printing paper on the inked plate, taping the paper to the top of the uninked side of the plate so it won't slip while you are drawing on it. Retrace the original drawing, which transfers the ink to the front of the paper. For a little tone, *lightly* rub around the edge. Lift to see if the drawing is completed.

FOR THE STUDENT

These instructions are for working on Yupo, a synthetic (plastic) paper. If you choose to draw flowers, make them as large or small as you want. Complete the background of the composition with color to make it contrast with the white paper on which it will be printed. Any area that is not colored will remain white.

Picnic
Charles Goolsby, dark field monotype, 24 × 18 inches. In the artist's words: "This is a good example of the subtractive process. I used a zinc printing plate and covered it completely with a layer of dark ink. Using paper towels and brushes, I lifted out the ink to reveal the medium and lighter value passages. The plate image was transferred to Arches cover printmaking paper using an etching press."

Trace monotype. Black line print made by placing the paper on an inked plate and drawing on the back of the paper. It lifts ink onto the paper.

1. Outline or fill in the design with water-based marker. Use watercolor to paint within the marker lines. Don't be afraid to blend colors. The bright colors of the markers will add to the excitement of the composition. Try to live with slight "mistakes," but true disasters can be wiped off with the corner of a paper towel dipped in water.

2. The markers and the paint will dry, but you will be working with dampened paper that will reactivate the colors.

3. The water will cause the marker to run somewhat, but that adds to the charm. Or you can paint the entire picture with watercolor marker. Some of the wild colors available in markers blend wonderfully with softer watercolors.

4. Paint a contrasting background or leave it blank. You can also add a border to define the edges of the paper.

5. Center the Yupo design face down on damp paper (examine the paper first to make sure there are no shiny spots). Turn it over so the Yupo is on the bottom. Place a sheet of copy paper or newsprint on top of the damp paper and, beginning at the center, use fingers or a brayer to rub firmly all the way to the edges. Remove the print and allow it to dry.

6. For a second, similar print, simply reapply colors over the image left on the Yupo plate and reprint. These prints can be accented (when dry) by using a fine-line black marker to loosely outline different values of color.

POP ART COLLAGRAPH

Time Needed: 2 to 3 fifty-minute classes

Materials: contact paper; polymer medium; brushes; tag board, chipboard, or mat board; string; paper; fabric; scissors; paper punch; art knife; polymer medium; water-based ink; brayer; plastic or glass sheet for rolling out ink

Goal: Students apply prior printmaking knowledge to create a collagraph printmaking plate using a variety of materials.

Goal: Students analyze and discuss themes in art that go beyond any one culture or place.

Objective: Students develop and refine a collagraph plate to create a print that reflects a feeling or personal experience.

FOR THE TEACHER

Art History Connection

The word *collagraph* comes from the French word *coller* (to stick) and the English word *graphic*. This semiabstract method of printmaking became popular in the 1950s, when permanent acrylic glues became available. Pablo Picasso (1881–1973) and Georges Braque (1882–1963) were early twentieth-century artists whose collages and collagraphs marked the beginnings of cubism. Other artists particularly well known for their collagraphs are Kurt Schwitters (1887–1948), Paul Klee (1879–1940), and Arthur Dove (1880–1946).

Preparation

Pop artists of the 1950s used commonplace subject matter like soup cans, letters of the alphabet, targets, or flags. Students can consider such ordinary images to get a head start on ideas for developing their plates. Suggest that they bring in texturally interesting items from home. The found materials and cutouts are glued onto the plate and varnished on the entire surface with polymer medium, allowed to dry, then inked. Successful plates tend to have more than one background material. Soft materials such as eyelet, lace, mesh potato sacks, perforated plastic ribbon, bubble wrap, yarn, and raffia can all be used to great effect. Letter or number stencils can be used as patterns for cutting lettering and shapes on tag board. This method of cutting, tearing, and pasting materials on the plate may be done with an idea in mind, but complete realism is unlikely.

Alternative Project
Stencil Letter Collage

If students use actual stencils to make a pattern, demonstrate for them how to draw the stenciled letters first, then cut them out. Remind students to paste letters backward so they will read correctly. Letters of any size can be made and printed on the computer on card stock, cutting them out to glue in place.

Gas
Water-based ink, 15 × 30 inches. Cardboard letters and numbers were traced from stencils on file folders and cut out with scissors. The back of the mat board was covered with clear contact paper.

Gas
Cutouts were glued backward onto mat board with polymer medium. A coat of polymer medium was applied on the front and sides.

Gas
The same print was printed three times with successively darker colors of water-based ink, working from light to dark.

Alternative Project
Nature String Print

Collect varied thicknesses of string. Make a complete drawing that will be transferred to mat board, with strong shapes outlined. Using scissors, string, and white glue applied with a brush, fill in outlines with white glue. It is not necessary to fill in completely because the mat board will have a pebbly texture for the background. When the string is firmly attached, the entire composition, including sides, should be "varnished" with polymer medium or thinned white glue and allowed to dry overnight before printing the next day.

Alternative Project
Tag Board Print

Cut up old file folders for a collagraph print. Use one half of a file folder (tag board) as a base, then make a design with scrap tag board. Even an abstract composition may have a recognizable object or subject within it. Cut two or three geometric shapes (triangle, rectangle, square, or circle). Repeat one of

the shapes and cut inside the shape with scissors or an art knife, making a ¼-inch wide "outline" shape. The cutaways, or negative shapes, add interest elsewhere within the composition. These must be securely glued in place with polymer medium or the ink will creep under the edges of the shapes. Flex the plate toward the back to make sure corners don't come up. Brush on polymer medium to preserve the "plate" for printing a number of times and prevent the printing paper from adhering to the plate.

FOR THE STUDENT

Pop artists of the 1950s thought that the subject was not important and consciously used such ordinary items as letters, numbers, comic book images, flags, maps, targets, advertising motifs, even Ben-Day dots (the tiny circles used in print illustrations in magazines and comic books). Some pop artists whose work endures today are Jasper Johns (1930–), Andy Warhol (1928–1987), Roy Lichtenstein (1923–1997), Robert Indiana (1928–), and Stuart Davis (1894–1964).

The collagraph is an ideal way to honor these artists' ground-breaking ideas, yet give a contemporary look to art through "layering" ordinary shapes and colors.

1. Think of some ordinary object that you often see (maybe in your home or on your clothing). Use varied materials or textures. Make several thumbnail sketches before deciding on a general idea for this print. Mat board texture is pebbly enough to show on the print.

2. Protect the back of the "plate" (heavy mat board or tag board) by covering it with polymer medium or clear contact paper. If you use mat board, also coat the edges with polymer medium.

3. Remember: *printing is reversed!* The final print will be the exact mirror opposite of your design on the plate.

4. Before gluing anything in place, put one layer of materials on top of another, arranging them to your satisfaction. Before you take them up to glue, you may have to draw a rough sketch to remember where things go.

5. You may have one layer or several. When everything is firmly glued down, go over all of it with polymer medium as a varnish and allow it to dry. The plate may be cleaned off after printing one day and used more than once.

6. Use a brayer to apply ink. Recharge the brayer often to make sure the plate is evenly covered. Make several prints if you intend to print second or third colors, as it is sometimes difficult to align the plate and the existing print perfectly.

7. To print with more than one color, apply a different color of ink to the cleaned plate. Carefully place the plate face down on the existing dry print, making sure it is facing the correct direction and matching the edges. Hold the print and paper in place to turn over before rubbing on the paper.

8. After printing, place the print someplace where it will dry flat. Clean the ink from the plate with a damp paper towel and dry the plate to be stored until another printing day. Sign the print and mat it.

PROJECT 5-4
NATURE COLLAGRAPH

Time needed: 2 to 3 fifty-minute classes

Materials: mat board, materials for gluing (raffia, leaves, tag board), polymer medium, gesso, brushes, clear acrylic spray, clear contact paper

Content connection: Science

Goal: Students will apply knowledge of elements and principles of design in a print that combines personal symbols or ideas.

Objective: Students will print and sign several prints to demonstrate knowledge of the procedures needed to make an edition.

FOR THE TEACHER

Preparation

Although texture is important in creating a collagraph plate, the composition can quickly become too busy. Remind students that as with any good composition, there should be a center of interest as well as someplace to rest the eye. Shiny surface materials such as Mylar or aluminum foil can give large, light areas. Suggest students avoid heavily textured materials that will absorb too much ink and tend to run when printed. This plate can be relatively small (8 × 8 inches).

Content Connection: Science

This could be the culmination of a leaf and weed identification unit. Encourage students to flatten a leaf in wax paper by placing it under a heavy book before attaching it to the mat board.

Alternative Project
Masking Tape on Mat Board

A simple printing plate for a collagraph can be made by creating a random design of masking tape on a piece of mat board and varnishing it. It might be particularly effective to use the intaglio technique, first inking the plate, then wiping most of it off.

Desert Living
Harriet Fisher Thomas, collagraph, 10 × 12 inches. A variety of materials is assembled on a mat board base that has had the back covered with contact paper. Materials are glued in place with gesso, and the collage is sprayed with matte polymer medium before applying colors for printing.

Redleaf
Harriet Fisher Thomas, collagraph, 10 × 12 inches. The artist often incorporates leaves and objects from nature in her collagraphs on mat board. Colored inks and oil paints are selectively applied to give a multicolored image in a single printing.

FOR THE STUDENT

The elements of art and principles of design are guides that may help you when you are working abstractly. You may sense that line is needed or that repetition in color or value (lightness or darkness) will give sparkle. Emphasis, variety, and rhythm may automatically become part of the composition. If you are working in color, you may find that a complementary color or an analogous color scheme will be dynamic.

1. After cutting the mat board to size, apply clear contact paper to the back to protect the plate. Use scissors or a cutting knife to trim the edges from the back.

2. Get out the materials. Begin with large shapes first, allowing the design to develop as you move materials around. Remember that the composition will be better if you leave enough space around some items. Build the composition, then place it on the floor and step away to look at it from a distance. When you are satisfied, attach materials in place with glue or gesso and allow them to dry. The gesso (a white liquid) you apply with a brush will give some texture.

3. If you use a leaf, place it facedown and remove the stem so it will lie flat. You may choose not to cover a delicate texture such as a leaf with gesso, but instead to protect it with acrylic spray.

4. Thin materials such as raffia, a leaf, or a mesh potato bag can be held in place with gesso. When the composition is finished, carefully paint gesso on top. When everything is fully dry, take it outside and spray-coat it with one or two coats of acrylic spray.

Fall Gatherings
Elizabeth Cavanagh Cohen, monotype collage on Sekashu paper, wood, wax-embedded leaves, 22 × 30 inches. A walk in the woods yielded the subject matter for this print. Leaves were dipped in wax prior to embedding them on the wood background. Leaves were individually colored with printing ink.

Gatherings
Elizabeth Cavanagh Cohen, monotype, 30 × 42 inches. The artist used natural materials to make negative patterns while applying ink to the weeds and the background cardboard. The weeds acted as a stencil. The inked weeds and cardboard were then reversed and reprinted (ink side down) to give positive images.

INTRODUCTION TO RELIEF PRINTING

Time needed: 10 fifty-minute classes

Materials: 4-inch squares of copy paper, rulers, soft pencils (4B), 4-inch square Safety-Kut printing material, masking tape, linocut tools, 12 × 12-inch squares of fadeless paper in a variety of colors, water-based printing ink, 14 × 14-inch black construction paper for mounting, spray mount

Goal: Students will create original works of art of increasing complexity and skill that reflect a unique approach and will challenge them to experiment and take risks.

Objective: Students will create a small relief print to be printed multiple times in more than one color on one sheet of paper.

FOR THE TEACHER

This introductory project to linocut printmaking was developed by Joan Larson of Oakville High School in St. Louis County, Missouri, and has been adopted by other teachers in her school. It introduces the concept of radial symmetry, and each student comes up with a successful yet totally unique design.

Vocabulary: radial symmetry, positive, negative, brayer, plate, proof

Preparation

To save time, precut 4 × 4-inch copy paper and 12 × 12-inch fadeless paper. You may have to cut 6 × 4-inch blocks down to 4 × 4-inch Safety-Kut or Soft-Kut blocks, but these 2 × 4-inch leftovers can be carved and used as borders. Discuss with students the ultimate goal, which is for each of them to repeatedly ink and use a single plate to come up with an original artwork. Show students how to find the center of the paper by measuring from each side and making a dot at the center.

FOR THE STUDENT

Safety note: keep your wrist and elbow locked. Always keep your hand behind the blade. If you need to make curved lines, rotate the plate as you cut, but always have the blade facing forward. When you are making a design for a linocut, approximately half of the design will be cut away. The uncut area (positive) will print as a color and the area that is removed (negative) will remain white.

1. Make a number of small sketches until you come up with a design that you think has possibilities and represents *you*. Fold a 4-inch square of thin paper diagonally. Use a soft (4B) pencil to draw a design on one of the two triangles that is formed. Refold the paper and firmly rub on the back of the design with a thumbnail to transfer it to the opposite triangle.

2. Although this would give a perfectly symmetrical design, two opposite corners must have different designs to make the print interesting. When you have altered one

corner design, widen and fill in the positive areas to remain dark (the lines must be wide enough that they will not break down when they are firmly printed), and put an X in each negative area that will be cut away.

3. Transfer the design to a 4 × 4-inch Safety-Kut block by firmly rubbing on the back of the paper with a thumbnail. After the design is visible on the printing plate, you may need to outline the design on the block with pencil to be able to see what you will be cutting away. Turn the printing block over. On the underside write the number 1 on one corner and the number 2 on its opposite (and differently designed) corner. These numbers are important to help you keep track of which direction you will place the plate to print.

4. Use linoleum cutting tools to remove the negative area that will show as white. If you do a proof of it (just use plain copy paper and lightly rub it with a pencil, like you used to do to make a penny rubbing). If you think your design needs improvement, you may want to trim a few lines or add more detail before inking.

5. To print, select a piece of 12 × 12-inch fadeless paper. Place a ruler to measure and make a tiny pencil mark in the center.

6. Add ink to a brayer, then transfer the ink to the printing plate. Put Corner 1 toward the center. Ink and repeat this step three more times, each time with the same color and the same numbered corner in the center. From here on you are free to try any number of the following experiments:

Begin with Corner 2 in the center.

Print with a contrasting color on the outside of the first four center prints. You can make an even border all the way outside or overlapping the center prints.

Use a ruler to lightly draw a two-inch border on the paper. Print the block in one color around the outside edges of the print and a different color starting at the center. Where prints overlap, you will find interesting patterns developing. Neatness counts.

7. Make a minimum of two distinct prints that show radial symmetry. Select the best print to mount on a piece of black paper for display.

Diana Dang. This illustration shows how the design is developed on half of the four-inch square. Oakville High School, St. Louis County, Missouri, teacher Joan Larson.

Diana Dang. The printing is done on fadeless paper by turning the plate each time ink is applied. Oakville High School, St. Louis County, Missouri, teacher Joan Larson.

PROJECT 5-6
RELIEF PRINT

Time needed: 4 to 5 fifty-minute classes

Materials: newsprint or copy paper, lino plate, lino cutters, bench hook, printing paper, brayers, ink, Plexiglas™ for rolling out ink, masking tape, pencil

Objective: Students will learn the importance of proper print registration by printing the same block with at least three colors.

FOR THE TEACHER

Art History and Cultural Connections

Relief printing is familiar to most students, as they remember earlier experiences with potato printing and linocuts made during elementary school. The materials may have changed slightly, but the technique remains the same. The woodcut, with its bold lines, had an emotional quality that was particularly appealing to northern European expressionists such as Edvard Munch (1863–1944), Käthe Kollwitz (1867–1945), Max Pechstein (1881–1955),

In Praise of Flower Hunting
Munakata Shikô (1903–1975), Japanese, 1954, impression-printed woodblock print, 56⅛ × 67¼ inches. St. Louis Art Museum, Gift of Munakata Shikô in memory of Leo Siroto. This woodcut demonstrates the idea of having 50 percent black and 50 percent white in a composition.

When Father Cast the Nets
Elizabeth Cavanagh Cohen, color woodcut hand-printed by the artist, 24 ×
32 inches. The artist based this print on a poignant poem written by the son
of how his father, a fisherman, had to cross a busy highway to cast nets, as his
family had done from their land for generations.

and Emil Nolde (1867–1955). Japanese woodcut printers of the nineteenth century such as
Katsushika Hokusai (1760–1849), Kitagawa Utamaro (1753–1806), and Ando Hiroshige
(1797–1858) had a major influence on the French impressionists. Painter-printmakers Mary
Cassatt (1845–1926) and Edgar Degas (1834–1917) were particularly taken with Japanese
prints, and their work reflected this
fascination. Postimpressionist Paul
Gauguin (1848–1903) created at least
forty woodcuts. The linocut came later
and was explored by Pablo Picasso and
many contemporary printmakers.

Preparation

Introduce students to linoleum printing by having them do a small print
(4 × 6 inches). If you have large classes
of many people who share colors, students probably should use ink straight
out of the tube. "Custom mixing colors"
might be reserved for advanced students
who have learned how to conserve ink.

Linocut materials: clockwise from upper left: baren, Soft-
Kut print plates, cutting knives, eraser for cutting a small
stamp, small battleship linoleum plate, bench hook.

Landscape with Squirrel
Mary Kate Kabbes, 12 × 18 inches, linoleum print. Villa Duchesne and Oak Hill School, St. Louis County, Missouri, teacher Christine Sarra.

Campus
Meghan Grojean, 12 × 18 inches. Villa Duchesne and Oak Hill School, St. Louis County, Missouri, teacher Christine Sarra.

Alternative Project

Embossing and Tissue Paper Color Transfer

If you have a printing press, embossed prints can be made from a linocut plate without inking. Use heavier, damp paper and increase the pressure for best results. The design and a plate mark (edges of the plate) will be visible. Another option is to place a piece of colored tissue paper between the linocut and the printing paper to transfer color and emboss the print at the same time. Test the tissue paper with a drop of water first to make sure it is the kind that "bleeds."

Alternative Project

Printing a Linocut on Other Materials

Cloth, plain or patterned, is a suitable background for repeated printing with a small linocut. By varying the direction of the block, interesting designs result. You can work this out in advance by making thumbnail sketches or allow it to evolve. Acrylic paint or textile ink might be more appropriate for printing on cloth.

Alternative Project
Reduction Relief Print

The reduction print allows printing in multiple colors using the same block. The technique does not differ significantly from normal linocutting except that when the student has finished, most of the surface of the block has been removed. To make several colors from the same linoleum plate, print several prints with a light color before carving away more of the plate and printing second and third colors.

Farm Daze

Susie Stopke, linocut, 18 × 28 inches. This student's linocut was made using three linocut printing plates on ordinary printed cloth (which had a farm scene, including animals). The design may be seen through the intricate designs created by turning and frequently reprinting the same three linocut plates.

FOR THE STUDENT

Keep in mind that the area that is cut away will be white, and the area that remains will be a color. As a rule of thumb in a relief print, approximately half the print will remain white, while the other half will be colored.

A tree branch or flower may be drawn exactly as you like. Remember artistic license. That means that because it is your work of art, you can make it look the way you see it. You put in, you leave out, and you add color or background exactly where you want it.

Make several thumbnail designs (these usually take only a minute or two each) roughly the same shape as the linoleum plate.

1. After selecting one design, draw around the outside of the plate and make a design on paper the exact size of the plate.

2. Put an X in the areas to be carved away, leaving unmarked the areas that will remain. You might refer to this master design from time to time.

Katy Trail. This 12 × 12-inch three-color reduction relief print was printed with the white background cut away first, leaving the darker (reddish) lines of cyclists, grain storage areas, and fence. These were cut away to enable printing of a lighter green grass, sky detail, and barns. If enough colors are printed on a reduction print, the plate's surface can almost completely disappear.

3. Tape the drawing to a window or a light box, and use pencil to draw over the design on the back of the paper. To transfer your design to the linoleum plate, tape the rectangle to the linoleum. Make sure the design that faces the plate is backwards (so the plate surface will be cut backwards—the reverse of the final print).

4. Redraw over the design to transfer it to the plate.

5. Carve the plate. If you have access to one, use a bench hook to assist you in safely cutting. Battleship linoleum may be heated slightly (with an iron or hair dryer) to make it easier to cut. Use a V-gouge to cut on the lines. When you make "mistakes" (and you will!), just shrug your shoulders and let that mistake be part of the charm of your linocut.

6. In relief printing, you can make a quick trial proof by holding a piece of thin paper on top of the uninked plate and rubbing it with the side of a pencil or crayon. Make a trial print, then if you are satisfied, make at least six identical prints.

7. Title, number, and sign your prints.

FINISHING TOUCHES

Time needed: 1 fifty-minute class

Objective: Students will examine prints made for this project, planning to change at least one print either by making a photocopy transfer, drawing on it in colored pencil, or cutting out pieces and pasting them onto another surface (perhaps a different print) to make a collage.

FOR THE TEACHER

From the beginning of printmaking history, artists have been known to "touch up" a print to make it just a little more effective. While purists feel that that the print as it is pulled is complete, other artists commonly use ink to disguise a hole they didn't intend to leave or pencil to accent areas that need it.

If a finished composition (print or collage) lacks "oomph," the simplest solution may be to enrich it by drawing directly on some areas. Pencil, watercolor or acrylic, charcoal, ink, Conté crayon, or pastel are all suitable drawing materials. Sometimes only a few lines are needed. I have mentioned before that rules in printmaking may be broken. Artists who are just coming to printmaking don't always know there are rules (printing traditions) and are doing some exciting things by cutting and pasting, combining, and drawing accents.

Prismacolor Pencil Drawing

The viewer is often attracted to the interesting and luminous effects that can be achieved with Prismacolor. The intense colors of these pencils make a dynamic accent. Use complementary colors (red next to green, for example). Or use several closely related colors to create a luminous line that gives the effect of roundness because it is light on the inside and becomes darker on the outside edges. As with any pencil drawing, controlled parallel marks—hatching or cross-hatching—are generally more effective than scribbles.

Photocopy Transfers

Time needed: 1 class period

Materials: solvent (oil of wintergreen, Citra Solv, or acetone), magazine photos or fresh photocopies, small brush or cotton swab, paper towels, small-mouthed plastic bottle, spoon, plastic bag in which to put used towels

FOR THE STUDENT

If your print could be enhanced with a little magic realism, burnish a photocopy image in black onto the print. To transfer the photocopy, place it upside down on a composition and burnish with a pencil on the back. The basic copies for this transfer may be made on either a laser printer or a photocopier; the toner on these copies is the magic ingredient. Place the photocopy face down on the surface to which you are transferring and burnish the back with a spoon or pencil. Several different solvents appear to work. *Caution:* if you use a solvent with a strong odor such as acetone (some types of fingernail polish remover are basically acetone) or oil of wintergreen, keep it in a small-mouthed bottle and keep it capped when not in use. Work in a well-ventilated area and use soap and water to wash any solvent off your skin.

Hidden Within
Joanne Stremsterfer, monoprint with spirit transfer and charcoal, 32 × 26 inches. In another version of this print, the artist transferred a photocopy of a buffalo to the print surface by using oil of wintergreen (available at drugstores) and rubbing on the back with pencil. The print was completed with the addition of charcoal. Collection of the artist.

Hidden Within
Buffalo detail that was added to Hidden Within in one version.

Looking for Cowboys
Joanne Stremsterfer, 2005, 9 × 12 inches. Watercolor monotype with spirit transfer (oil of wintergreen) and collage. The artist first printed a watercolor base and then built layers of colors, printing various shapes. Collage (using portions of old prints) gives additional interest. Collection of Anne Stupp.

PROJECT 5-8
COLLAGE WITH PRINTS

Time needed: 2 fifty-minute classes

Materials: heavy 8 × 10-inch watercolor or mat board as a base; leftover prints (the ones you couldn't throw away); miscellaneous papers of all types; YES! glue, polymer medium, or PVA glue; covered container for thinned YES! glue; scissors; brush; envelopes or small plastic bags to store small scraps for reuse; old catalogs or magazines

Goal: Students will engage in experimentation and risk taking.

Objective: Students will use sensitivity and subtlety to create an abstract collage, using extra prints of their own or others that may be combined with other materials.

FOR THE TEACHER

It is a big decision for a printmaker to tear a print to incorporate it in another work of art. However, once the decision is made, students will have wonderful material to combine with other prints. Collage is where the amateur printmaker is rewarded for keeping all those prints gone wrong.

Materials that are appropriate to combine with prints in a collage are thin Asian papers; decorated, handmade, or found papers; mesh onion or potato bags; wrapping materials; corn husks; raffia; cloth; and string. Greeting cards and gift bags yield fabulous textured and shiny paper.

The collage can be any size or shape, but a small collage of 6 × 8 inches mounted on an 8 × 10-inch piece of heavy paper allows for many manageable experiments. It happens to be the size that several international collage exchanges have adopted, because the 8 × 10-inch format easily fits into a mailing envelope. Another option is for students to make a larger collage, then use a viewfinder (a 6 × 8-inch opening cut into a piece of copy paper) to isolate the "sweet spot."

Art History Connections

Over the years many artists have incorporated collage into their work, in particular Henri Matisse (1869–1964), cubists Pablo Picasso (1881–1973) and Juan Gris (1887–1927), Kurt Schwitters (1887–1948), Tom Wesselman (1931–2004), Romare Bearden (1914–1988), Eric Carle (1929–), David Hockney (1937–), and Robert Rauschenberg (1925–2008). Students can see the potential of collage by researching one or more of these artists online or in books.

FOR THE STUDENT

There is no right or wrong way to begin. You may decide to make a realistic collage such as a cityscape or landscape or work on a theme such as an animal in an imaginary jungle or a garden. Or simply make a total abstraction and give special emphasis to one area. Everything in the collage leads your eye to that one spot because of its color or complexity.

1. Select parts of the leftover prints that have interesting detail and tear or cut them out. Find related or complementary colors in other papers such as Asian mulberry paper, magazine pages, advertising brochures, paste paper, ticket stubs, or wrapping paper. Move things around until you come up with the final design. Look for relationships: repetition, shapes, line, color, and value. Remember that leaving uncomplicated, open areas can make a composition interesting.

2. When you tear paper, a white border will be left either on top of or underneath the torn edge, depending on whether you are right- or left-handed, or tear toward or away from yourself. Experiment! For complete control, place fingers from both hands close to the edge you are tearing and work slowly. Or cut with scissors.

3. Hang on to any small slivers of paper that you are not planning to use in this collage, since they may be used later to emphasize a line or become part of the next collage. Strips of shiny paper, string, printed words, or found photos can add sparkle and wit to your collage.

4. When you are satisfied that the collage is complete, carefully remove the layers and set them aside.

5. Paste the bottom layer first. Work on an old catalog or magazine to apply glue to the edge of the piece. Place a sheet of copy paper on top and rub hard, making sure each piece is attached before applying the next piece. Turn the catalog page to avoid getting glue on the front of the next collage piece. Keep a damp towel handy to wipe your fingers.

Tribute to Philip Johnson, Architect
The print that was the base of this collage was based on a sketch made while waiting for a plane in New York City. The print was a little "off" (as was the sketch, for that matter), but when cut up, it became a good beginning for a collage.

6. This collage can be mounted on a piece of heavy paper or mat board. When it is finished, it should be mounted onto a piece two to three inches larger on all sides.

7. If the collage is smaller than the mounting paper, consider deliberately letting something "spill" over into the blank border.

Preprinting Possibilities

Brayer-printed paper and paste paper may be done before any printing is done at all or can be done after students have an understanding of the potential of printing a linocut on paper that already has a design. Both of these techniques are also useful for collages involving leftover prints. If large sheets of thin drawing paper are prepared, the designed paper is useful for making book covers and cards. It makes a beautiful background for prints.

BRAYER-PRINTED PAPER

Time needed: 1 fifty-minute class

Materials: drawing paper, all sizes; brayers of several sizes; water-based printing ink in a variety of colors; inking slabs (Plexiglas or glass); water for cleanup

Goal: Students will prepare paper in advance for later printing projects or collage.

Objective: Students will create movement and decorative patterns with the use of at least three different colors and a variety of marks.

Brayer-printed paper can be made either at the beginning of a printing session or at the end, when students are using up ink that has already been rolled out.

FOR THE TEACHER

Most students are familiar with brayer use, but this is good preparation for printing with other methods. Brayer-printed paper is wonderful for later use in collages because of its lush texture or as base paper for another type of print such as a linocut or woodcut.

Interchangeable patterned roller heads for brayers are available through art supply stores or catalogs. You can add pattern to existing old brayers by carving simple designs with a lino cutter, gluing string on the roller to make patterns, or temporarily placing rubber bands in patterns over the brayer. These enable students to make patterns such as dots, waves, linen, mesh, or speckles.

Monotypes with Art Paste and the Brayer

Although I prefer using printing inks for brayer printing, acrylic or tempera colors that have been mixed with Elmer's Art Paste will work too. The best method I have found is to use a teaspoon to drop a small amount of one or more of the color mixtures on a sheet of paper at intervals. Use the brayer to spread the colors on the entire sheet. If you have too much paint on the sheet of paper, you can cause a happy accident by placing a clean sheet of paper on top of the paint-laden paper. Use your hands to smooth the new paper, working from the center outward to get rid of air bubbles. Separate the two sheets, and you have made not just one, but two monotypes.

FOR THE STUDENT

Brayer-printed paper is simple to do and offers infinite possibilities. It is done by inking a brayer and rolling it on a large piece of paper. It is possible to use only one color, working with natural patterns, but it is irresistible to experiment with layering one color over another. When a brayer runs out of color, it leaves just traces of the new color, allowing the first coat(s) to show through. In painting, it might be referred to as letting the grandfather show through.

1. Put a small amount (enough to fill a toothbrush) of each color of ink on separate inking slabs (or if you are working on a large inking slab, simply space different colors at intervals). Roll the ink out until it makes a *shhhh* sound and looks velvety, then apply it to the paper. You can work in an uncontrolled manner simply by starting anywhere on the paper, working in different directions, and continuing until you run out of ink.

2. Reink and repeat the procedure, perhaps using a different color. I recommend applying ink right up to the edges of the paper so you can use the entire sheet either as a work of art or as a book cover or liner. Scraps, naturally, are perfect for collages.

3. Circular designs can be made by holding one end of the brayer in place and moving the other end of the brayer around in a circle. Circles can be combined with wavy designs.

4. You can make straight lines by placing the brayer, lifting it, and placing it down a half inch away. Experiment!

PROJECT 5-10
PASTE PAPER

Time needed: 1 to 2 fifty-minute classes

Materials: 12 × 18- or 18 × 24-inch medium-weight drawing paper, methyl cellulose glue (Elmer's Art Paste), 1- to 2-inch sponge brush, containers with lids for paste colors, acrylic paint (liquid or tube), plastic spoons, sponge, container for water, paper towels, tub for dampening paper, mark-making tools (such as plastic credit cards, wide-spaced combs, hard plastic bread clips, or rubber painters' graining tools (available at a paint store), scissors, iron

Goal: Students demonstrate the ability to make pattern by informed decision-making and experimentation.

Objective: Students produce several sheets of paste paper that will be used for later projects.

FOR THE TEACHER

Paste paper makes an ideal background paper for relief printing or stamping. It may be used as cover or lining paper for handmade books or collage. You can use many different tools for mark-making, from a plastic fork to a purchased triangular graining comb (available at paint stores), a hair comb with widely spaced teeth, small plastic bag tabs (from the grocery store), serrated pen tips, or plastic toys. Make tools from old credit cards by cutting ¼-inch deep "teeth" on the long side with scissors.

Elmer's Art Paste (methyl cellulose polymer in powder form) is available at art supply stores or through catalogs, and one package makes a gallon of paste. To mix smaller amounts of paste, use approximately 2 teaspoons to 1 cup of water. There are many formulas for cooked paste, but this one is fast and easy. I prefer it because it is not organic, does not develop mold or unpleasant odors, and appears to last indefinitely (unrefrigerated), even when mixed with acrylic paint.

Vocabulary: graining

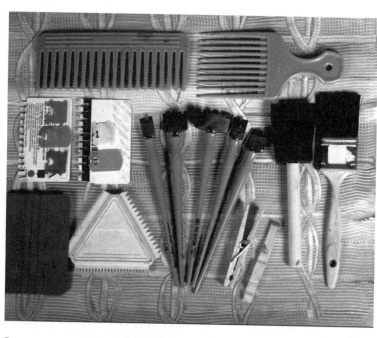

Paste paper tools. These items are used to make designs in paste that has been applied with foam brushes. Included are combs, clothespins, calligraphy pens, a painter's graining triangle, and credit cards with scissor-cut edges.

A Paste Paper pattern.

FOR THE STUDENT

These regularly patterned papers are effective, but experiment by using contrasting colors side by side or spread several different colors evenly on a paper and try using several different types of "markers" to combine designs on a single sheet of paper. The process is fast and easy, and extras may be used for covering boxes, lining dresser drawers, or wrapping gifts.

Hawaiian tree linocut printed on paste paper.

1. Mix acrylic paint with paste, spread it on paper, and manipulate it to make beautiful patterns. To mix specific colors, pour approximately ½ cup of paste into a container that has a lid. Add approximately 1 to 2 tablespoons of acrylic paint to the paste and stir well. The amount of paint needed depends on its intensity. If kept covered, the colors will last a long time.

2. Work on a clean plastic surface (a tabletop or a piece of Plexiglas larger than your paper). Dip the paper in water briefly and quickly remove it, allowing excess water to drip off. After placing it on the

nonstick surface, lightly sponge it from the center outward to remove bubbles and excess water. If there are ridges on the surface, they will affect the pattern or might cause the paper to tear when you apply pressure. Working on dry paper also works reasonably well.

3. Using a brush or sponge brush, apply paint to the paper in smooth, even horizontal strokes from edge to edge. It will get ink on the plastic surface around the edges. You can clean it with a sponge later. Avoid applying paint thickly, as it may flake off later when you want to make folds in the paper. Metallic powder can be sparingly sprinkled on the surface before graining.

4. Press the graining tool (even fingers can be used as a tool) firmly into the wet paint, making horizontal marks over the entire paper, then go over it vertically with a tool with slightly different spacing. Or make diagonal marks across the vertical lines. Try making waves of various lengths, first horizontally, then vertically. On the next piece of paper, make deeper waves, perhaps working on a diagonal.

5. Make designs on the paper while the paste is wet. If the pattern appears to run together (either because your paint is too thin or the paper is too wet), wait about ten minutes to allow the paint to thicken and try it again.

6. Remove the paper from the surface and either place it flat on a drying rack or the floor to dry. Or hang it on one-inch PVC pipe that is suspended by a clothesline run through the center. You can allow the paper to dry normally or use a hair dryer. If the paper is buckled after drying, it may be ironed on the wrong side to smooth it.

6

Photography

Students love photography! It is immediate and highly personalized. The history of photography is interesting to students. Many of them have old family photographs and cameras, and enjoy learning about them. Have an "old camera day," when students bring in family photographs and old cameras. Encourage them to bring the oldest photo and oldest camera they can find. Even if they bring in only their own baby photos, at least they have looked through family albums and talked about photography with parents and grandparents.

The first hundred years of photographic history featured mostly black-and-white photos. A rich legacy has been left by the thousands of journalists, fashion photographers, and amateurs over the 170 and more years that photography has existed. Those photographers recorded exploration and war, daily life, family, Hollywood, and news events. Some subjects still seem to almost *demand* to be printed in black and white. Darkroom film photography in this medium continues to be taught, even in advanced courses in some high schools and universities. This chapter includes information on changing digital color photos to black and white and instructions for developing film and printing black-and-white photos in a traditional darkroom. It isn't enough to simply deluge students with information; you need to give them opportunities to apply the things they have learned. They will be taking photos long before you have really taught them everything they should know about composition. Build skills over a period of time by repetition and practice.

The first three projects in this chapter are suitable for either black-and-white film photos or digital work.

Technology in cameras changes rapidly and varies greatly between camera brands and styles. Specific information about computer programs is quickly outdated, but some standards remain much the same in programs such as Photoshop Elements, Photoshop, GIMP (a free download from the Internet that works on PCs), and others.

Numerous tutorials are available on the Internet that will reinforce what you are teaching in class. Wonderful books on programs such as Photoshop exist that will be valuable resources. No attempt is made here to be encyclopedic in the discussion of digital graphics, as there is enough material for a lifetime! Instead I have tried to include assignments that can enrich your courses, based on the assumption that you, the teacher, already have some knowledge of digital graphics.

A vocabulary list at the end of the chapter will be useful for this and the next chapter, on computer graphics.

Camera drawings

It's a Digital World (Almost)

Few students will own *film* cameras now (just visit a camera store to discover how little film is available), and most new photographers are using digital cameras. Using a digital camera allows the photographer to take an almost unlimited number of photos, discarding poor photos and taking another photo if the result isn't quite what was expected. Although many so-so photos can be fixed on the computer, and part of what students will learn is how to improve minor imperfections, the greatest favor you can do for your students is to motivate them to be selective in the images they take and keep. Set a minimum and maximum number of photos to turn in for a shoot (approximately twenty-four to thirty-two). Ask students to give this file a name and turn in their memory cards (which contain metadata about each photo).

Cameras

Ideally, the photography class should have enough quality cameras to give all students the opportunity to take high-quality photos. You will have to work out a schedule giving them equal access so that they can take photos outside of the classroom.

Cell Phone Photos

Although cell phones and tablets are not considered *cameras* to be used for a photo class, they do give most students ready access to take a snapshot almost any time, any place. Many cell phone photos are of publication quality if they are not overenlarged. And they are adequate for some uses: posting on the Internet or remembering events such as family gatherings or trips.

Rules of composition can apply even with cell phone photos. The elements of art and principles of design are of special importance in photography. Your students will benefit from looking at historic photos and discussing their *visual* appeal in *art* terms, in addition to the subject matter. What is special about some photos that cause them to become *icons* of photography?

COMPOSITION TIPS FOR GREAT PHOTOS

These are tried-and-true ideas for *composition* that are applicable for darkroom black-and-white or digital color photography.

Use the rule of thirds whenever possible (imagine a rectangle divided by thirds vertically and horizontally to make an imaginary ticktacktoe grid). Place the subject at one of the intersections or show the horizon either on the upper or lower third, rather than in the middle.

The center of interest (focal point) is usually not in the center. Try to avoid the "bulls-eye" photo.

Closer is usually better. Let the viewer see what attracted you to this subject originally.

Eliminate all background clutter. Change position or move in close. Simplicity is important. A birds-eye view or worm's-eye view may eliminate unnecessary detail and make even the ordinary subject look more interesting. Deliberately make your eye go to one corner of the viewfinder and follow the outline of the picture all the way around the viewfinder.

Include a distinct focal point such as a tree, a rock, or a person, even when you are basically shooting a landscape (such as the Grand Canyon). Sometimes shooting low and including a subject in the foreground will add needed impact.

Work a subject. After deciding *what* you will take, concentrate on *how* you take it. Use various camera angles (horizontal, vertical, and diagonal); maximum f-stop for sharp depth of field; minimum f-stop for sharpness on the focal area; fast shutter speed or slow shutter speed; double exposure; normal exposure or underexposed or overexposed—you may want to make an HDR (high dynamic range) photo later.

Photos of children. Try to get down to eye level with children, rather than shooting them from above.

Leave space in front of a moving subject or face. For example, a person should be walking into the picture rather than out of it, and if a person is looking one direction, leave space in front for looking, rather than centering the face.

Vertical subjects. People and faces are vertical. You can make the best use of space by using the camera vertically for individuals or couples.

Cropping. If you are not shooting the entire body, crop (cut off) at the shoulder, waist, hips, knees, but not usually at the neck, ankle, or wrist. Hands often are an important part of the composition.

Large-group shots. For a formal large-group photo, have some seated on the floor, some on chairs, and some standing behind. Or take the photos with people standing on a staircase. If you are taking a group photo, take three quick photos without people changing position, as usually someone will have eyes closed or mouth open. That way, you can later make improvements to that image on the computer. Look at each face before exposing to make sure you can see the entire face, even if you have to move people around to make them visible.

Look for leading lines, which are lines merging in a hallway, looking straight up on buildings, or down a city street. Diagonal lines that lead the eye to a subject are strong. Horizontal lines tend to be restful.

Balance can be formal, with the subject in the middle and objects on either side roughly the same size. Informal balance has the center of interest to one side, but smaller objects and lines keeping the composition from seeming to tilt from the weight.

Repetition is dynamic in photography, with the artist being sensitive to objects that are frequently of the same shape (circles, for example). The repetition of similar shapes can provide rhythm that makes a photograph "sing."

Things to Avoid

Avoid shooting all photos at eye level.

Mergers, such as a tree from the background growing out of the subject's head.

"Kissing"—when part of the subject is just touching the edge of the photo—either let it run off or move it in.

SOME PHOTO ASSIGNMENTS

Here are some ideas for taking photographs. You may already have a subject in mind, but these might also be useful when thinking about *how* to take the picture.

- Create a mood through the lighting you choose.
- Make three separate photos by selecting three elements or principles of art to illustrate (for example, value, line, shape, repetition, pattern, emphasis, or contrast).
- Take a series of photos to tell a story (something like "a day in my life").
- Photograph a classroom activity (such as sewing, cooking, dissecting, or playing music).
- Make a portrait of one friend that includes hands.
- Make a portrait of three friends together (be sure to *fill* the frame—not just a line-'em-up-and-grin photo).
- Use an unusual camera angle to create a mood.
- Make a black-and-white photo of a human condition such as joy, contentment, disappointment, loneliness, despair, poverty, or exhaustion.
- Take two photos to later combine showing a student either tiny or huge in comparison to an object being held in the hand or in relationship to a building. Humor helps here.
- Take photos to make actual postcards on postcard paper.

Abstract	Nature	Everything in focus (f/16 or f/22)
Animals	Pattern	Family portrait
Architecture detail	Reflections in parts of cars	Food (make it good enough to eat)
Blurred action	Rhythm	Groups in uniform
Boats	School life	I'm just crazy about _____
Children	Shadows	Music (instruments and musicians)
Close-ups	Shape	Nighttime, with only existing light
Cornered	Signs	*Subject*-only in focus (f/2)
Downtown	Space	Panned photo (1/30 second; follow the action)
Faces (real or not)	Sports	Photojournalism (tell a story in one picture)
Flash	Stop-action	
Flowers	Strong emotion	School building (strong light and shadow)
Framed	Sunset	
Hands	Texture	Silhouette (backlighting)
High contrast	Trees	Black against black
Humor	Value	White against white
In the park	Water	
Line	Weird	
Machinery	Double exposure	

Camera Controls

For cell phone photos or point-and-shoot cameras, the controls are automatic. It is still useful for students to understand that when the light is too low, they will either end up with a flash photo or *camera shake* that results in an out-of-focus picture.

Urge your students to read the manual that came with their cameras or read about that particular model on the Internet to get the most out of it. The number of megapixels that the digital camera has (usually written on the outside of the camera or the box it came in) is critically important to the pixel count available with each photo taken. Generally, the higher the pixel count, the better the quality of the photo.

Exposure

Although many cameras are of the "point-and-shoot" variety or may be used on automatic setting, students should still understand how the controls—the aperture and shutter—affect the appearance of a photograph. The effect of the controls remains the same, even on a complex camera. The aperture, shutter, and ISO (film speed) work together to allow the correct amount of light to enter the camera for proper exposure.

ISO, or Film Speed

The film speed rating indicates the sensitivity of the film (or camera sensor) to light. The higher the ISO (International Standards Organization) number of real film, the more sensitive it is. The recommended general-purpose film for use in school is 400 ISO. It is sensitive enough to use indoors, but still has reasonably fine grain. One disadvantage to higher-speed film is that there is more grain (clumping of particles of silver), which some do not find as attractive as a finer-grained film.

In digital photography the same general rules apply, although there is no *film*. In digital photography, the ISO number measures the sensitivity of the camera's sensor. Rather than clumping of silver particles that causes *grain* in film, the higher ISO number in digital causes *noise* (random color specks), which is visually similar to grain. The lower the ISO number, the finer the quality of the photo. A higher ISO number might be useful if you were shooting indoor sports and needed to stop action or were in an extremely low light situation. If your digital camera has such controls, set it for super-fine quality (or raw), which will increase the pixel count in each photo. This allows you to later enlarge it in a computer program such as Photoshop without lowering the quality.

Lenses

Cameras with a nonmovable (fixed) lens are usually set at a normal lens opening of 55mm (which is also what the human eye sees when looking straight ahead). A lens opening number of 18mm gives *wide-angle* vision (and sometimes distortion), but is useful for group, cityscape, and indoor photographs in a tight space. A fish-eye lens of 12mm gives extreme wide angle and distortion. A *telephoto* lens of 80mm to 200mm brings a subject closer and narrows the field of vision. A*djustable* or *zoom* lenses give a field of vision range that is listed on the front of the lens. Most digital cameras that students use have a zoom lens with the equivalent of 28mm to 100mm, plus a macro (close-up) setting.

Shutter

The shutter determines how long the lens is open. The *shutter speed button* indicates the speed at which a photo is taken. Numbers such as 2, 15, 30, 60, 500, 1,000, 2,000, or 4,000 represent fractions of a second that the shutter is open. Number one represents one second; number 500 is 1/500 of a second. A *shutter priority* setting gives preference to movement (such as sports or action).

To control camera shake, a good rule of thumb is that the shutter speed should not be slower than the focal length of the lens. For example, a 125mm lens should be exposed at 1/125 of a second (125), and a 200mm lens should not be exposed at less than 1/250 of a second (250). There is not a 200 on the shutter release. If a photo must be taken at 1/30 of a second or less (30), the picture is likely to be blurred, so you must become a "human tripod." Brace against something, hold the camera firmly against your forehead, take a deep breath and release the shutter.

To *pan* (stop action while blurring the background), set the shutter speed at 30. For example, a bicycle is going by: follow the bicycle with the camera, expose, and briefly continue following the action.

To *stop action* (freeze everything in the picture), a shutter speed of 1/250 or faster is preferred.

Aperture

The *aperture* is an opening in the lens of the camera through which light passes to expose the film. The size of the aperture controls *depth of field* (the area in front of and behind the main subject is in focus). The aperture openings are called f-numbers and range from f/2 through f/64. In antique and inexpensive cameras, a fixed aperture is usually f/8, offering a photo that is neither extremely sharp nor extremely out of focus. The smaller the f-number, the larger the opening on a standard camera. The sharpest depth of field in a standard camera is f/16. A group of photographers in the 1930s were known as the "f/64" photographers because that was the smallest lens opening on their large view cameras, and using it guaranteed that everything in the photo would be in the sharpest focus possible.

Aperture priority is selected when it is desired to have more of the photo in focus (such as taking scenery or a subject closer than two feet). If using this *macro setting*, identified by a flower symbol on the camera's setting, it is advisable to use a tripod. *Smaller lens openings* such as f/11, f/16, and f/22 will have more of the picture in focus (greater depth of field) and are best for normal photographs of people, places, and things. With a *larger lens opening* (such as f/2, f/2.8, or f/3.5), the *subject* on which the camera is focused will be sharp, whether it is close or far away. Choose a large lens opening if you wish to blur out the foreground or background in a photo (when making a portrait or flower photo, for instance).

Flash

On automatic cameras a flash is activated as needed to provide light. The flash is synchronized to work with the shutter speed. When a flash is used, the shutter speed is normally synchronized at 1/60 to 1/125 of a second. The lowest *safe* handheld shutter speed is 60 (1/60 of a second). The range of a built-in flash on a camera is normally from six to about ten feet. Beyond that, the light falls off sharply. You can shoot in almost any lighting situation without a flash if you have the camera on a tripod. Museums request that flash be turned off, as it can seriously affect the colors in a painting. A larger, separate flash such as those used by professionals may be attached to the camera or used off-camera for photographs of events or at locations where you cannot be as close to the subject as you would like. With digital cameras, it is often best to turn the auto flash off. If unsure, shoot one picture with the flash and a second without the flash.

Make Light Work for You

Light is the king in photography. An almost completely dark photo catches attention with pinpoints of light and subtle variations. The contrast of darks and lights in black-and-white photography explains its continuing appeal. Notice that many of the great old photos were muted or had strong shadows. Teach students to see things photographically, envisioning in advance how they will look. Most photographers continue to find that photos taken in early morning or late afternoon give the best results, as the light isn't quite as harsh as it is midday.

Backlighting

Remember—the camera is just a *machine* that records the light coming through the viewfinder. If a subject is backlit (light behind the subject, light coming through a window from behind, or theatrical lighting), the camera can be fooled, and the subject may be too dark, giving a silhouette effect. Compensate by opening the aperture one or two stops (plus 1 or 2 on an automatic camera—deliberately overexposing) or using a flash (even outdoors in daylight). Models are sometimes side-lit by the reflected sunlight from a large white or silver placard held by a photographer's assistant.

Bracketing

If you're unsure of the lighting, take photos at several different exposures. One special type of photograph called HDR (high dynamic range) requires that you take photos at several different exposures, later combining the images on the computer to make an exceptionally detailed, richly colored photo.

Photo Floodlights

Photo floodlights with reflectors supported on tripod stands may be used to artificially light a subject such as artwork or a model. The bulbs are specially balanced for film and allow you to get greater detail with a digital camera. Students should experiment by using photo flood-lights to get more dramatic photographs than overhead lights provide.

Taking Photos for a Portfolio

Take photos with an SLR (single lens reflex) camera if possible, filling the lens with the picture to avoid having to crop later. If you have distortion, it will be noticeable when brought up on a computer screen and may be adjusted by using the Transform Tool and cropping. Some teachers simply place the artwork on the floor where the lighting is even and get very good results.

To Photograph Artwork Indoors

Set the digital camera to the type of light available in the room, usually fluorescent. Attach the artwork to a neutral black, white, or gray background with pins or a dab of restickable glue. If the camera has the capability, set a digital camera to *vivid color* to capture brightly colored artwork or to *black and white* for pencil or ink drawings. Ideally, you will use a tripod whether you take the photos indoors or outside. Have the camera at the same height as the artwork, shooting straight on to avoid distortion. Photo floodlights also work well, but watch for bright hot spots. For even lighting with floodlights, place them between the artwork and the camera at a 45-degree angle at the same distance from the artwork. Both bulbs should be of the same age to provide equal lighting.

To Photograph Artwork Outdoors or by Sunlight Coming through a Window

Use a camera with a standard lens of 50mm, and have the sun at your back. If the sun is too bright, you may prefer to be in a "cloudy-bright" location out of the wind.

LEARNING TO LOOK: PHOTO APPRECIATION

Time needed: 1 fifty-minute class

Goal: Students research the work of one or more photographers to comprehend the complexity of the subject and to analyze *why* one photo endures visually while most are forgotten.

Objective: Students write about and participate in classroom discussion about composition, using formal terms.

Objective: Students compare and contrast photographs, examining images and symbols that might reflect psychological content.

The Steerage
Alfred Stieglitz, American (1864–1946), 1907, photogravure, 13⅛ × 10⅜ inches.
The Nelson-Atkins Museum of Art, Kansas City, Missouri. Gift of Hallmark Cards, Inc., Photo: John Lamberton.

FOR THE TEACHER

Ask students to find a photograph that appeals to them, allowing one week to bring in a photo to be scanned if it is in a book or they may give it to you on disk or flash drive. Part of the assignment will be a short written paragraph about why the student has selected this work and what elements and principles are seen in the photo. Make a digital slideshow of the photos to encourage involvement by the entire class. The written work will give them advance preparation for a discussion.

An alternative is for you to project a Photo of the Day, getting students accustomed to seeing great photos. Occasionally they can write about what they see in the photo at the beginning of the class.

Many art museums and school districts have adopted a learning method for looking at art based on research findings by Abigail Housen and described in Philip Yenawine's book, *Visual Thinking Strategies (VTS)*. The system involves the discussion leader asking three open-ended questions: What's going on in this picture? What do you see that makes you say that? What more can we find? Facilitation when using this technique and suggestions for encouraging writing through looking at art are further explained in Yenawine's text.

Art History Connection

To cover the range of photographic history, assign different students to select a historic period or famous photographer to investigate, and try to avoid having students duplicate an era or group of photographers.

- Early photography (1824–1870)
- Group f/64 (1932–1936)
- Farm Security Administration photography (Great Depression years, 1935–1941)
- Wars since the advent of photography (1861–present)
- Famous fashion photographers
- Famous contemporary photographers

In leading a discussion about photography, try to avoid asking any question that calls for a yes-or-no or single-word answer. Following are a few conversation starters. Expect that students have enough understanding of elements and principles at this point in their education that they will use some of these terms:

Elements: color, line, shape, space, texture, value

Principles: contrast, emphasis, repetition, rhythm, variety, balance, unity

- Where do you see the center of interest in this photo?
- What are some types of contrast that you see in this photo?
- How has the photographer used repetition in this photo to lead your eye across it?
- How does this photographer achieve balance?
- Why do you think this photo is famous or has the potential to be famous?

- Where might you crop this photo to make it better?
- What f-stop do you think was used on this photo? (Sharp focus or some areas sharper than others?) Can you identify different areas of focus?
- What shutter speed do you think the photographer used in this photo? (Stop action or blurred?)
- What in this photo gives you the idea about the time of day it was taken?
- What is the emotion that you feel this photo best expresses?

FOR THE STUDENT

You will have the opportunity to look online and in a library to find one photograph from any time period that appeals to you enough that you want to talk about it.

1. If you have found the photo on the Internet, download it on a flash drive or disk to be turned in as part of a classroom slide show. If you see a photo in a book and you cannot find it online by name or the photographer's name, bring in the book to be scanned.

2. Write a short paragraph giving the title, date, size, and name of the photographer. If a term is used that is unfamiliar such as daguerrotype or cyanotype, look it up to explain to the class.

3. Be prepared to talk about your selection, giving the name of the photographer, the time period it was printed, and why its subject matter appealed to you.

PHOTO ESSAY: FAMILY CELEBRATION

Time needed: 10 fifty-minute classes

Materials: digital camera, computer access, printer, photo paper, 14-ply mount board, spray mount

Content connection: Literary arts

Goal: Students become aware that most famous photographers became known for a recognizable subject matter or style such as fashion, landscape, interior, or portraiture.

Goal: Students research a famous photographer such as those of the 1930s Great Depression or *Life* magazine war photographers and later share information with the class.

Objective: Students demonstrate creative problem-solving skills through preplanning, creating photos, and exhibiting a finished, mounted, related group of photos.

FOR THE TEACHER

Few of your students are likely to become commercial photographers, but most will gain an interest in photography that can last a lifetime. A year tends to go from celebration to celebration, including national and religious holidays, birthdays, and family recognition of something special—at all of which photos will be taken. Challenge your students to think how they can tell a story of such an event in five or more pictures. Discuss with students the difference between a snapshot and a *photograph!*

Content Connection: Literary Arts

This project will be much better if students write a journalistic essay to accompany the photographs. The writing needn't be simply factual, but might include a brief story or a poem to illustrate the personality of one of the people included in a picture.

Preparation

Find examples of photo essays in newspapers and magazines, pointing out to students the layouts, which usually include varied photo sizes. Students can find wonderful photo essay examples on the Internet by going to *Life* magazine (life.time.com).

Alternative Project

Personal Experience

If a few students seem less than inspired by this *family* assignment, ask them to think about something where they are personally involved and are allowed to take photos, such as a job, sports, music, or theater rehearsal. This is a good opportunity to remind them of the courtesy of asking nonfamily members if they may take a photo. Another option is to take photos of an ordinary family event such as meal preparation or a day in a life of a little sister.

Alternative Project
Digital Photo Essay

If displaying photos on large mount board is too expensive, students may elect to make a digital photo essay by placing all the photos together on one printed page in a *photo composite*. Or students may use Power Point or Movie Maker with still photos and transitions.

Alternative Project
One Picture Tells a Story

Some photos such as a flower, tree, or baby are just beautiful to look at. Others, such as Albert Stieglitz's *Steerage,* make you wonder what the story is about: they make you want to ask questions of the photographer. One can sense the anxiety felt by new arrivals to the United States. Students can take just such a photo by being alert and open to tell a tale (a cell phone photo might be acceptable here).

Alternative Project
Writing and Photography

Students select their *best* photograph and write a journalistic short essay related to a subject or the emotion felt when looking at this photo. The poem doesn't have to rhyme, but at least needs to have enough substance to it that it is meaningful to viewers. It may be easiest to begin by jotting down single words or phrases that come to mind as you look at it. The poem and photo might be displayed on the same piece of mount board.

Content Connection: Literary Arts

Write an essay to be mounted with and included in the photo essay.

FOR THE STUDENT

Birthdays, graduations, anniversaries, new jobs, reunions, holidays—families celebrate these *occasions*. Sometimes such celebrations display a single photo that is printed in the local newspaper or online local news with a caption that identifies the people in the photo. Notice that in photo essays, the photos relate closely to each other in color or value, complementing rather than detracting from each other. Also note that some include the overall scene; some, individual figures; and some, close-ups or textures.

1. Whether it is a national holiday or family celebration, you are the photographer who needs to tell its story in three to five pictures.

2. Is there one person or several who are the center of the celebration? How would you take a photo so that anyone looking at it would know whose special day it is?

3. If you are taking a photo of a group, think how you can fill the frame to make an interesting photo. Be aware of what is in the background that might be used to make

the photo more interesting. If the background might detract from the story, *eliminate* it, by moving in close or changing locations.

4. After the photos have been taken, decide which photos to use and whether they should be in black and white or color. It can be a combination of both, but usually one or the other. The photos may be different sizes and shapes and may be *cropped* to eliminate unnecessary, distracting detail. Consistency in *value* is important.

5. Although you can use a caption under each photo, you might also choose to write a short journalistic essay to mount with the photos that includes the who, what, where, when, why, and how that describe the event.

6. On a large piece of poster board, move the photos and a printed-out version of your essay around to best display them or instead put printed captions under each photo. If you prefer to mount the photos individually to display next to each other, use pencil to sign at the bottom of the mount board, including your name and a title. Neatness counts: nothing should be crooked, poorly trimmed, or poorly printed. Whether on a small or large mount board, leave a border around all edges of the mount board of at least 1½ inches.

IMPROVE YOUR DIGITAL PHOTOS

Time needed: ongoing

Materials: digital camera, CD and flash drive, computer access, digital program printer, photo paper, 14-ply mount board, spray mount (optional)

Goal: Students demonstrate willingness to take risks, even without knowing in advance the end result.

Objective: Students modify an image using camera or art software controls.

FOR THE TEACHER

At the end of this chapter is a handout of digital terms that apply to photography *and* computer graphics that will also be applicable in Chapter Seven. Some of these terms are specifically explained in the next few projects.

Although most students are computer literate, computer graphics is a new approach to photography, and if you pour on too much information at once, you will overwhelm them. After you have demonstrated something to your students, you may want to recommend a specific *tutorial* that they can access on the Internet. Although a few students may grasp everything instantly, most will benefit from *repetition, review, hands-on guidance,* and *experience.*

The vocabulary may include words students already know, but the words have slightly different meaning as applied to digital photography. Many digital cameras have built-in processing that includes automatic color correction, exposure, white balance, tint, and compression of images in JPEG file format. Students can be introduced to ways to improve their digital photographs through using a few basic in-camera tools and import programs for transferring photos from the memory card to the computer.

One professional photographer recommends always copying *all* original photos onto a CD before making any changes and to always work with a *duplicate* of the original photo because once changes are made to an original, you can't go back.

Remind students that there are many ways to accomplish the same general effect, and that being open-minded, keeping notes, and experimenting may be the best ways for them to learn. Assure them that the only dumb question is the one they didn't ask.

Have students take all photos in color, rather than changing to black and white in the camera. This allows them the option of a color or black-and-white photo to print. A program such as Photoshop Elements, Photoshop, or Gimp allows complex changes in the computer, and the screen's larger size makes them far easier to do.

Introduce students to a few simple *key commands* that will save them considerable time as they work. In PC key commands, the Control key is used with a letter, and in the Macintosh, the Command key has the same function. To indicate key commands, I will give (CTRL-J or CMD-J), for example. The ALT key on a PC is the same as the OPTION key on a Macintosh, and in this chapter will be written (ALT or OPTION). Demonstrate how to import photos into the computer and organize them, how to make duplicate images, and how to use a few simple tools. Students can duplicate a layer to save the original or they can duplicate the original to make a copy.

FOR THE STUDENT
Things to Remember

1. Always copy your photographs onto a CD or flash drive to keep the original image, just in case. Rotate the direction of any photos in the batch that are not right side up.

2. After you have imported your photos into a program such as GIMP, Photoshop Elements, or Photoshop, you will find that you can sometimes improve a photo through a few simple changes.

3. If you are about to make a change that cannot be reversed, make a duplicate photo first by going to EDIT>DUPLICATE. Or you can make a duplicate layer in the Layers Panel. Go to the Applications Bar at the top of the screen, then to FILE>SAVE AS, and put the original into a folder on the computer's *desktop.* Name the original photo and any other photos on which you make improvements so each will be easier to find the next time you want to work. It is also a good idea to place it on a flash drive so you can make changes any time.

4. Select one photo to work on. If you make changes, they are sometimes easily lost, so remember to *save early and often!*

Changes to Try

Crop the photo to eliminate anything that doesn't seem to belong in the picture. You can control the size of your cropped images by typing a size number (such as 4 × 6 inches) in the Options Bar.

Straighten the photo by using guides on which to align it. Use the move tool (arrow in the toolbar) to drag the guideline from the left side or top. If the photo is obviously bigger or smaller on one side than another, hold down the shift key to avoid distortion and use EDIT>TRANSFORM>SKEW (CTRL-T or CMD-T) to align it to the guidelines. Click Enter when you are satisfied. Crop when you are sure the photo is straight.

To use the crop tool, draw a rectangle over the photo. Rotate it so it lines up with a horizon line and click OK. It's straightened and cropped all in one move. After lining it up horizontally or vertically, you should drag the corners to the edges so it fits inside the picture. Then click OK.

Filters. The use of filters offers infinite changes. Experiment with a few to see the differences that can be created in a photo.

Contrast. If the photo lacks contrast, there are several ways to improve it. You will find that most of the controls listed under image adjustments allow you to make an auto adjustment, which is the same as an automatic processing enhancement at a film developing shop.

Levels (CNTRL-L or CMD-L). Improves contrast, tone, lightness, and darkness. This allows you to improve contrast by lightening or darkening the photo, improving highlight, midrange, and dark areas.

Curves (CNTRL-M or CMD-M). The Curves box offers many options for change. Experiment with the sliders on the diagonal line to see the changes you can make in this mode. Auto Curves removes unusual colorcasts. It gives much the same effects as Levels.

Clone (CNTRL-S or CMD-S). This allows you to repair a blemish or speck by selecting an area nearby to replace the original spot. Repair flaws by using ALT or OPTION-CLICK on a good area, then going to the flaw. Click to replace it with the good area. Adjust brush size as necessary.

Anger
Brittany Riegert, digital composition, 8 × 10 inches. This "anger" image was one of several taken by Brittany that expressed emotions depicting the steps in the grieving process. Two portraits were "cut out" using layer masks. She took scans of handwritten notes that expressed her emotions to be used in the background. Transparency in the layers was used to interact with the portraits. Oakville High School, St. Louis County, Missouri, teacher Brian Crawford.

Ghostly Park
Dory Kennon, digital photo, 8 × 10 inches. This digital photo was altered by using a Neon Glow Filter that turned the day sky into night. A Blending Mode set to Darken combined the glowing layer with natural colors, and the final effect was enhanced with colors using Hue and Saturation and Levels. Oakville High School, St. Louis County, Missouri, teacher Joan Larson.

Patch Tool. The Patch Tool is also a great way to correct blemishes.

Mask. Highlight a layer and click on the square with a hole in it (a mask) at the bottom of the Layers Panel. A blank white box appears next to the original icon for the highlighted layer. It is linked together with the photo unless you unlink it by clicking the chain at the top of the Layers Panel. Paint black on the mask to hide distracting details in the image that you wish to eliminate. If you make an error, use the brush with white to correct (CTRL-X or CMD-X allows the brush to easily switch between black and white).

Black hides, white shows. You may find it helpful to make a new layer under the photo mask and fill it with any color (OPTION-DELETE) so you can see your corrections.

Red-eye correction. The pupil shows as red because the iris was wide open when the photo was taken, and the red is blood in the back of the eye. New programs in GIMP and Photoshop have a Red Eye tool. Enlarge the photo to work on the iris. If you're using an older program, use a light green color at approximately 50 percent to paint on the iris area with a brush.

PROJECT 6-4
CHANGE YOUR COLOR DIGITAL PHOTO TO BLACK AND WHITE

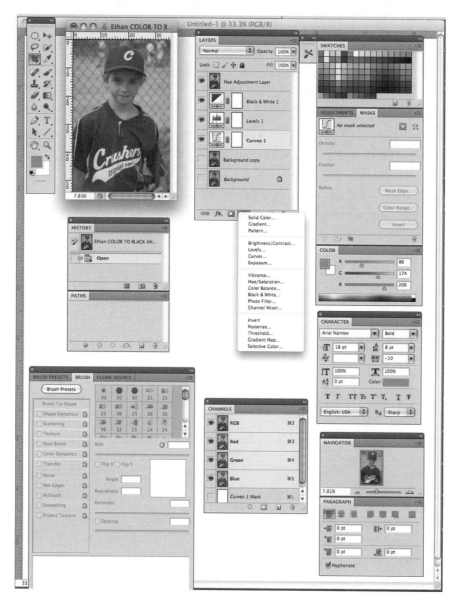

This screenshot of a digital color photo changed to black and white includes (clockwise from top left): the Tool Bar; photo of student; Layers Panel; Swatches; Character Panel; Navigator; Channels; Brush Presets; the History Panel; and Paths.

Time needed: 2 to 3 fifty-minute classes

Materials: digital camera, computer access, digital program printer, photo paper, 14-ply mount board, spray mount (to use if you do not have a dry mount press)

Goal: Students investigate and practice several methods of changing color digital photographs to black-and-white images.

Objective: Students demonstrate sensitivity and subtlety in selecting an appropriate photo to change from color to black and white.

Antigua, Guatemala. Color was eliminated by experimenting with several methods listed in this project for the best results for an original photo that had low color contrast.

FOR THE TEACHER

Until color photography came along, photographers used various methods to add color to *monochrome* photos (black and white) to make them more appealing. Now that black-and-white film and darkroom photography is being taught less and less, there is a present-day resurgence of interest in the appeal of black and white, and there will always be a place for it.

John Nagle, a pioneer in the field of digital photography, insisted that his advanced digital graphics students spend the first half of a semester experimenting with ways to change color photographs to black and white. This exercise forced students to become aware of value differences that might not have been apparent in color and to try to *think* in grayscale (to visualize black-and-white photos before taking them).

Point out to students that there are many ways to achieve the same effect. They

Earthquake victims, Guatemala.

can use Blending Tools in the Layers Palette or IMAGE>ADJUSTMENT commands in the Options Bar at the top of the screen. The instructions here are for Photoshop, but the process is similar in other programs.

It is worthwhile to give your digital photography students information on how to change a digital photo from color to black and white. Close-up portraits of themselves or friends are particularly fun for students to use for experimenting, and to find out how to improve skin tones and eyes through cloning, blending modes, and adjustment layers.

Alternative Project

Spot Color on a Black-and-White Photo

Color can be removed from the entire photo using one of the methods discussed here, but color may be reintroduced in one or more areas. To add in color again, paint on the white mask in an Adjustment Layer. Enlarge the picture to make painting easier. Use the brush from the Tools Panel, with the color on black to paint over any area where you want color to reappear. Change the brush size to large or small as needed. If you change your mind, change the brush color to white (and remember that *black hides, white shows*).

Adjustment Layer. Make a duplicate color layer (CTRL-J or CMD-J). Highlight the layer. Click on the black and white yin-yang circle at the bottom of the Layers Panel, holding it down to check Vibrance to make an Adjustment Layer, or go to the Applications Bar to open IMAGE>ADJUSTMENT>VIBRANCE. In the Adjustment Layer box, move the Saturation Slider all the way to zero to change the image to gray. Or go to IMAGE>ADJUSTMENT>BLACK AND WHITE.

Dragon
Tammy Ho, 8 × 10 inches, black and white with spot color. Oakville High School, St. Louis County, Missouri, art teacher Joan Larson.

Vocabulary

Applications Bar. The bar that runs across the very top of the screen lists locations of controls that will be used in computer graphics.

Options Bar. The options bar is also across the top, below the Applications Bar, and it changes each time a different tool is selected.

Tools. WINDOW>TOOLS. Photoshop and other operations are accomplished through using such tools as crop, brush, or eraser.

Background. This is the bottom layer in the Layers Panel, and it is locked and can't be altered. Some minor changes such as levels can be made while it is locked, but usually you will want to make a duplicate layer (CTRL-J or CMD-J).

Layers. WINDOW>LAYERS. These are like layers of tracing paper. You can make a change in a layer that affects the layer below it, but you can also throw it away if it doesn't do what you want (highlight it and click on the trash can or drag it to the trash can at the bottom of the layers palette). You may find it helpful to make an empty layer under the photo with the mask and fill it with any color (ALT/OPTION delete) so you can see your corrections easily. Layers may temporarily be turned on or off by clicking on the eye to the left of a layer.

Channels. WINDOW>CHANNELS brings up the Channels Palette, which has four layers named RGB, Red, Green, and Blue. Each of these color channels gives a different appearance to the final photo and are useful when working in black and white.

CMYK. Cyan, magenta, yellow, and black, which are found in IMAGE>MODE, are mostly used for color images that will be commercially printed.

FOR THE STUDENT

If you know in advance that you will print these photos in black and white, *think* before you take the photos, being aware of pattern, sharp edges, simple details, and contrasts. A scene that has little difference in value seldom looks wonderful when changed to monochrome (black and white).

Before beginning any conversion from color to black and white, take the time to copy the original photo to avoid losing it (IMAGE>MODE>DUPLICATE). Save and name the original color photo, putting it in a *folder* on the *desktop*.

Methods for Changing Color to Black and White

Here are several different ways to change a color photo to black and white. Remember to name each layer to help yourself see differences as you experiment.

Grayscale. IMAGE>MODE>GRAYSCALE. While this is the fast and easy method, it seldom gives the best results. However, it is useful if you simply want to preview a photo to see if it is worthwhile working on it in black and white. Grayscale can be improved by adding a Curves Adjustment layer (IMAGE>MODE>CURVES).

Desaturation. ADJUSTMENT LAYER>HUE/SATURATION. Remove color from a photo to make it monochromatic (black and white). The black and white circle at bottom of the Layers Panel gives many possibilities. The Applications Bar has another approach: LAYER>IMAGE>ADJUSTMENTS>HUE/ SATURATION>DESATURATE. Red, Green, and Blue Channels are individually converted to grayscale, then evenly merged back together for a total of 100 percent. Changes you make in each channel should still total 100 percent.

Adjustment Layer>Black and White. IMAGE>ADJUSTMENTS>BLACK AND WHITE. If you use the Default mode, your photo automatically becomes black and white. Experiment with other adjustments such as Vibrance. If this is a little flat (lacking value differences), use Levels or Curves to adjust.

Lab Mode. WINDOW>CHANNELS>IMAGE>MODE>LAB COLOR. The Lab Mode has three channels: the lightness channel, which has image details, and two channels that have red to green and blue to yellow. Working in the Lightness channel, drag (a) and (b) channels to the trash at the bottom of the Layers palette. If you are not satisfied with the contrast, experiment with IMAGE>ADJUSTMENTS>LEVELS to make changes.

Channel Mixer. IMAGE>MODE>RGB *or* IMAGE>ADJUSTMENTS>CHANNEL MIXER. In the Channel Mixer box, check Monochrome. Check Preview, then check Preserve Luminosity (to keep the sliders automatically at 100 percent). When you have made all the changes, go to the upper right of the Layers Palette to MERGE/ FLATTEN, if you want to change this to JPEG to send to someone on the Internet.

DIGITAL COMPOSITE

Time needed: ongoing

Materials: digital camera, computer access, digital program printer, photo paper, 14-ply mount board, spray mount (optional), CD and flash drive

Goal: Students experiment while taking photos, keeping notes to turn in this information with the contact sheets.

Goal: Students make changes with filters, adjustment layers, and other changes to further personal understanding.

Racing with Man's Best Friend
Caitlin Knipp, digital combined photo. Caitlin panned the background to give the effect of a downhill race. The dog posed while seated on the stationary skateboard. Oakville High School, St. Louis County, Missouri, teacher Joan Larson.

Objective: Students select an appropriate background for a photo composite, using masks, arranging layers, and making color adjustments to make an almost believable photo.

FOR THE TEACHER

You might choose to select one of these ideas to assign to an entire class of students so they are all working on roughly the same thing and experiencing the same problems, though their photos will all give a different result. Any of the projects here may be selected by advanced students. Depending on their comfort level with the computer, a composite could take from one day to a week. Introduce mask making, opacity, adjustment layers, and transformation (size, orientation, and skew).

One Photo, Different Sizes. Use a single photo repeatedly, changing it by scaling (making larger or smaller) or color changes. Or you can combine many different photos.

Mix Black and White with Color. Before the advent of the computer, Romare Bearden (1911–1988) made exciting collages by combining solid, brightly colored paper with his own black-and-white photographs and prints of Harlem. You can easily use the computer to make your own statement about your life and surroundings. Combine several related photographs in black and white or color, overlapping and interspersing them with bright color in geometric or random shapes.

An Impossible Photograph. Consider combining pictures together in a composition to *look* as if it is a single original photograph. Coordinate value, color, contrast, and shadows to make it believable. Then make a change or include something bizarre in the photo that makes the viewer realize it can't be real.

Underlying Theme. Develop an underlying idea for pulling several photographs together. Seascapes, cityscapes, a collage of a pet, shots taken from different angles, vacation or sports photos, or old family photographs can be combined to make a composite.

Panorama. Stand in one place and take a number of photographs while turning to overlap each shot by one-third with the previous one. Keep the horizon line on the same spot of the viewfinder. After downloading, open two or three side-by-side photographs onto the desktop. Make a new horizontal document—approximately 17 × 22 inches—and use the move tool to place your photos appropriately, with each photo on a separate layer. Carefully align them (adjusting opacity on a layer to see the underneath layer and adjusting the size as necessary). Using a large soft brush in black, hide the vertical line where they are joined. Crop to make an even border around the entire composition. FILE>AUTOMATE>PHOTOMERGE may be used in Photoshop to blend the photos. Some new digital cameras set to Panorama can automatically stitch together two or three frames. They show an edge of one frame to align with the next one.

One Subject, Twenty Photos. Think of what is around you. If you live in a small town, you may have historic buildings that are worth photographing for a photomontage. Or perhaps you live near the water, and the boats or ships can be photographed individually, then combined to make your own version of a harbor. Some towns have transportation museums that include period cars, trains, or airplanes. When you take photographs specifically

Fire Lane
John Dyess, 2005, digital composite on photo paper, 14 × 11 inches. Judicious cropping is necessary in any composition—leaving traces, and in this case, showing "scorched" areas. Digital artwork must go beyond simply exposing photographs and printing them together. It is the unexpected, the "aha" factor in Dyess's prints that makes them art.

with the idea of combining whatever you "find," you will look at your surroundings differently.

Signs. Take a walk down "Main Street" or your nearest shopping center and photograph signs of all kinds. Isolate each one on a separate layer with a mask and move them around, adding, eliminating, and resizing to make a composite. Or assign yourself to take only circular shapes one day—or mailboxes or doorways!

FOR THE STUDENT
Getting Started

A photo composite is done on the computer on one page and may derive from one group of photos. Or you may choose to scan new or old photographs for use in the composition.

1. For a standard-size print, make a new horizontal or vertical document 8 × 10 inches with 300PPI (pixels per inch) in U.S. paper, with a white background and Adobe RGB color profile. This will be the background layer. To see how well your masks cover, make a duplicate blank layer just above the background layer (CTRL-J or CMD-J). Fill this layer with a light color of your choice (ALT or OPTION>DELETE).

2. Place each photo on a separate layer to facilitate editing.

3. Select the photo you think is going to be the center of interest (not necessarily the center of the composition, but the one that will be the focus). Use the Lasso tool to select an area to make a Quick mask. You can go back and forth using the Q key to see where you have painted. Go to the bottom of the layers palette to add a mask to that area. Paint around the area you want to save with a brush in black, adjusting the brush size using CTRL-B or CMD-B. Remember that you can adjust the size at any time to make changes (CTRL-T or CMD-T). And you can adjust the intensity with Levels (CTRL-L or CMD-L). Navigator allows you to quickly zero in on a specific area (WINDOWS>NAVIGATOR).

4. Consider what might be used as your background for this composite. It could be a plain color or an overall view of a place you visited. Put that on a separate layer. Perhaps you will have to drag the background layer to the bottom of the layer stack so it will be behind the center of interest, then decide how dark or light you want it to be.

5. You may add one or two more photos onto layers that will go on top of the background photo. Size them appropriately and make tone adjustments so the result looks as if it were one photo. To change only one layer, choose LAYER>ADJUSTMENT LAYER.

6. As you add photos to the collage, consider changing the opacity of the pictures so some pictures show through others.

7. Use only your own photos in a composition (*no* copyright images), because images that you might enter into a competition require that the entire composition be original. Some teachers allow students to use original sketches made from Internet

research, listing the specific web page address on the sketch as a reference. Free pictures from the Internet are often of very low resolution and would need to be adjusted to match a file (which is not worth it).

Information: Black-and-White Film Photography

Although most secondary schools and universities are now doing digital photography, there is still magic to being in a darkroom and watching the image emerge from blank paper in a developing tray. Some schools and districts continue to include black-and-white photography and printing as part of the learning process in both beginning and advanced classes. Although a darkroom with separate enlarger stations is ideal, black-and-white photography can be done in any room that can be made completely dark where you have an enlarger and can set up trays. After photos have been fixed, they can be placed in a water-filled tray to be carried to another room for washing. In a situation where this was the only solution, I have covered windows with black plastic attached by Velcro so it can be put up and taken down easily, and used a red night-light as a safelight (as long as it is not too near the paper).

A darkroom ideally would have enough enlargers for half the class. Vertical dividers between enlargers will allow you to put them fairly close together and not have the light from one enlarger affect the enlarger next to it. Darkrooms should have a dry area and a wet area, with the enlarger(s) on the dry side and the chemicals on the wet side. The darkroom should have counter or table space for one or two sets of developing trays (three trays to a set), one or two sinks, and adequate ventilation. Be willing to sacrifice working space to install a light trap so you and the students can enter and leave the room without having to worry about light exposing prints as you go in and out of the room. Teacher Joan Larson had a small window with red glass installed in her school's darkroom so she could observe her classroom while she was working with students in the darkroom.

PROJECT 6-6
DEVELOPING FILM

Time Needed: 1 fifty-minute class

Materials: photographic thermometer (must be accurate); film changing bag; light-tight developing tank with reel; beverage-type can opener to open purchased film; scissors; darkroom chemicals: film developer, stop bath, fixer, hypo clearing agent, wetting agent (such as Photo-Flo); plastic negative sleeves (holder for up to 35 negatives); clips or clothespins for hanging film to dry

Goal: Students learn to expose pictures on film and develop them, experiencing the thrill of watching photos emerge in a developing tray.

Objective: Students turn in a proof sheet, test strip, and photo, listing exposure time and f-stops.

FOR THE TEACHER

Setting a schedule beforehand to indicate when students will mix chemicals will make your job easier. Write explicit instructions for mixing each chemical on 3 × 5-inch cards and post them near the area where chemicals are mixed. When you assign a number of people to be responsible for each chemical, someone is usually there to do it when needed.

Vocabulary: spindle, leader, developing tank and reel, cassette, negative sleeve

FOR THE STUDENT

1. *Load film in tank.* The film must be taken from the cassette in absolute darkness and placed on a reel inside a developing tank.

   a. Place the following items into a changing bag or on a counter in a totally dark place: scissors, reel, spindle, light-tight developing tank, and lid.

   b. For bulk-loaded film, hit the extending spindle on a tabletop to force the lid off. If you are using purchased film, remove the end with a beverage can opener. Remove the film.

   c. Cut the curved leader off the film before beginning to roll film onto the reel. Begin with a straight edge on the film.

   d. Put the loaded reel(s) into the tank and close the top securely, being sure the spindle is in the tank to prevent light leaking in.

   e. The tank may now be taken out into daylight.

2. *Develop.* Before beginning to develop, take the temperature of the chemicals. Film developing time is dependent upon the type of *film*, type of *developer*, *dilution*, and *temperature* of the chemical. Follow directions for developing time given with the film.

   a. Mix a proper dilution of film developer and water and take a temperature reading. Begin timing as you begin pouring the chemicals.

b. All chemicals should be from 68 to 70 degrees Fahrenheit. If the temperature is lower or higher, adjust the developing time according to the manufacturer's directions.

c. Tap the tank on the countertop (to dislodge bubbles). Agitate for the first 30 seconds (by inverting it several times to make sure the chemicals don't remain on the bottom), then agitate for 5 of every 30 seconds for the entire developing time.

d. At the end of the developing time, discard the developer.

3. *Wash.* Fill the tank with water, then empty.

4. *Stop bath.* Pour stop bath into tank, agitate for 15 seconds, then empty back into the stop bath jug. Stop bath may be reused. "Indicator" stop bath will turn purple when exhausted. Some teachers use water instead of stop bath to stop developing.

5. *Wash.* Fill the tank with water, then empty.

6. *Fixer.* Pour fixer into the tank.

a. Tap the tank on the table, agitate first 30 seconds, then agitate 5 seconds out of every 30 seconds for 8 minutes.

b. Pour the fixer back into the jug. Open the top of the tank and lift out the spindle and reel, making sure that the film is a translucent dark purplish gray. If the film looks opaque, it has not fixed long enough and should quickly be returned to the fixer. A simple test to see if the fixer is still good is to put a small piece of film into the fixer. If it turns clear, the fixer is still good. *Note:* In some classes, fixer is poured into a "Used fixer" jug and the teacher checks the solution with Hypo Check before reuse.

7. *Hypo clear.* Leave the tank lid off; rinse in water, then fill the tank with hypo clear. Soak the film in hypo clear for 2 minutes. Pour hypo clear back into the jug.

8. *Wash* in running water for 5 minutes.

9. *Photo-Flo.* This is a wetting agent used to eliminate spots; soak in Photo-Flo solution 1 minute. Pour Photo-Flo back into the jug.

10. *Squeegee.* Remove film from the reel. Either use a film squeegee or use the first two fingers of your hand as a squeegee. Pull the film through them one time, gently, to remove excess water. It is possible to scratch the wet film because the emulsion is still soft. *Handle film only by the edges. Never touch the emulsion.*

11. *Drying.* Hang the film in a dust-free locker or cabinet or attach to a line or clothes hanger with clothespins or clips. Put a clip on the bottom end to help film dry straight. Allow it to dry at least 1½ hours before using to avoid damaging the emulsion.

12. *Negative storage.* Cut the film into strips of five frames each and place them in a plastic negative sleeve to keep from scratching images.

BASIC BLACK-AND-WHITE DARKROOM PRINTING

Time needed: ongoing

Materials and equipment: enlarger; safelight; negative carrier; grain focuser; timer; easel; scissors; pieces of heavy 8 × 10-inch white cardboard; heavy glass (11 × 14 inches), either with polished edges or edges bound with masking tape; developing trays; tongs; sponges; paper towels; darkroom chemicals: developer, stop bath, fixer.

FOR THE TEACHER

Darkroom Magic

Enlarging one's own negatives is one of the most exciting moments in photography. Routinely following directions such as the ones given here will give consistently good photos and economically achieve the best results. To "encourage" students to follow routine procedure, require a proof sheet and test strips to be paper-clipped onto each mounted photo that is turned in. If these are missing, make deductions for each. Looking at these helps you find out quickly if they understand the procedures. Use variable contrast filters to add or reduce contrast in a print. Students should use a grease pencil to write the f-stop and exposure time used on the back of the photo paper before developing.

Vocabulary: grain focuser, cropping, proof sheet, emulsion, safelight

FOR THE STUDENT

In the Darkroom

- Be thoughtful of others who are working in the darkroom with you. Don't use bright light to examine negatives that might expose or *fog* someone else's photo paper.
- Keep your photo paper carefully wrapped or inside a drawer to avoid accidental exposure.
- Leave your work space clean—papers picked up, counters wiped off with a sponge, and sponges rinsed.

Developing

Always move prints from one tray to the next by using tongs (these are *chemicals*—you don't want your hands in them). Hold the photo over the tray for a moment to drain excess chemicals before dropping the print into the next tray.

1. Developer: leave the print in for 1 to 2 minutes. If the photo was properly exposed, you should not see an image before 20 seconds. Gently agitate the tray. If not properly agitated, the print will be "muddy" with partial development.
2. Stop bath: 5 seconds; continuous agitation.

3. Fixer: immerse print. Agitate for 2 to 4 minutes.

4. Wash: 5-minute wash is recommended. Discoloration may show up later if the print is not well washed.

Proof Sheet

1. Make a proof sheet: remember "emulsion to emulsion." Lay all the negatives (still in negative sleeves) dull (emulsion) side down on the shiny (emulsion) side of paper. Place a clean sheet of glass on top to hold them flat. When a negative is held in place in this way, it is called contact printing.

    a. For a 5 × 7-inch print, expose the paper at f/11 for approximately 5 to 7 seconds.

    b. For an 8 × 10-inch print, expose the paper at f/11 for approximately 15 seconds.

2. Develop the proof sheet.

3. Select the best negative from the proof sheet. Sometimes it is best to do this in daylight.

4. Clean the negative with a negative cloth. Don't wipe your hands on the cloth, as chemicals will ruin the negatives.

5. Put the negative in the negative carrier. *Never drag your negatives across the carrier to look at them, as they will get scratched.*

6. Place the white cardboard on the easel to see the negative clearly, and focus.

7. Open the aperture all the way (the numbers are the same as on a camera, with the smallest number being the largest opening on an enlarger).

8. Focus the enlarger. If available, a magnifying glass or a focusing aid will help in getting it as sharp as possible. If desired, the picture may be improved by cropping.

9. Reset the aperture. Normally try to print from f/8 to f/16. In order to get all the detail, an ideal exposure would never take less than 10 seconds.

10. Make a test strip. Place the negative you have selected in the carrier and focus it.

    a. Cut a one-inch wide strip of photographic paper and place it emulsion side up in the easel.

    b. Expose the entire strip for 3 seconds.

    c. Cover all but one inch with cardboard.

    d. Set the timer for 2 seconds (for a 5 × 7-inch print). Move the cardboard one inch and reset the enlarger for 2 seconds. Repeat this process several times to make clear separations in the test strip.

11. *Develop the test strip.* Use tongs to move the test strip from chemical to chemical. Remember to use separate tongs for each chemical and put them back into the proper tray to avoid contamination.

12. *Evaluate the test strip.* Look for whites, black, and intermediate grays. If there is not much contrast, a filter is needed.

13. *To use a polycontrast filter:*

    a. Choose the proper exposure time from the test strip.

    b. If there are no strong blacks and whites, use a high-numbered filter.

    c. When using a filter, add exposure time to your white-light time. Instructions for exposure time come with the filters.

Printing

14. *Make a trial print.* Use a filter when making the print. At this point evaluate the print under white light for any dust spots or scratches. If some areas of the print are too dark or too light, you can "burn" or "dodge" the print by using your hand to hold back light in some areas while adding more light in others.

15. *Make the final print.* Follow regular developing procedures. Remember to wash the print with running water for five minutes.

16. *Dry the print.* Resin-coated paper may be dried with a hair dryer or air-dried for a short time by hanging with a clothespin on a clothesline in the classroom.

Adjust. Allows enhanced color, exposure, contrast, highlights, shadows, saturation, temperature, tint, sharpness, and noise.

Background. This is the bottom layer in the Layers Panel that is best to keep locked. It should not be deleted. Make duplicate layers (CTRL-J or CMD-J) for all changes.

Blending Modes. At top left of the Layers Panel. You can cycle through to see the effects of Blending Modes by holding down Shift as you touch each one (for example, Normal, Multiply, Darken, or Hard-Light).

Boosted color. Color throughout the photo is intensified. Use IMAGE>ADJUSTMENTS>HUE> SATURATION.

Brightness or Contrast. IMAGE>ADJUSTMENTS>BRIGHTNESS/CONTRAST. Check Preview, use default or legacy, or move sliders. This is usually used for black and white. Curves is preferred by some teachers for working in color: IMAGE>ADJUSTMENTS>CURVES.

Channels. WINDOW>CHANNELS brings up the Channels Panel, which has four layers named RGB, Red, Green, and Blue. Each of these color channels gives a different appearance to the final photo, and they are especially useful when working in black and white.

Clone. (CTRL-S or CMD-S). This allows you to repair a blemish or speck by selecting an area nearby to replace the original spot. Repair flaws by using OPTION>CLICK on a good area, then going to the flaw; CLICK to replace it with the good area. Adjust brush size and sharpness as necessary.

CMYK (cyan, magenta, yellow, and black). These colors, which are found in IMAGE>MODE, are mostly used for color images to be commercially printed.

Color balance. Allows correction of the color of the photo, adding red, green, or cyan.

Contrast. If the photo lacks contrast, there are several ways to improve it. You will find that most of the controls listed here allow you to make an auto adjustment, which is the same as the automatic processing enhancement at a camera developing location.

Cool color. Color is changed to the cool end of the spectrum (blue, green, violet).

Crop the photo to eliminate unnecessary detail. You can control the size of your images by typing a size number (such as 4 × 6 inches) into blanks in the Options Bar. Save as the cropped size. To undo a crop, a cancel symbol is top right in the Options Bar.

Curves (CTRL-M or CMD-M). The Curves box offers many options for change. Experiment with the sliders on the diagonal line to see what changes in this mode can do. Auto Curves removes strange color casts.

Cyan. Color term in *light* that describes blue.

Cyanotype. Historic method of printing a photograph that gives a photo in shades of blue.

Default. Many adjustments are preset. Unless you change these, the default will be used.

Desktop. A computer desktop is a place to name and move your photos to a folder for easy retrieval.

Dodging and burning. A darkroom term used to improve a photograph by adding light (burning) or holding back light (dodging) to achieve desired results. A Dodge, Burn, and Sponge tool is useful for the same effect on a digital photo. Teacher Beth Goyer suggests dodging and burning (on a layer above the original) of 50 percent gray overlay blending mode to leave the original unchanged in case you want to go back. The layers can be merged or flattened later.

Download. Import photos from a digital memory card into the computer.

Drag. Many changes can be made by putting the Cursor or Selection Tool on something you want to move or copy, then simply dragging it to a different location.

Edit. Allows you to make changes either in a camera or computer.

Effects. While changing the photo, you can try to see (within a complex camera) how it looks in black and white, sepia, antique, faded color, boosted color, faded edges, or vignette (rounded edges).

Enhance. Improve the contrast in a photo.

Export. Photos are moved from the memory card into a folder on the desktop of a computer where they can be easily accessed.

Filters. Filters can do magic. They can make photos look like paintings, with large selection of different effects.

Flash drive (sometimes called a thumb drive or portable external hard drive). A small device that enables you to store and transfer data between computers. Unlike CDs and DVDs, it is possible to make changes on data stored this way.

Folder. Folders are crucial for sorting and retrieving photos. Although you will name them, you should also include a four-digit year and a two-digit month to sort them easily (for example, 2014. 02).

Grayscale. When a photo lacks colors, it is considered black and white (or monochrome).

Grid. A temporary set of guidelines throughout the photo that help in straightening.

HDR (high dynamic range). Combines several different exposures to capture extreme detail.

Highlights. The lightest areas in a photo.

Histogram. A slider that is used to show pixels ranging from white on the right side to black on the left and in-between. A normal picture will have pixels relatively evenly spread. To improve a light or dark area, move sliders, also watching how it affects the photo.

Import. Photos are taken from the memory card and brought into the computer.

Intensify. The colors in a photo are made darker and brighter.

ISO number. Measures the sensitivity of the camera's sensor.

JPEG. Compression of an image file so it takes up less space and may be sent by Internet. JPEG is an acronym for Joint Photographic Experts Group. Layers in a photo must be merged or flattened to a single layer to be saved in JPEG.

Kerning. In the Character Panel, Kerning allows making changes in the spaces between letters.

Keyboard shortcuts. Learning to use combinations of keys with SHIFT>OPTION>ALTERNATE plus and minus and brackets greatly increases efficiency.

Layers Panel. WINDOW>LAYERS are like layers of tracing paper. When a photo is opened, it automatically goes onto a layer that is locked. Make a duplicate layer on which to work (CTRL-J or CMD-J). Layers may be turned on or off by clicking on the eye on the left column.

Leading. In the Character Palette, Leading controls the space between a line of type and the one above or below it.

Levels (CTRL-L or CMD-L). Improve contrast, tone, lightness, and darkness. This allows you to improve contrast by lightening or darkening the photo, improving highlight, midrange, and dark areas. Move the sliders while watching the histogram and the photograph. You may find the midrange slider will be the one you use most often.

Main Menu (also called the Applications Bar). The bar that runs across the top of the screen lists locations of controls that will be used in computer graphics.

Mask. At the bottom of the layers panel, on the left side, is a square with a hole in it (mask). If you click on a highlighted layer, a white blank comes up. Paint black on the mask to hide distracting details in the image that you wish to eliminate. If you make an error, use the brush with white to correct. CTRL-X or CMD-X allows the brush to easily switch between black and white.

Memory card. A small recording device used for photos in a digital camera.

Menu Bar. The menu bar lists applications that can be opened such as Bridge or Photoshop.

Monochrome. A one-color picture that ranges from light to dark.

Multiply. This blending mode will darken the photo. With two layers, you can multiply more than once.

Navigator. This box enables you to enlarge within specific areas in the image to get extreme detail if necessary to make changes or a mask.

Opacity. In the upper right of the Layers Panel, a slider allows you to control transparency from 100 (completely opaque) to 0 (completely transparent). A 100 percent opacity could give the effect of tempera or oil paint, whereas a lesser opacity (35 percent or so) looks like transparent watercolor.

Options Bar. The options bar is across the top, below the Menu Bar. Changes that can be made with each tool are visible in the Options Bar, and you should refer to it as you change tools. The last change you made will always remain in the bar and will be used the next time you open the tool, unless you change it.

Pixels. Pixel comes from a contraction of *pix* (pictures) and *el* (element) and represents dots per inch. More pixels per inch give a higher resolution and affect the print size of the image. These are referred to as PPI—though some still prefer the term DPI—dots per inch.

Raw mode. Images taken in raw mode are completely unprocessed and uncompressed, with all processing done within the computer.

Red eye. If the eye's iris is wide open, a flash reflects on the blood in the back of the eye. New programs in Gimp and Photoshop have a Red Eye tool to correct it.

Resolution. The number of pixels per inch (PPI) determines the level of resolution. For something to be published or printed, it should be 300 PPI or higher. To send something on the Internet, a resolution of 72 PPI is adequate.

Retouch. The size and opacity of the *spot-healing brush* are controlled to disguise a blemish.

RGB. Represents the normal coloration of photographs (red, green, and blue).

Rotation. Turning a photo so it appears in the correct position.

Saturation. The intensity of the colors in the photo, whether black and white or color.

Scan. Almost anything flat (photo, magazine cover, antique letter, or cloth) can be scanned (copied) and imported, then combined with other images.

Sepia. A brownish tint on photos. On old black-and-white photos this was accomplished with sepia toner. To do this with digital art, use LAYER ADJUSTMENT>PHOTO FILTER>SEPIA.

Shadows. The darker areas of an exposure.

Single-lens reflex camera (SLR). The image you see through the viewfinder is the image you get.

Skylight filter. Intensifies photos taken in bring sunlight.

Straighten. Straighten the photo by using guides on which to align it. Use the selection tool (arrow in the Toolbar) to drag the guideline from the left side or top. If the photo is obviously skewed (bigger or smaller on one side than another), hold down the Shift key to avoid distortion and use EDIT>TRANSFORM>SKEW to align it to guidelines. Click Enter when you are satisfied. Crop when you have straightened the photo. Or use the ruler tool on a vertical or horizontal line, then IMAGE>ROTATION>ARBITRARY.

Tools Panel. WINDOW>TOOLS. Tools such as *crop, brush,* and *eraser* are used to make changes on an image.

Tutorial. A demonstration of how to accomplish operations when using the computer; often found on the Internet.

Vignette. An oval white or dark space around an image.

Warm color. The color is moved toward the red end of the color spectrum.

HANDOUT
DIGITAL KEY COMMANDS

Keyboard shortcuts. Students will use only a handful of the many keyboard shortcuts available, so it isn't necessary for them to learn or memorize the vast majority. However, students will find themselves going to certain tools or adjustments often, so learning to easily access these will increase their efficiency. I have found the shortcuts listed here to be useful.

CTRL-A or CMD-A: select all

CTRL-C or CMD-C: copy

CTRL-V or CMD-V: paste (with Move Tool active)

CTRL-I or CMD-I: invert selection

CTRL-J or CMD-J: make new, identical layer

CTRL-L or CMD-L: levels box

CTRL-X or CMD-X: cut

CTRL-Z or CMD-Z: undo last move (with Move Tool active)

CTRL-+ or CMD-+ (plus): enlarge your photo

CTRL-– or CMD-– (minus): shrink your photo

CTRL-Alt-Shift-E or CMD-Option-Shift-E: merge all visible layers into a single layer without losing previous layers

Brackets: left bracket ([) makes brush smaller; right bracket (]) makes brush larger

Alt-Delete or Option-Delete: fill layer with color

V Move tool

M Marquee tools

L Lasso

Q Quick Selection

C Crop and Slice

I Eyedropper, Ruler, Color sampler

J Spot healing brush, Patch Red Eye

B Brush, Pencil

S Clone stamp

Y History brush

E Eraser tool

G Gradient tool, Paint bucket tool

O Dodge tool, Burn tool, Sponge tool

P Pen tool

Q Quick Mask Mode

T Type tools

A Path Selection tool

W Quick Selection, Magic Wand

C Crop and Slice Tools

U Rectangle, Rounded Rectangle, Ellipse, Polygon, Custom Shape

H Hand

R Rotate View

Z Zoom

D Default Colors

X Switch Foreground and Background Colors

Shortcuts
for Selecting
Tools

Ashlyn Ball, *Drinking Tiger*

Ashlyn Ball, *The Winding Staircase*

Sarah Rauls, *Think We can Make It?*

These five photos from Joan Larson's photo classes at Oakville High School, St. Louis County, Missouri, demonstrate the use of computer tools to clone out unnecessary items and increase contrast (top two figures); make a background more painterly (middle left) use a gradient map (middle right) and change color to black and white with the adjustment layer (lower right). All photos are 8 x 10 inches.

Lauren Vandemore, *Friends*

Emily Jackson, *Henna Hands*

Computer Graphics

7

Computer graphics opens infinite possibilities for students, ranging from using personal photos to scanning personal drawings. The capacity to combine many techniques is an integral part of all the software. Many artists working today are experimenting with taking photographs beyond the "snapshot" and making them into fine art or using them as inspiration for a different medium.

This chapter is written with the assumption that the teacher has access to computers, a software program, and is already familiar computer graphics. Because computers and software programs are constantly being changed and updated, this chapter gives ideas for composition and approaches to graphic design that will always be timely.

Scrabble

Kelsey Boyle, 8 × 10 inches. This imaginative composite involves a Scrabble message illustrated by the attitudes and actions of the students. Oakville High School, St. Louis County, Missouri, teacher Joan Larson.

That said, some computer graphics programs may be in use, with upgrades and adaptations, for a long time. Adobe Photoshop, a leader in the field, allows the artist to work in layers and make changes to photographs. An infinite number of effects can be achieved with this workhorse program. A free Internet download, GIMP, offers many features that are similar to Photoshop.

A computer graphics class should cover how to design using photos, text, and drawn images. Adobe Photoshop is a wonderful application to use for work involving photographs. Adobe Illustrator (often sold in a package with Adobe Photoshop) or another type of vector-based program is best suited for assignments using text and/or drawn images.

iPads, or tablets, are popular in computer graphics classes. Some schools expect every student to have a digital device that can be used for Internet research and drawing. Some school districts allow and encourage secondary school students to "Bring Your Own Device." One St. Louis area school district has made plans to provide an iPad for every student within two years. Plans are under way in some districts to purchase "loaners" that may be taken home by students who do not have a digital device. Teachers in some districts are challenged to design a curriculum that offers possibilities for the new generation of computers.

Teacher Marilyn Palmer recommends that the teacher's seat in a computer lab ideally be placed to the side of the room, so that students' screens may be seen and the teacher quickly notices when a student needs assistance.

I recommend that students should all have a flash drive so they can work at home or the local library as well as at school. Each student should also create a folder (digital portfolio) to place inside the teacher's folder on the school's computers so you can keep abreast of their progress in class. This will also enable them to send work to your folder from home.

Don't Slow Children
John Dyess, digital print, 15 × 19 inches, private collection. This composite includes signs and in addition displays lettering of various sizes. The brilliant coloring combined with a running child add drama.

PROJECT 7-1
DRAWING SIMPLE SHAPES

Time needed: 2 days

Materials: computer, printer, printing paper, software such as Adobe Photoshop and Illustrator, Photoshop Elements, or GIMP (a free download from the Internet)

Goal: Students develop and refine skill in the use of digital tools by experimenting and learning key commands.

Goal: Students use a draw or paint software program to make simple graphic designs.

Objective: Students print and label six to ten options with which they have experimented.

FOR THE TEACHER

These simple exercises serve to introduce students to a few possibilities they might use in later projects, while giving them experience in using some of the tools and locating them.

FOR THE STUDENT

Milk or Coffee?

Hannah Judd, 13 × 19 inches. This photo, transformed and simplified in Adobe Illustrator, proves again that it doesn't matter what the subject is, it is how you see it. Parkway West High School, St. Louis County, Missouri, teacher Katy Mangrich.

1. Make a new document (CTRL-N or CMD-N). Set it at 8 × 10 inches, as most printers won't print to the edge of the paper, and clipping occurs. Set the resolution at between 200 and 300 PPI (pixels per inch). IMAGE>MODE can be RGB (red, green, blue), which is what is normally seen on the screen.

2. *Marquee and Shapes Tools.* It is possible to make varied shapes with the Marquee Tool (CTRL-M or CMD-M), Shapes Tool (CTRL-U or CMD-U), or the Straight Line Tool for geometric shapes (found in the Shapes Tool). The Option Bar at the top of the screen allows you to quickly select various possibilities.

   To make a circle, hold down the Shift key while selecting a sphere from the Elliptical Marquee Tool or Shapes Tool.

   To make a square, hold down the Shift key while selecting a rectangle from the either the Rectangular Marquee or Shapes Tool.

   Shape variety. While in the Shapes Tool, click on the white Shapes box in the Options Bar to bring up a box of standard shapes such as arrows, light bulb, hearts, and patterns.

3. *Duplicate a shape* by holding down the ALT or OPTION key and (while in the Move Tool) dragging the shape to another spot. You can do this an infinite number of times.

4. *Rotate* the shape using IMAGE>ROTATION: options are 180 degrees, 90 degrees CW (clockwise), 90 degrees CCW (counterclockwise), and arbitrary. You can also flip the *entire canvas* horizontally or vertically.

5. *Resize a shape* by using the EDIT>TRANSFORM option to make something larger or smaller. Or you have the ability to "skew" a shape or use perspective with it.

6. *Gradient.* Use the Gradient Tool (G) to make gradations of color across the shape.

7. *Add color.* If the shapes you have drawn are completely enclosed, it is possible to pour color into a shape with the paint bucket (on the tools panel). Other ways to color a shape are to use a brush to paint each shape or use the EDIT>FILL command (OPT or CTRL>DELETE or ALT or CMD>DELETE). If you are using the Shapes Tool, it will fill in whatever color the foreground color is in the Tool Box.

8. If you are working in Illustrator, color automatically fills with the color you have selected in the Fill Box at the bottom of the Tools Panel and is outlined with color selected in the Stroke Palette.

9. *Scan a photo into one or more shapes.* Either scan or directly transfer a photograph to this drawn composition, disguising it slightly with size, opacity, color, or texture to allow the viewer to find it almost accidentally. Any photograph can be repeated many times by holding down the ALT or OPTION key to drag it wherever you want it to be.

10. *Extension: composition with geometric shapes.* Keep this first simple drawing as the basis for an actual work of art, incorporating these simple shapes into either a total abstract composition or a standard realistic subject such as a bowl of fruit, the human form, or a landscape.

PROJECT 7-2
POP ART SELF-PORTRAIT

Time needed: 4 class periods

Materials: photo of self, computer, software, printer access

Goal: Students compare and contrast similar styles of works of art done in electronic media to those done with traditional visual arts materials.

Objective: Students research and explain how art and artists both reflect and shape their time and culture.

Objective: Students take a simple assignment and make it their own by transforming a personal photo on the computer.

FOR THE TEACHER

A portrait captures a person's personality, just as a word portrait might also describe a person's inner being. Even after the advent of photography, formal portraits were still precious possessions, recording a unique moment and time. Portrait artists have been challenged for hundreds of years to go beyond just showing a face, features, clothes, and other visible characteristics of a subject. They include clues about the subject's livelihood, personal interests, and personality. Historic painted portraits might reveal a seated man reading a book, while visible through an open window one sees a ship in a harbor. A desk might feature a navigation instrument or map. A portrait should convey a magic *something* that causes the viewer to think about the subject's personality or lifestyle.

Vocabulary: font, font size, character panel, kerning, tracking, margin, guides, opacity, upper case, lower case, typeface

The Twenty Marilyns
Andy Warhol (1928–1987), 1962. © Copyright The Andy Warhol Foundation for the Visual Arts/ARS.

Preparation

Show students portraits by pop artist Andy Warhol (1928–1987), who was using darkroom photography in the 1970s (precomputer) to capture celebrity personalities. From his amazing straight photographs, his ultimate transformations were memorable. He exaggerated or swapped color, created collages, and made multiple copies of the same portrait on one page (*The Twenty Marilyns*, for example)—and his work became some of the most memorable of his time. The Internet has many fine examples of his work that can be used as inspiration for this project. Another artist whose self-portraits are distinctive is Mexican painter Frida Kahlo (1907–1954).

Alternative Project

Digital Self-Portrait

Students might consider a possible use for a self-portrait (even if imaginary). It can be put on a Facebook page or another website, used in letterhead stationery, put on a poster to advertise a one-person exhibit or candidacy for office, or e-mailed to a friend. Students should incorporate the same storytelling criteria used for a portrait made of someone else. Remind students that parents or grandparents may see it and send it to their friends.

Teacher Joan Larson's students create multiple-image Warhol-inspired portraits by using Threshold to create high contrast, then change color in each layer.

Portrait Image Flat
Ashley Webelhuth. This portrait was created in Adobe Illustrator. Oakville High School, St. Louis County, Missouri, Art teacher Tom Lutz.

Apple-stair
Lauren Vandemore's imaginative self-portrait shows her friend coming down a staircase as she is waiting at the bottom. Oakville High School, St. Louis County, Missouri, teacher Joan Larson.

Alternative Project
Nine-Photo Grid

Art teacher Marilyn Palmer assigns her students to take a photo of an everyday item (such as a box of McDonald's French fries), then make color changes on it eight times, lining them up like a grid. They are to make the following: monochromatic, cool colors, warm colors, complementary colors, black and white, the original photo, split complementary, neutrals, and analogous colors.

 FOR THE STUDENT

This project challenges you to create a portrait that has enough descriptive information about you that a viewer pauses to look at it for a time or do a "double take." The portrait might include more than just your face, and you can be seated or standing. You have many options for making changes, and you might want to try several versions before settling on a final composition.

1. Begin with the photo. *Plan!* Look around your home or room for a prop or costume such as a hat to see if there is some way you might like to present yourself that would be completely different from school photos. You may have a uniform that you wear for sports or band or a costume for a play.

2. Ask someone to take your picture with a digital camera. If you choose to scan a school photo into the computer as an alternative project, you will need to make significant changes. If you have a distinguishing feature (extra curly hair, for example), you can exaggerate it with the colors and treatment you choose.

3. You might try to reproduce a historic style in the photo or include your hand near your face. To give an expression that is less "set" and more natural, turn your head away from the camera then quickly turn back, and ask someone to snap the photo at that moment of action.

4. Imagine that you are having your photo taken by a painter who plans to do a formal portrait for posterity. (You're the president of a university, and this will be made to hang in the hall, for example.) Will you smile? Look stern? Be seated? Standing? Holding a book? Consider that your portrait might be on a dollar bill, like artist Gilbert Stuart's famous portrait of George Washington.

5. Remember to make a duplicate layer of the original photo before making changes (CNTRL-J or CMD-J). You can temporarily turn any of the layers off or on by clicking on the Eye to the left of the Layer.

6. Improve contrast and color and eliminate any distracting background with a mask. It is your choice whether you would like the portrait to be in black and white or color. There is always the opportunity to return to the original photo color as long as you made a duplicate layer and have saved and locked the original.

7. Try to get in the habit or making Adjustment layer changes by using the circle in the bottom of the Layers Panel. These are temporary, while IMAGE>ADJUSTMENT changes in the Options Bar are permanent, unless you have first made a duplicate layer.

8. If you have a perfect "backdrop" for the photo, you can import it by scanning and placing it on a separate layer behind your subject.

9. You can become playful with color, making the portrait any color(s) you wish. CURVES (M) gives an almost infinite number of options. You can dye your hair (on the computer) and change the background completely. As you *paste* or draw it in, think about what you are trying to say.

10. If your portrait is in color, you can change it by loosely drawing around edges with the computer Pencil Tool in any color. The Pencil and Brush Tools (B) are in the same spot on the Tool Bar. Control the size of the pencil in the Options Bar or by using CNTRL or CMD right bracket or left bracket ([or]).

11. Remember you can undo a "mistake" by using CNTRL-Z or CMD-Z or EDIT>UNDO or EDIT>REDO to go back as many as thirty steps. To go back more than one or two steps, repeatedly use ALT-CNTRL-Z or OPTION-CMD-Z. The History Brush on the Tool Bar allows you to go back to a point, or all the way to when you opened the file, but once something is gone from the history brush, it is *gone*. With Undo, you can always Redo if you change your mind.

Phantasmagoria
Maya Mironova, surreal digital design. Although this is not a personal advertising poster, the student took advantage of stock images on the Internet, combining them with personal photographs to create a fascinating composition. Parkway North High School, St. Louis County, Missouri, teacher Clint Johnson.

12. *Mounting digital prints.* As with any work on paper, digital prints may be placed inside a mat. Sizes such as an 8 × 10-inch mat for a 5 × 7-inch photo, or an 11 × 14-inch mat for an 8 × 10-inch print fit inexpensive standard-size frames. Any artwork looks best with a two- to three-inch border all around. Another possibility is to *bleed mount* a digital print on black or white mat board or foam core, eliminating a border entirely. A dry mount press (if you have one) is the easiest way to attach a photo to mat board, but a print can also be attached to mat board with spray mount adhesive.

ADVERTISING POSTER OR FLYER

Time needed: 1 to 2 weeks

Materials: computer, color printer, disks, printing paper, card stock, scanner (for photographs and drawings)

Goal: Students investigate and report on emerging technologies that affect how information is disseminated.

Goal: Students apply advertising principles developed on paper to contemporary digital ads seen on the computer.

Objective: Students develop and refine a poster or flyer advertising a school event such as a theater or dance production that includes images and specific information.

Kids

Fast food

Upscale

Eric Michalak, logo for kids, fast foods, upscale. Oakville High School, St. Louis, Missouri, teacher Tom Lutz.

FOR THE TEACHER

Advertising posters created during the late nineteenth and early twentieth centuries by European artists are considered serious artwork today. Their simple designs that advertised nightclubs, steamships, trains, travel destinations, or chocolate were prime examples showing that the image and lettering must complement each other.

To introduce poster (or flyer) making, show students

Kids

Fast food

Upscale

Austin Westolich, logo for kids, fast foods, upscale. Oakville High School, St. Louis, Missouri, teacher Tom Lutz.

examples of posters made by Toulouse Lautrec (1864–1901), Erté (1892–1990), and Alphonse Mucha (1860–1939), as well as those by unknown artists. Point out how simple they are. The most eye-catching posters have broad areas of color and lettering that is large and clear. Simple divisions of space are a good beginning point, with the largest words being the reason for the poster: an event, an artist's name, a country, or the brand name of a soft drink.

The typical school year is filled with events that everyone in the school's community needs to know about. Flyers can be distributed in the school and posted at other nearby locations. Even as schools become more green, relying on the Internet for getting out information, there is still the need for dynamic "advertising" for events on school or district websites. Students may also be called upon to design a school phone book cover or curriculum guide cover. The same general guidelines for a poster apply when designing a flyer. It needs to be eye-catching from a distance. Students may design a flyer for something in which they are specifically interested: a play, concert, art show, prom, or yearbook.

Alternative Project

Business Advertisement

Regional businesses often feature ads in the local papers and onscreen in local theaters. You have nothing to lose by approaching a local theater and asking if they can suggest businesses that already do advertising onscreen or approaching the local business first to discuss what you can do for them. Make a list of what such an ad needs to say and how best to say it without being trite or boring. Websites and Facebook pages featuring local or neighborhood news might also welcome visually exciting ads.

Alternative Project

Advertise Yourself

Consider that someday you will have achieved your dream—perhaps you are that artist who is getting ready for an exhibition, the ballerina, the owner of your own bank, the pilot for your own airline, or the inventor of the newest innovation for the Internet. If you choose to advertise an imaginary product, you will naturally call it by your own name and use appropriate colors, perhaps even a slogan.

Alternative Project
Magazine Cover or CD Cover

Many appropriate digital projects for high school students incorporate lettering and photography. Art teacher Joan Larson challenged her students to either create a cover for a magazine that doesn't (yet) exist or design an album cover for an imaginary musical group.

Alternative Project
Poster for a Cause

Students can select something that is especially meaningful to them, such as world hunger, cancer awareness, or animal abuse, and create a poster to call attention to their ability to help financially or otherwise.

Alternative Project
School Website

Students should look at their school's existing website and think how they might come up with appropriate designs for each day of the week or month, logos representing specific departments, or sporting events. The art department section can certainly use a fresh heading each month.

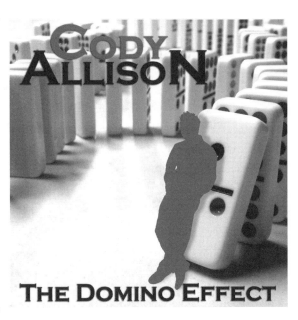

Domino Effect
Jordan Schlechte, front of CD cover. Oakville High School, St. Louis, Missouri, teacher Joan Larson.

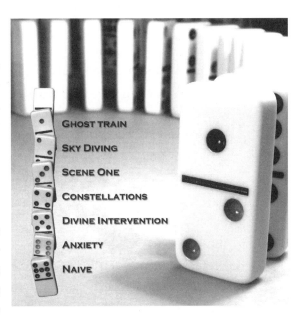

Domino Effect
Jordan Schlechte, rear of CD cover. Oakville High School, St. Louis, Missouri, teacher Joan Larson.

FOR THE STUDENT

The purpose of a poster or flyer is to advertise something. It is not usually expected to be a permanent, framed work of art. Advertising billboards are usually horizontal, but posters and flyers are normally vertical.

A poster can have a top line, a waist line (between one-third and one-half down from the top), and a base line.

1. Keep it simple, to make it eye-catching and interesting to look at. Leave comfortable margins on all sides. The main element of the design should dominate the poster, with everything else being subordinate. One important message should appear in the largest print. Limit the font selection to no more than three.

2. The background space is often a problem. Sometimes dividing it diagonally or vertically to have slight value differences can make it dynamic. If the poster will be in color, a Gradient (G) can be an effective background.

3. People should be able to tell at a glance what the poster is about: who, what, where, when (and why, if it is for a special cause). It should be easy to read in a few seconds. Simple lettering of the same size and color is for the main message, leaving enough space around the design so that it is easily seen and understood.

   • If the poster is vertical and the size font you have selected is too large to go across, then use a smaller font.

   • Darker (saturated) colors show up better from a distance. The purpose is to have this easily readable. Never split a line of text, stack letters, or make diagonal lines of letters.

   • Avoid alternating colors in lines of text. Keep in mind that yellow does not carry well at a distance unless it is outlined.

   • People can read lowercase typeface more easily than capital letters, so while the main message might be in capitals, the incidental information could be in lowercase. Words written in caps read like yelling.

   • The lettering should be appropriate to the message (bubble or circus-style lettering fonts are for happy occasions, not serious performances).

4. Balance is an important consideration when designing a poster. Avoid a top-heavy effect. If the major lettering is at the top of the poster, give "weight" and balance to the entire composition by putting color or an image near the bottom.

5. Poster size may be limited by the size of the school's printer and the ability to print in color. You may decide to take the file to a print shop to be printed larger.

6. To make a large *hand-lettered* poster from your design, you can print the design onto an 8 ½ × 11-inch clear overhead projector sheet and use an overhead projector to enlarge it onto a large sheet of poster board, drawing it first in pencil, then filling in with marker.

PROJECT 7-4
DESIGN AN AREA RUG

Time needed: 5 fifty-minute classes

Materials: computer, computer software such as Photoshop, quality paper for printing, mount board for display

Goal: Students solve a visual arts problem demonstrating effective use of color, shape, and texture.

Objective: Students plan and create a computer graphic design that reflects complex ideas such as distortion, scale, and color theory.

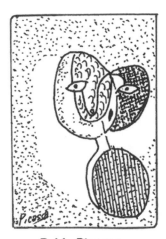

Pablo Picasso

Pablo Picasso

Alexander Calder

Joan Miro

FOR THE TEACHER

This computer design assignment has infinite possibilities for students as you invite them to design an area rug for their bedroom or other room in their home. The Internet abounds with contemporary rug design ideas, and magazines are filled with inspiration for both traditional and contemporary rugs.

An ongoing "Student Rug Design Competition" sponsored by the Hagopian World of Rugs, in collaboration with Detroit's College for Creative Studies, has featured an annual theme such as Color as the Focus, Graphical Elements for Contemporary Decor, Folk Art for Generation X, or The Essence of Michigan.

An assignment such as this gives students an opportunity for further exploration on the computer, letting them experiment with DUPLICATING LAYERS, LAYER OPACITY, FILTERS, BLENDING TOOLS, COLOR SELECTION, and GRADIENTS. Students will use tools such as the Shapes Tool and EDIT>TRANSFORM>SKEW. It most assuredly calls on them to put into practice what they know about the elements of art and principles of design.

This assignment is well suited for Adobe Illustrator or other vector-based programs because the drawing tools are more easily handled.

Art History

Many famous artists designed rugs, including Sonia Delauney (1885–1979), Alexander Calder (1898–1976), Joan Miró (1893–1983), Pablo Picasso (1881–1973), and Wassily Kandinsky (1866–1944). These designs closely related to their painting styles.

Preparation

Let students be *owners* of this assignment by allowing them to select an overall class theme. Write their suggestions where all can see them and ask them to vote. Students may want to confine themselves to a limited color scheme (monochromatic, triadic, or neutral) to have time to explore a design fully. Some may want to begin with a few small thumbnail drawings. Others may want to design in black and white, adding color later.

These instructions are based on Adobe Illustrator, so if you are using another program, it is strongly advised that you make a rug design using *your* program first so you can anticipate any problems students might experience.

Skateboard Bottom   Skateboard Top

Hannah Roedner

Hannah Roedner, skateboard designs (top and bottom), Adobe Illustrator. Oakville High School, St. Louis County, Missouri, teacher Tom Lutz.

Alternative Project

Skateboard or Snowboard Design

Teacher Tom Lutz finds his students enjoy designing a skateboard or snowboard using their computer skills in combining images and lettering.

FOR THE STUDENT

Although this is likely to be an abstract design, it might still be helpful if you can base it on a *subject* that you find interesting such as cell structures, geometric designs, algebraic formulas (or animals, flowers, flag designs, a favorite sport, a peacock feather, stripes, tire treads, cars—but no rainbows, please). Keep scratch paper next to the computer to work out a few things.

1. Make a new document—8 × 10 inches, 300 PPI; check VIEW>RULER. Use the Move Tool to pull a guide to the top, bottom, and both sides, leaving ¼ inch on each edge and a horizontal and vertical guide at the middle. Make a duplicate layer (CTRL-J or CMD-J).

2. Remember that you can undo anything you don't like by clicking CTRL-Z or CMD-Z (or ALT>CTRL-Z or OPTION>CMD-Z). You can undo up to thirty times.

3. Make a New Layer for a background color. Touch the cursor to the black or white patch at the bottom of the Tools Panel. This brings up the Color Picker from which you may select a color. When your selected colors show at the bottom of the Tools Panel, go to the new layer and use the key command ALT>DELETE or OPTION>DELETE to fill the layer with your color. Label the layer and lock it by clicking the lock at the top of the Layers Panel.

4. Go to the Shapes Tool in the Option Bar. Notice that whichever shape you select has a number of options. In Photoshop there are a number of premade shapes, and you can select one or more of these to combine, sizing them appropriately.

EVERYBODY NEEDS A BUSINESS CARD

Time needed: 2 fifty-minute classes

Materials: Clean Edge Business Cards from office supply store, visual examples of great business cards

Goal: Students design and print a personal business card, applying knowledge of elements and principles of art.

Goal: Students explore a potential career in the arts as they learn about graphic design.

Objective: Students reflect complex ideas such as distortion or arbitrary color in a personalized business card.

Johanna Prinz recently designed a business card that has images showing what she does, a personalized signature, and contact information.

FOR THE TEACHER

As a teacher, you may already have your own business card. Some may be ordered for you by a district, and they are usually pretty straightforward black on white: simple *business* cards. This challenge is for your students to create a card that contains all the important information such as name,

Susan Hume. Callooh Callay. The artist selected a stock black-and-white image, colorizing and using it to enhance standard information.

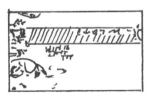

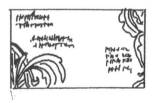

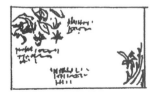
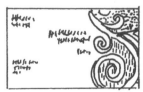

Drawings of card designs from the Internet.

address, phone number, cell phone number, and e-mail address—and for it be *personal* and look good! It is a nice chance for students to work within a specific size and shape format and to investigate fonts.

Vocabulary: arabesque

Preparation

Go online to the Internet and search on "business cards." You will find hundreds of examples that students might also like to see. You can project those on a whiteboard to introduce students to the concept or print out a few pages so they can see possible ways to break up space and still include the pertinent information. For starters, design your own card.

Discuss symbols, logos, and personal beliefs with students. If they see themselves as environmentalists or scientists, or if a primary interest is art, music, or the military, any of these could serve as a starting point for a design. Some students have never given thought to what might happen in the future and might be content just to have a good-looking imaginative design. Although part of the assignment will be for students to actually print out ten cards, the design might also be used on stationery or at the top of a personal website.

Alternative Project
Return Labels

Students can design "return" labels and print out a full sheet of them. If the label sheets used are fresh (not dried up), they are great for labeling books, cell phones, cameras, flash drives, umbrellas, golf clubs, and other personal items. They may be covered with clear postal mailing tape to keep them clean and firmly affixed.

 FOR THE STUDENT

If you already have given some thought to what your career might be some day, envision yourself giving the card you have designed to a client. You may not feel the need for a business card for yourself yet, but perhaps you would like to design one for a family member.

1. Make a new document, 2 inches high × 3½ inches wide and 300 PPI.

2. Your name is the most important feature of the card and can be in almost any font. If you wish, you can write it by hand and scan it for placement on the card. If you choose not to use handwriting, try different fonts with this shortcut. Type out your name and highlight it, holding down the Shift key to try different fonts for a style of lettering that you think shows off your name well.

3. Your name is the dominant feature of the card, usually in the center and often with a title or description of what it is that you do (or what your career might be). If you want to use only your name, that is fine also. Approximately one-fourth of your card will have other information such as postal address, phone number(s), and e-mail address.

4. On most business cards, there is a design element of some sort vertically along the side. If it is on one side, sometimes a small portion might be repeated on an opposite

corner. This can be anything from straight lines to simple curved designs called arabesques (decorative designs that are inspired by Islamic art).

5. Think about appropriate colors for background and lettering. If you choose to have a dark background or a portion of the background dark, the lettering on that portion can be white or in a light color that would contrast against the dark color. It will probably be most effective to limit yourself to two or three colors.

6. If you use a photo you took, select one that has a large enough light area (such as an area of water) that dark lettering will contrast with it.

7. When finished, the card is ready to print on purchased business card forms.

PROJECT 7-6
ANIMAL ALPHABET BOOK: GROUP PROJECT

Time needed: ongoing; 5 days of fifty-minute classes

Materials: computer, computer graphics program, printing paper

Goal: Students take individual responsibility to complete a portion of a joint class project following discussions as to general style.

Goal: Students analyze and discuss the aesthetic value of all contributions to their joint work of art and defend their position after considering other students' views.

Objective: Each student completes a portion of a joint class project, meeting deadlines and agreed-upon guidelines.

FOR THE TEACHER

An all-class Alphabet Book can be magnificent, whether it is seen only on disk, transferred to a digital slide presentation, displayed in alphabetical order on a wall, or is printed out as a booklet with each student having a copy. If you do not have twenty-six students, you may carry over some letters until another semester. This project was developed by Michael Swoboda.

Vocabulary: format, gradient

Preparation

Each student selects one letter of the alphabet, which will be the basis for his or her page. If this is an animal alphabet book, students ideally take their own animal pictures for the page by photographing family pets or taking photos at a pet store or the zoo. If you have school cameras, students may have to check cameras out for two nights to complete this process. They can even do a drawing of an animal and scan it to the computer.

G Is for Giraffe
These brightly colored giraffes are arranged to fill the space comfortably.

Alternative Project
Set of Fifty-Two Face Cards

A group of St. Louis artists, Thirteen Squared, made and published a deck of cards that featured the number, suit (spades, hearts, diamonds, or clubs), and artist's name in each corner (showing upside down on the opposite end, just as real playing cards do). Some of the face cards featured collage, and some of the *number* cards were imaginatively transformed. Shuffle a deck and let students draw "their cards" from a regular deck of cards until all have been distributed. Each person will write his or her name on the card and give it back to you. Standard cards are vertical, 2 ⅝ × 3 ⅝, and a predesigned format for students to use will give uniformity to the playing side of the deck. One design can be used as the "back" of the deck.

Alternative Project
Class Calendar

Students work together to design a calendar to be published by the class and possibly sold as a fundraiser. Small groups can share the work by being responsible for one month. This might include holidays with special designs and a calendar cover.

FOR THE STUDENT

Making one page of an alphabet book may sound pretty easy, but if you do it right, it will take some time.

1. Make a new document, 8 × 10 inches, 300 PPI. If the class decides it wants a different shape or size from this one, everyone will need to work in the same format. Decide first on the letter you have chosen and list animals with names that begin with that letter.

2. Consider where you might be able to get pictures of that specific animal and plan to work from your own photos. Could you take photos of your own pets? Zoo photos? A nearby pet store? Visit to an animal park? A last resort might be the Internet or *National Geographic* or conservation magazines.

King of Clubs
Elizabeth Concannon, 2013. This king of clubs was one of a set of fifty-two cards designed as a fundraiser by a group of thirteen St. Louis artists called Thirteen Squared. Each artist, using a personal style or medium, created square designs for four cards.

King of Clubs
Thirteen Squared. This spread deck of cards shows how thirteen artists collaborated, with each artist taking responsibility for four of the cards, using a personal style.

3. Type the letter you have chosen on the page. By holding down the Shift key, you can cycle through various fonts until you find one that you think relates to your page. Where will you place the biggest letter? How many more times might you repeat it?

4. Place the animal(s) on the page. You can have one large image (perhaps just a face), or several different views and sizes. The colors can be whatever you have in mind; they don't have to be realistic, and you can make your own pattern to fit within a recognizable shape, such as a moose or elephant.

5. The background may be one color, or you can use a Gradient layer to make it multicolored. Rather than using a completely plain background, you can fill it with the names of other animals in that species (consider all the variations of breeds among dogs).

6. When your page is done, print it and put it in a mat for display. Give the file to your instructor to be "alphabetized" and perhaps actually printed as a booklet.

CREATE YOUR OWN REALITY (CITYSCAPE)

Time needed: 10 fifty-minute classes

Materials: computer, software, printing paper

Goal: Students compare and contrast similar styles of work done digitally with those done in traditional media.

Objective: Students apply elements of art and principles of design as well as development of personal style to complete a unique cityscape.

FOR THE TEACHER

Artists have always found buildings to be an interesting subject, whether painted or photographed, viewed close up or farther away. Challenge students to take photos of buildings in the region, creating their own "reality" by how they combine or group buildings to make a cityscape. The beauty of computer graphics is that the size, color, and orientation of the buildings do not have to be accurate. These can be changed as needed to make an interesting composition.

Show students cityscapes by American impressionist Childe Hassam (1859–1935), Lyonel Feininger (1871–1956), Charles Sheeler (1883–1965), and Benjamin Edwards (1970–).

Preparation

Be certain students understand how to isolate a single item from a layer by using a selection tool. The LASSO, MAGNETIC LASSO, and POLYGONAL LASSO in Photoshop allow one to isolate a building with precision by Zooming in and following the outside edges. The NAVIGATOR

Roman Holiday
Digital composite print, 13 × 19 inches. This composite, made using Photoshop, involves approximately twenty digital photographs, masked, repeated, and manipulated in scale to give an impression of Rome.

St. Louis Quilt #1
Digital composite, 13 × 19 inches. This composite, made using Photoshop, is an approximation of the city of St. Louis. It was composed as a reference for a large oil painting.

tool allows students to be selective. It may be necessary to create a Mask to further refine a selection.

Show them how to turn the layers on and off, how to move a building in front of or behind others by dragging a layer up or down, and how to duplicate and resize a building (ALT or OPTION) to repeat it in a different place. Demonstrate the many uses of EDIT>TRANSFORM, such as changing size, and FLIP>HORIZONTAL.

 ## FOR THE STUDENT

It is interesting to improvise on reality, adjusting everything to make an interesting composition, rather than concerning yourself with what actually exists. You are building your own reality here, and you can make buildings and people any size you want them to be. The background of your "skyline" can be a view toward a group of mountains far in the distance or an existing group of buildings such as you might see in a port, looking up from a river.

1. The sky can be copied from a real photo or can be "imported" from another of your photos or even a single building or landmark (such as an Eiffel Tower photo you have found online) that will make people question your cityscape's reality.

2. Isolate each building or small group of buildings onto a separate layer. After it is selected, it can be pasted into a new blank layer and labeled to allow you to move the layer if necessary. Put a mask around the building.

3. Change buildings by improving color or contrast, or soften by eliminating some detail. You can make them any size by using EDIT>TRANSFORM from the Options Bar, or by using the Move Tool (CTRL-V or CMD-V), to place them anywhere you would like.

4. Experiment with filters for interesting effects.

5. You can place a building in front of or behind another building by slowly dragging the layers above or below each other. This is another reason to label each layer and isolate each building with a mask.

6. If you include people or cars, just remember that any composition usually has larger objects in the foreground, with objects becoming smaller the farther away they are. Closer objects are lower in the composition, and distant objects are higher up in the frame. Then again, this is your own take on reality. If you are looking for something in your composition that obviously doesn't belong there, go ahead and try it.

7. The final composition can be printed in color, or can be changed to grayscale and printed in black and white.

ILLUMINATED MANUSCRIPT: VECTOR-BASED DRAWING

Time needed: 15 to 20 fifty-minute classes

Materials: computer, printer, printing paper, software such as Adobe Photoshop and Illustrator

Goal: Students learn to control straight- and curved-line vector drawings through preliminary exercises with the Pen or Straight-Line Tool.

Objective: Students create an original illuminated manuscript page with a design consisting of a border, corner design, and central letter.

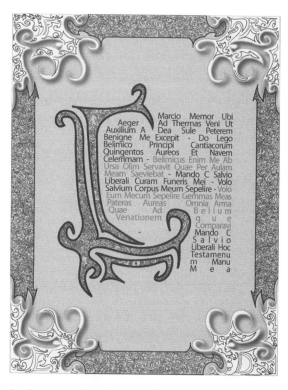

Student work. This illuminated border has the student's initial and corners that give the illusion of floating in space. Parkway West High School, St. Louis County, Missouri, teacher Marilyn Palmer.

Student work, illuminated manuscript. This student chose to complete the border with medieval lettering in Latin and a dragon image. Parkway West High School, St. Louis County, Missouri, teacher Marilyn Palmer.

FOR THE TEACHER

In this project, developed by Marilyn Palmer, students adapt one of the oldest known forms of art (manuscript illumination) to digital graphics, one of the newest. This project, done in Adobe Illustrator, assumes that students have some familiarity with Adobe Photoshop. Students will create their own designs, drawing with the Pen or Straight Line Tool. The emphasis is on intricate hand-drawn detail in three areas: the central letter, the corner design, and the border design, all of which need to fit together as one cohesive design.

Art History

The Egyptian *Book of the Dead* was the first known *illuminated manuscript*. Papyrus was used until about AD 300, when vellum and parchment were introduced. Fine-grained lambskin, kidskin, or calfskin specially prepared for writing was used into the Middle Ages in Europe. Until printing came into use during the 1440s (Gutenberg's Bible was printed in 1454), handwritten manuscripts had been the chief records of history for 4,500 years. The vast majority of western manuscripts were religious and were produced in monasteries. Even though he was illiterate, Emperor Charlemagne was a patron of the arts, supporting the copying of classical manuscripts by monks and nuns.

Distinctive illumination styles developed in different parts of Europe: Anglo-Irish, Byzantine, English, and French. All used six basic forms of decoration: animals and people, branches, geometric designs, ornamental letters, braids, and scrollwork. Many handwritten books were decorated with intricate borders and embellished lettering.

Preparation

Introductory exercises making straight line shapes will improve students' confidence and skills. This is a good place to teach students how to match colors with the Eyedropper Tool or to use gradients, because the shade of a color changes as it retreats into space.

As an introduction to using the Pen Tool to make curves, demonstrate for students how to make simple curves, spirals, and curved shapes before moving on to more complex drawings. Practice will increase their confidence.

FOR THE STUDENT

Straight-Line Vector Drawings

1. To prepare for this project, take photos of a corner of a room or hallway or even an exterior view of the school, in which all lines are straight.

2. Bring the photo into Adobe Illustrator (FILE>PLACE) as the bottom layer. Reduce the opacity of this background layer to about 65 percent and lock it (while the layer is highlighted, touch the lock icon at the top of the Layers Palette).

3. On a new layer, begin to draw each shape in the photo, using the Pen Tool or the Straight Line Tool, setting the Fill and Stroke colors to match the colors in the photo (use the Eyedropper Tool to match the colors). Or you may use any color you prefer. Be sure to enclose each shape so it will fill with color.

4. Some shapes can be filled with textures or pattern as well as color for more contrast.

5. Keep different objects on different layers for easier editing.

6. Turn the visibility of the photo layer off occasionally as you work so that you can see only the drawing. Turn the photo layer off when completed.

Curved-Line Vector Drawings

This method is similar to straight-line vector drawing, except that you are working with curved objects.

1. Take photos of curved objects such as cars, musical instruments, even faces! FILE>PLACE a photo as the bottom layer. Reduce the opacity of this background layer to about 65 percent and lock the layer.

2. Parts of the objects will be drawn on new layers using the Pen Tool. Set the Fill and Stroke colors to match the colors in the photo. Or you may use any color you prefer. Be sure to enclose each shape so it will fill with color.

3. Move anchor points and manipulate the handles of the curve to adjust the curve as desired. This will take practice.

4. Keep different objects on different layers for easier editing.

5. Some shapes can be filled with textures or pattern as well as color for more contrast.

6. Use gradients and/or the gradient mesh tool to help show roundness of form.

7. Turn the visibility of the photo layer off occasionally as you work so that you can see only the drawing. Turn the photo layer off when completed.

8

Fine Crafts

Fibers, Book Arts, Ceramics

Fine crafts, sometimes called applied arts, is the creation of beautiful objects that may also serve a practical, everyday purpose. Ceramics, weaving, knitting, batik, basketry, pottery, jewelry, handmade books, and combinations of materials are both artistic *and* practical. Not all students love to draw or paint, but many find enormous satisfaction in the manipulation of materials.

Museums are filled with beautiful objects—applied art from cultures around the world. The most enduring, of course, are made of glass or metal, ceramic, shells, and stone. Soft fibers such as cloth or string that held these objects together seldom endure, yet if care was taken, examples do exist. Books that have been in a dry desert climate such as that of Egypt go back at least two thousand years.

Fiber arts materials and processes have ancient traditions, as people learned to dye fabric and apply ornamentation to their clothing. Native Americans added dyed porcupine quills for color before glass beads became available. They have a long tradition of weaving that is also found throughout other cultures. African mud cloth and adinkra cloth were both special methods of adding pattern to plain cloth, using special, representational symbols.

This chapter will include ceramics and give an introduction to fiber arts and book arts.

Underfoot
Helen Moore, low-fire red earthenware, press-molded and sculpted. Installation dimensions variable. Art teacher Helen Moore says, "This work grew out of my curiosity with scientific illustrations of diatoms and diatomaceous earth. Each individual piece in the installation started from one particular diatom and then 'grew' into its own set of similar sculptures. Collectively, the pile is reminiscent of earth drifted into a pile in the corner—'underfoot,' so to speak."

Fiber Arts

TRASH QUILT (GROUP PROJECT)

Time needed: 5 fifty-minute classes

Materials: rulers, scissors, canvas (80 × 80 inches on which to attach all nine squares), Elmer's glue or polymer medium, wooden curtain rod or PVC pipe 1 inch × 82 inches long

Goal: Students use elements of art and principles of design to create original artworks that communicate the concept of ecological responsibility.

Goal: Students work cooperatively so that each will complete a portion of a large artwork.

Objective: Students demonstrate imaginative use of found objects in a carefully constructed design section that complements the entire finished hanging.

Trash, Really?
76 × 76 inches, mixed media. This "quilt" was made of discarded and recyclable items found in and around the Missouri Botanical Garden by its Green Team. Each of the nine squares represents an area of focus.

FOR THE TEACHER

This group project can be exciting—to your students, your staff, and your district. The idea originated with the Green Team of the Missouri Botanical Garden and is used with their permission. The quilt was assembled by environmentally conscious individuals who worked together to make a beautiful work of art. The quilt won a prize at the opening of an exhibit called Sustainability and the Built Environment of St. Louis.

Vocabulary: quilt, quilt block, fiber, piecing, embellishment, embroidery, found objects, pattern

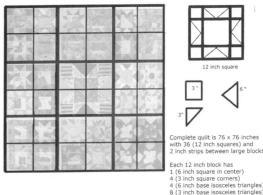

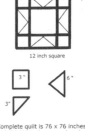

12 inch square

3″

3″   6″

Complete quilt is 76 x 76 inches with 36 (12 inch squares) and 2 inch strips between large blocks

Each 12 inch block has
1 (6 inch square in center)
4 (3 inch square corners)
4 (6 inch base isosceles triangles)
8 (3 inch base isosceles triangles)

Trash, Really?
Trash quilt pattern. This "pattern" allows you to see how each group worked within the same format to create completely different 24-inch squares, yet because of the pattern there was unity throughout.

Preparation

Introduce students to awareness of "quality junk" that can be recycled as art—materials that have been discarded, but have artistic potential because of their color, reflective quality, texture, and "message." I suggest that students work in groups of four to make one *large* 24 × 24-inch square, composed of four 12 × 12-inch squares, each by one student, for a total of thirty-six 12-inch squares. This enables them to coordinate colors for their one-ninth of the quilt.

To make this approach work visually, the students should all be working with the same "quilt" pattern as the one shown in the illustration here or you may select one that will serve the same purpose. If students can bring in a "family quilt," this is a good opportunity for them to see some examples of the traditional craft of quilting.

In your discussion, ask students to name items that they know are discarded or thrown in landfills. Begin collecting items for this project a week before actually beginning the quilt. Here is a list of some items used in the Botanical Garden's trash quilt: magazine pages sorted by color (such as green and brown) to cut into patterns and strips, tightly rolled up and glued magazine pages cut into lengths to be assembled in a pattern, drinking straws, aluminum foil, packing peanuts, leaves of native plants, thin cross-slices of a small tree limb, plastic spoons, colored bubble wrap, bottle caps (matched or unmatched), red bottle lids, pop tops, potato sack mesh, flattened aluminum soda cans, cellophane, raffia, cloth.

Prepare the canvas support for hanging by folding under and sewing (on a machine if possible) a 3-inch wide tube to accommodate a sturdy wooden curtain rod for hanging. To save time, you may have one student cut all the 12-inch poster board blocks and patterns in advance. An alternative would be to hang this in three 24-inch wide strips, with three composite blocks on each strip.

FOR THE STUDENT

This project is going to involve some research and "gathering" ability on your part. Get together with a group of four people and begin by reading about environmental concerns. Perhaps as a group you can decide which of several issues you would like to represent in your large square: Choices might be recycling, wetlands, composting, plastic pot recycling, sustainable building and construction, humans and animals in the same habitat, landfills, or many other environmental issues of which you are aware.

1. Measure and cut carefully to make tag board patterns. Each 12-inch square block will have

    One 6-inch square to go in the center

    Four 3 × 3 × 6-inch triangles to be centered on each side

    Four 3-inch squares to be placed in each corner

    Eight equilateral triangles, 3 inches on each side

2. After materials are assembled and your group has discussed a general color scheme or idea, each person will be responsible for making one individual quilt block 12 × 12 inches square. You can include photocopies of a photograph (easier to glue) and words that describe some of your concerns.

3. Each quilt block square should have one or more printed words in one of the squares, some of which you can find in magazines or online.

4. Each member of your group of four is responsible for carefully *piecing* the quilt block and embellishing it with found objects in a repetitive pattern.

5. When the four squares are complete, group them together on a piece of poster board, 24 × 24 inches. These will then be attached to a background piece of canvas for display.

Alternative Project
Friendship Quilt

The friendship quilt is just that—an expression of appreciation for a friend—someone who might be moving out of town, getting married, or a favorite teacher who is going to another school. It is lovingly made, often with an embroidered sentiment, and certainly with the donor's name. These are put together to make a large quilt. Older friendship quilts must have been cherished, as so many museums have them in their collections. Quilt squares can be made if you are doing a batik unit or painting on fabric. Perhaps a parent would be willing to sew them together for display.

Although real quilting is a nicety, there are shortcuts that can be made by tying the quilt at intervals with yarn. Or this friendship quilt can be composed of student portraits transferred to fabric squares.

PROJECT 8-2
YARN BOMBING (GROUP PROJECT)

Time needed: 6 fifty-minute classes

Materials: fibers of all types: yarn, old wool sweaters, beads, dyes, camera

Goal: Students plan a cooperative artwork, demonstrating engagement through experimentation.

Goal: Students research and discuss fiber arts in different times and cultures.

Objective: Students work together to apply different fiber art materials to an object in the environment. Each student's portion will become part of the whole.

Slipcovered tree. This tree was slipcovered as part of the Floriade festival that happens every ten years in Venlo, Netherlands, near Amsterdam. This particular pieced slipcover is made with colorful nylon fabrics that are impervious to fading. Photo by Carl Schumacher.

FOR THE TEACHER

Yarn bombing, sometimes also known as knit graffiti, began in about 2005 and involves covering many different surfaces with woven or knitted patches loosely joined together with yarn. Notable yarn bombings seen on Internet video sites include a yarn-covered *bus*, motorcycle, parking meters, tree trunks at the National Mall in Washington, D.C., and a gun! Knitting would consume too much teaching time to be practical as a class project, but students can combine fiber creations of other types to make a *temporary* slipcover for something indoors or on the school grounds.

Mention to the administration that you are planning to do a temporary environmental public art project that will be photographed to memorialize it. To avoid vandalism or damage, this project should be in a highly visible, protected place, and be left up only a few days, unless you have it in a safeguarded area such as a courtyard. Many environmental artists preserve their (often temporary) work with photographs. Display the photographs after students have reclaimed their portion of the work.

This project should be completed during a season when it is warm enough to be outside.

Vocabulary: embellish, appliqué, batik, weaving, wrapping, posterity, unity, pattern, variety, texture

Yarn-bombed tree, the Weavers' Guild of St. Louis. This small tree was covered by a collaborative group of knitters who planned which portion would be done by each. This group also considers their work "knit graffiti."

Preparation

This is an opportunity to introduce students to fibers of all types, as well as to recycle found objects. As in the previous project, this is obviously a group project, with each small group of four coming up with a pattern for their part of the project, which will contribute to the whole. Students may even have a piece they have knitted or woven previously that can be included. Students will need a week to locate found fibers—wool sweaters, socks, yarn, clothesline rope, buttons, and decorative *stuff*.

A tree can be decorated with one kind of fiber project that is done by every student in the class. Or small groups of students can create one type of fiber, and each group work on a different object. If students are going to join their individual artwork together, they will want to be able to take it apart and take home their section later. Whether students are working on one tree or several, if a variety of techniques are used, *unity* is created by working within an agreed-upon color scheme. Here are some fiber project options to consider.

Felting. This can be done with old 100 percent (or at least 85 percent) *wool* sweaters with labels that say Dry Clean Only. Wash sweaters of similar colors inside a pillow case in *hot* water (tie the pillowcase at the top to keep lint from clogging the washing machine, and to contain a few golf or tennis balls that you've put in the pillowcase to improve the process). Use a normal amount of liquid detergent and have a hot water rinse. Dry on high heat in dryer. Cut them apart at the seams, possibly using these seam strips elsewhere as decoration.

Cutting apart acrylic, polyester, and cotton sweaters. Advice from experienced "knit graffiti artists" is to buy *non*-wool sweaters (at a by-the-pound thrift store, for example) because they *won't* shrink or fade outdoors. The felting project above needs wool sweaters precisely *because* they will shrink!

Cardboard loom weaving. You can introduce an entire class of students to cardboard loom weaving with yarn, joining all the pieces before sewing them together to encircle a tree.

Knitting. If someone in the class or a parent knows how to knit, that person could teach a small group of students to do it and they could plan knitted bands to go around a tree. Many students know how to make long knitted "strings" by knitting using a wooden spool with four nails on the end.

Wrapping. Ordinary clothesline rope can be wrapped with colored yarn to make coiled circles to attach or dangle from branches.

Beading. Although this can be done only on a small scale because of cost, a few students might like to learn how to string beads and sew them onto fabric in a design.

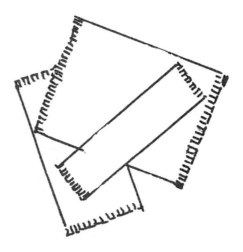

Cardboard looms come in a variety of sizes.

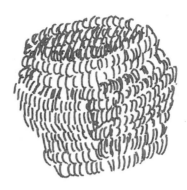

Wrapping cords for wrapping with yarn or raffia are available from art supply houses.

Batik. The tree could be covered entirely with small multicolored batik pieces that are sewn together as patchwork before sewing them into place on the tree.

FOR THE STUDENT

Much environmental art is temporary, and the only way anyone ever knows it existed is to keep a photo record of it. An important part of this project is taking photos of the entire project so each member of the group will have a portfolio photo as a record of the work. Know in advance that you intend to take a photo of the finished project and possibly do a video of the fiber art process.

1. Depending on the material your class chooses to make or adapt, each person's or group's contributions will be added together to make the final environmental public art on your school's grounds.

2. Measure the circumference of the tree or other object to be covered and make a paper pattern to guide you as you join projects together. If you do not have a tree nearby, cover an object with fibers to be displayed near the office or on a column in the library.

3. Some materials just do not go well with others. For example, if part of your class chooses to do felting, and another group chooses batik, these would probably not go well together on a single tree. But if similar techniques were applied to different trees, they would look great.

4. When everyone has completed the project and they are sewn together and laid out on the pattern, think how you might finish them. Some of the sewing together might work best if done with a sewing machine. Decorative materials such as yarn, buttons, sewing trims, and zippers might make wonderful embellishments, and repetitious patterns can be made of them.

5. Tassels for a fringed skirt as seen on the Floriade tree shown at the beginning of this project can be made in a variety of colors of yarn.

Book Arts

The instructions given here are simply the mechanics of making a few simple books. If your students really love bookmaking, books exist that contain detailed instructions and photos. The covers and inside cover papers can be made of wrapping paper, paste paper, marbleized papers, or brayer-printed paper. A handmade book is a treasure to be saved or given.

These fiber art projects may not seem like *fiber* to most students, but without question paper is made of fiber, and variations of *paper* are made all over the world. Many wonderful resource books have been written about how to make a book, so the instructions given here are minimal. (*Cover to Cover: Creative Techniques for Making Beautiful Books, Journals, and Albums,* by Shereen LaPlantz, is one of my favorites.)

This project will deliver better results if students have time to reflect on what the book's use is and what they want to include in it, rather than plunging in headfirst.

Students might choose to use this handmade book to present an original poem or story that they have written in another class. It might be a glossary of terms that they have learned in a foreign language. It doesn't have to be handwritten (though that also would make this book unique), as students can print out or photocopy words, such as the lyrics to a favorite song. If they want to use photographs as illustrations, I strongly recommend using photocopies or digitally generated pages, as some photos are too heavy to glue well, and once glued, are difficult to remove.

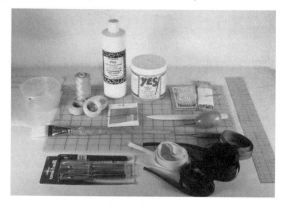

Definitions

Awl. Sharply pointed instrument for making holes for sewing signatures

Archival. Acid-free paper and other materials that will not disintegrate over the years

Bone folder. A flat plastic knifelike object for neatly flattening folds

Book board. Heavy board used for covers that will not warp, unlike mat board, which is made of several types of paper fibers held together with glue

Book tape. Specialty tape for binding the side of a signature-sewn book

Cover paper or cloth. Various materials can be glued to book board: marbleized paper, textured pastel paper, paste paper, canvas, or cloth

End paper. Inside cover of a book (such as brayer-printed, marbleized, plain, or paste paper); in ancient books, marbleized paper was the standard

PVA glue. Polyvinyl acetate glue is archival, quick drying, and dries flat; unfortunately, it is relatively expensive and might be too costly for class use—white glue is an adequate substitute

Signature. A group of pages sewn together, then combined with other groups to form a book

Special folds. Mountain fold (fold that goes outward) or valley fold (inward)

BOOK 1: ACCORDION-FOLDED BOOK

Time needed: 2 fifty-minute classes

Materials and equipment: X-acto knife, scissors, 6 × 6-inch squares of mat board or book board (two per student), two to three pieces of drawing paper cut 5½ × 18 inches, two pieces of end paper 5½ × 5½ inches for inside cover, two pieces of cover paper 8 × 8 inches, one or two 36-inch long ribbons, white glue, bowl for glue, brush, ruler

Goal: Students consider and discuss the evolution of bookmaking, relating traditions of the past to modern technology that will affect visual artists.

Objective: Students create a book in at least one of three different methods to demonstrate skill in the mechanics of assembling paper and sensitivity in the manner of finishing it.

Objective: Students complete the assembled book with some form of communication such as pictures, a written story or poem, or a combination of both in an illustrated story.

Basic accordion-folded books; student work.

FOR THE TEACHER

Art History

The long history of books goes back well over five thousand years, when important knowledge was recorded by scholars on incised stone or bones, wax tablets, wooden writing boards, cloth, bamboo, papyrus, and paper. Because of the dry climate of the Middle East, three-thousand-year-old examples of papyrus scrolls such as *Book of the Dead* and the *Dead Sea Scrolls* exist today. The oldest book in the Americas is a Mayan codex from ca. AD 1500. Parchment and vellum were used to hand-copy important knowledge until the invention of the printing press ca. 1440. The *Book of Kells* is a wonderful example of an illuminated manuscript. The *Bible* was first printed ca. 1454. Today's students are going through another period of major technological change, with electronic books replacing printed copies.

Vocabulary: archival, awl, bone folder, codex, accordion fold, mountain fold, valley fold, mitered corner

Preparation

Although this project will create a simple book, it is important for students to follow the steps in the order given for the best results. Before they glue the accordion-folded paper to the cover, walk around to make sure the ribbon used for closing is correctly placed and have them show you what and where they will glue. (Having also taught this to university students, I saw much greater success rates after such inspections.) The inside cover page (the end paper) is the last step to completing the book and can mask a multitude of errors.

To anticipate any problems students might have, you should make a book first and demonstrate the process for them.

FOR THE STUDENT

This simple book can be made as a gift for someone, with printouts of photos, a poem, found paper objects, and so forth.

1. *The covers.* Make the two cover pieces before beginning the center section. Coat a 6 × 6-inch book board piece on one side with glue. Center the glued side of the cardboard onto the underside of the 8 × 8-inch cover paper. Turn it over and smooth the paper, starting at the center to eliminate bubbles. Before gluing the edges to the inside, make folds around all four sides.

2. *To miter the corners on the inside,* use your thumbnail or a bone folder to make sharp folds on the sides. Fold the corners of the cover paper straight toward an imaginary dot in the center of the board, then glue the center of each corner down before firmly creasing the four sides inward and gluing each in place. Complete both covers in this way and set them aside.

3. *To make the accordion-folded paper,* overlap by 1 inch and glue the lengths of paper that will form the book end to end. Fold the paper approximately in half, allowing the glued seam to go on one side of the fold. Use a ruler to measure 5½ inches outward from the center fold, then make a tiny pencil mark. From this valley (inward) fold continue to carefully fold the paper back and forth, making a 5½ × 5½-inch accordion-folded book. The last folds that will be pasted onto the inside of the covers will have slightly different lengths (no problem), and will be glued to face toward the front edge of the book. Do not glue yet, but set the folded portion aside.

4. *Assembling the book.* To make a codex book (a book that opens from a single spine), lay the two covers side by side with approximately a ⅛-inch space between them. Fold the length of ribbon in half, center it on the covers, and glue it in place across the insides of the two covers, allowing ribbon to hang from each cover. Glue the ends of the accordion-folded paper facing forward so the book opens frontward.

For a book to be displayed open and upright. If you intend to decorate both sides of the accordion-folded pages and display the book standing open, each cover will have ribbon(s) extending across and hanging from both sides. Glue the accordion-folded paper closer to the bottom of the two covers, rather than centering it. To ensure that the book will stand upright, as a rule of thumb the cover should be only ⅛ inch larger than the inside of the book.

5. *The end paper.* After the ribbons and accordion-folded interior are glued in place, the last step is to glue the end paper to cover both the ends of the folded interior and the ribbon. This paper can be plain or can be brayer-printed, marbleized, or paste paper.

6. This is the plain book. It is up to you to fill it with appropriate words, photocopies of photographs, prints, collages, or digitally produced pages. It is a lovely gift for yourself or someone else special.

BOOK 2: SEWN SIGNATURE BOOK

Time needed: 2 fifty-minute classes

Materials: X-acto knife, scissors, paper, ruler, awl or sharply pointed instrument for making holes, darning needle, string, waxed linen thread, book board, cover paper, end paper, bone folder

FOR THE TEACHER

Signatures are the standard bookmaking format for a book style that has existed for centuries. A signature consists of folded pages sewn together, then combined with a number of other signatures. All are bound together to make a codex book (a standard book with two covers heavier than the inner pages and a spine, as opposed to a scroll or other style). If students are making a one-signature book, select a soft cover that is larger than the signature by ½ inch vertically and horizontally. It is best to have all paper and cover materials cut in advance. Talk with students about the history and evolution of bookmaking. Have them examine even their textbooks to see how signatures are joined at the spine.

Vocabulary: signature, codex book, spine, end papers, marbleizing

FOR THE STUDENT

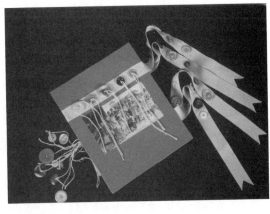

Watermelon Feast
This family picture book was sewn in several signatures, allowing the string to hang on the outside of the spine. Vintage buttons were chosen as accents.

Watermelon Feast
Family album with sewn signatures.

1. *Preparing a signature for sewing.* To make a signature, use four pages folded in half individually, carefully creasing them in the center with a thumbnail or bone folder, then placing one inside the other.

   Make a guide for punching holes on a piece of paper 2 inches wide, the length of the signature, folded in half lengthwise. Poke holes at measured intervals so all the signatures will have exactly the same spacing for sewing.

   Place the signatures on a folded towel or magazine and use an awl, pushpin, or large nail to punch holes in the crease of the signature and the cover so they will line up perfectly.

223

2. To sew a single signature and soft cover:

   These instructions are given for three and five holes. After punching holes, begin sewing from the outside at the center hole (3), leaving a tail end of approximately 6 inches hanging outside the signature.

   From the inside (3), go up and outside through the next hole (2) and back to the inside at (1). Now go to the next hole down (2) and back inside again at hole (4), skipping hole (3), and back outside at hole (5). Go to hole (4) and bring the needle back inside, go outside at (3). Tie the tail ends together with a square knot, catching in the long piece of thread that skipped hole (3).

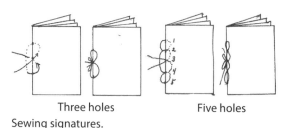

   Three holes   Five holes

   Sewing signatures.

3. There are many decorative possibilities for a book cover. Almost anything can be used, if it is done before the signatures are attached to the insides of the covers. The cover can have an opening cut in it to make a frame, giving a hint of what is inside.

4. Long ribbons can be placed to go around both covers to hold the book together. The ends would be hidden by the end paper (inside cover paper).

5. The last step in making a book with signatures is to glue the end paper in place.

BOOK 3: STAB-BOUND BOOK

Time needed: *4 fifty-minute classes*

Materials: X-acto knife, scissors, book board for the cover pieces, cover paper or cloth, paper ½ inch smaller than the cover dimensions, book tape, PVA glue, brush

FOR THE TEACHER

The traditional stab-bound book originated in Japan and is composed of single sheets of paper bound together on one end and folded back on the unbound end to enclose and protect the sheet underneath. Glue is not used because it can cause the pages to warp. The pages are grouped together and bound in a cover with a cloth hinge that allows the book to open flat so pages can be easily viewed.

FOR THE STUDENT

Your adaptation of this form of bookmaking may include single sheets of regular-weight paper, perhaps for a journal or to reproduce a collection of drawings.

1. *Making the covers.* The back of the cover is one flat piece and is ⅛ inch longer than the front cover. The outside of the book board may be covered with cloth or paper. Cut the front cardboard cover with a 1 ½-inch strip on one side (to allow it to open easily). Measure and cut the outside cover paper 2 inches larger all around than the cardboard covers.

2. Cover the two front book board pieces with glue. Place them on the cover paper, placing the end (narrow) piece ⅛ inch apart from the front piece. Add book tape inside between the two pieces to reinforce this hinge.

3. To finish the covers, make mitered corners by turning in one corner and gluing it down. Glue an adjacent corner, then glue each side until the edges are finished.

4. If ribbons are to be added, they need to be glued in place before the end papers are glued.

5. Place the inside pages between the covers, holding the entire group together with clamps (remember to put clean pieces of paper between the clamps and the book to protect the book from clamp marks). Depending on how thick the book is, you may use an awl or hammer and nail to make holes. If the stack is too dense, use an electric drill. To determine where to make holes, decide first whether you will form them in a single line or at varying measured distances from the edge.

6. *Stab-binding* is done by sewing through a hole from back to front, allowing a tail to hang from the back hole. Take the thread around the outside and once again sew from back to front. One hole might be approached from three different angles to give a geometric design. Many variations of design are formed on the outside of the book—some simple, others complex, depending on the whim of the artist. Because knots should be inconspicuous, they may be tied inside the book and trimmed.

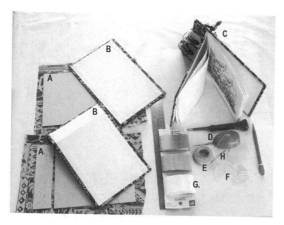

Finished stab-bound book.

Materials and examples of a stab-bound book in process: (a) cover before fabric is glued (front cover of book is in two pieces); (b) book covers with mitered corners and end papers; (c) covers and inside of book clamped in preparation for drilling holes with awl; (d) awls; (e) linen thread; (f) wax for thread; (g) bookbinding tape; (h) needle.

Ceramics

Ceramics is an ancient art form that is both craft *and* fine art. As a craft, it often involves practical objects such as bowls, vases, and teapots. As fine art, ceramic sculpture and bowls, vases, and teapots are beautiful to look at and might never be used except as ornament. Although most modern potters are trained in throwing pots on a wheel, many of them choose to hand-build to give an expressive, personal quality to their ceramics. Some may combine several methods such as slab building, coiling, and wheel throwing in one object.

When students are asked what they loved most in their elementary and middle school art classes, the large majority reply that they loved painting and ceramics. When a student brings home a glazed ceramic piece in whatever form, that piece is displayed for years.

Get students excited about working with clay. Talk about it, showing examples and perhaps making a digital slideshow of objects made by your former students. Pots relate to human anatomy, sharing body parts such as the lip, neck, shoulder, waist, belly, and foot.

Although this chapter is primarily about working with fired clay, there are many self-drying clays on the market that can at least give students the experience of modeling a pliable material.

CERAMICS DEFINITIONS

Bat. A flat circle sometimes made of plaster or Masonite that serves to absorb moisture from clay; often used for wheel-thrown pottery

Batten. Flat sticks ¼ or ½ inch thick × 1 ¼ inch wide × 12 inches long, used for slab rolling

Bisque fire. The first firing of a piece, sometimes with underglazes; the fired clay is called bisque ware or biscuit ware

Bone dry. Unfired clay that is free of water and ready for firing; if it feels cool against your cheek, it may still be damp

Burnish. To polish clay while it is in the green ware stage

Casting. To pour clay slip into plaster molds; allows mass reproduction of one form

Ceramic. Clay products that have been fired for permanence

Clay. A moist earth of decomposed rock; used in products such as pottery, bricks, tiles, and sculpture

Coiling. A method of creating pots by building up the bottom and walls with even ropelike coils

Cones. Small clay pyramids that automatically turn off a kiln when a certain temperature is reached

Decal. Designs that are transferred to ware before firing; often used in china decorating

Drape. Thin slabs of clay may be draped over a bowl or mold to form soft folds

Earthenware. Low-fire pottery, usually red or tan, that has been fired to below 2000 degrees F

Egyptian paste. Low-fire, self-glazing body fires to a gloss or crackle finish

Engobe. A glaze made of clay diluted with water that is painted on greenware

Extruder. A shaped tube (available in various sizes and shapes) in which clay is placed and forced through to make a uniform tube shape

Firing. Making clay products permanent through baking at high temperatures in a kiln

Glaze. Pulverized glass suspended in water that is painted on bisque ware; when fired at high temperatures, it adheres to the clay and becomes molten

Greenware. Clay in an unfired state; it is quite fragile at this point

Kiln. The "oven" that is used to fire clay

Kiln wash. Powder-water liquid solution applied to kiln shelves for protection from glazes

Knife. Tool for cutting off excess clay or for scoring

Leather-hard. Unfired clay that isn't quite dry, yet firm enough to carve or burnish

Loop. A tool with a handle and a heavy wire used to trim clay

Matte finish. A glaze that is not shiny when it is fired

Modeling. Clay is molded by hand to change its form; mostly used for sculpture

Mold. Soft clay can take any shape when pressed into a mold; liquid clay (clay thinned with water to liquid consistency) can be poured into a mold until the outer ¼ inch hardens; the remaining liquid clay is poured out for reuse

Paddle. Flat wooden stick (sometimes textured) used on the outside of a pot while supporting it inside with the hand to add firmness; a ruler is a good substitute

Plaster of paris. Gypsum used to make bats on which to dry clay or used for molds

Porcelain. High-fire translucent ware fired at 2205 degrees F, sometimes called "china"

Potter's rib. Thin metal tool held with the straight edge next to the palm, used as a scraper to refine pottery

Potter's wheel. Electrical or foot-operated flat plate that turns as a potter uses both hands to form a pot from a lump of clay

Raku. Low firing of clay pots often done outdoors that produces dark areas and iridescence

Reduction firing. Firing with insufficient oxygen causes interesting color changes in glazes

Rolling pin. Used for slab rolling; a 1-inch diameter dowel cut to 12 inches length is a good substitute

Scoring. Making marks with a pencil on two pieces of clay before joining with slip

Sgraffito. Scratching designs through slip to allow the contrasting body color to show through

Slab. Clay evenly rolled and formed

Slip. Clay diluted with water to the consistency of cream; used for joining or as an engobe (glaze)

Stilts. Small "stars" used to prevent clay pots from touching the kiln shelf

Stoneware. Gray, reddish, or tan clay that has been high-fired (cones 5 to 10)

Talc. A compound added to white clay

Terra cotta. Reddish clay that contains grog, commonly used for ceramic sculpture

Test tiles. Small flat geometric tiles that are made to test glazes and used as examples

Throwing. Creating vessels on a potter's wheel

Turning. Completing a piece of pottery by rotating on a wheel and trimming the bottom with tools

Underglaze. Liquid, crayon, or pencil colors applied on greenware or bisque ware before firing; usually a clear glaze is used for a second firing

Wax resist. The application of melted wax to the foot or body of a clay object to resist the glaze

Wedging. Kneading moist clay to eliminate air bubbles and produce a uniform texture; students can wedge clay by forming a ball and firmly slapping between the hands for about ten minutes to force out bubbles

Wire clay cutter. Wire with small wooden toggle on each end that allows slicing through large blocks of clay easily

Ceramics tools include glaze samples, a decorating wheel, and various loop tools.

General Suggestions

Safety note. Ideally the kiln should be in a separate room, with a kiln venting system that goes to an outside vent. Do most of your firing overnight to allow the room to be free of odors during the daytime. Tell students never to touch anything that may be drying on top of the kiln, nor to open it unless you are there.

The Ceramics Room

Keep your room as dust-free as possible by expecting work tables to be washed twice with clean sponges, then dried. Have your room mopped each evening. To make cleanup easier, students can work on old bath towels brought from home, newsprint, 12-inch squares of Masonite, heavy linoleum, or even thick wallpaper samples. Keep lots of sponges at the sink. Keep a bucket of water in the sink for sponges to be rinsed in to avoid clogging the drain. When enough clay settles to the bottom, the water can be poured off and the clay recycled on bats.

Assign a different table or group of students each week to be responsible for wiping counters and making sure tools are clean.

Tools such as loops, knives, and kidney-shaped scrapers should be kept clean. Check them out to students at the first of the hour and don't accept them back until they are spotless and dry.

Behavioral expectations. Announce that if anyone throws clay, he or she will lose points on a grade and will be allowed to scrub down the room for an hour after school. It works!

Teaching Methods

- Teach students the vocabulary of ceramics from the very beginning. Distribute the preceding handout of Ceramics Definitions.

- Your students may not have seen many professionally created ceramics. To expose them to good design, suggest some online resources and offer many ceramic books and magazines from the school library for students to look at in class.

- Insist that students design their projects in advance. They may make a number of thumbnail sketches, then enlarge the design onto graph paper. Have them draw all views: bottom, top, and sides.

- If you announce that you will not fire a piece unless it is of high quality, students will take the time to work carefully.

Glazing, Firing, and Conditioning

Glazing. Glaze is applied by brushing, pouring, dipping, and spraying. Before applying glaze to a bisque-fired pot, either use a wet sponge to dampen the pot or pour warm water inside and outside.

Make test tiles. Roll out clay ¼ inch thick. Cut into 1 × 3-inch rectangles or triangles. Fire them, then apply a different glaze on top of each to show the effect of color on different clays. Print the name of the glaze on the back of the tile with underglaze. Use a pencil to make a hole in the tiles for hanging either on cup hooks on a board or strung together on jute twine, knotted between tiles.

Painting. Acrylic paint will cover ceramics nicely and sometimes allows the artist to use colors that could not be achieved with glaze.

Nonglaze finishes. Reddish clay is attractive in its natural state. Apply wax, polymer medium, or shoe polish to give it a sheen. Spray paint in closely related colors gives the effect of slightly uneven firing.

Underglazes. Colored underglaze designs can be painted directly onto leather-hard or bisque-fired clay. Light colors need more coats, as they tend to fade after the clear glaze is applied.

Slip glazing. Slips (engobes) are made by thinning clay to the consistency of cream and applying it to the pot. Sgraffito (scratching designs through the layer of slip) gives some beautiful effects.

Commercially prepared glazes. Commercially prepared glazes are painted onto bisque-fired pieces. Reds and oranges easily become overfired, turning brown or clear. Experiment with glazes on test tiles for best results.

Glaze formulas. Making your own glazes allows you to pour or dip pots into glazes for interesting effects. To mix your own glazes, obtain a book with glaze formulas. Mix them by weight with an accurate scale. Store the dry chemicals in wide-mouthed food jars from your school cafeteria. Keep liquid glazes in glass jars; they will last indefinitely if well covered. *Safety note:* Most glazes in school supply catalogs specify that they are lead-free. This is an important consideration when teaching young people.

Firing. Be sure the bottom has been wiped clean of glaze, and protect the kiln shelves by setting the work on stilts for firing. Protect new shelves by painting a "kiln wash" on top of them. Don't allow glazed pots to touch each other, or they will stick together.

Conditioning clay. To recondition quantities of clay that have dried out, use a wooden spoon handle to punch deep holes and fill these with water. Cover and store the clay overnight, and it will absorb the water. If clay is totally dry, it can be put into a barrel or bucket and covered with water until it becomes soft enough to work, then excess water poured off and lumps of clay put on bats. Wedge before using.

Test clay for elasticity by rolling a ½-inch thick coil. If it can easily bend around a finger without cracking, it is perfect for many different projects. It is far better to work with properly conditioned clay than to use water on the outside of a piece to smooth it. The water dries more quickly than the clay and can cause cracks.

Storing clay. Until work is ready for firing, students must be responsible for keeping work in progress in working consistency by carefully putting a couple of barely damp paper towels around the clay and around the bottom and wrapping in plastic.

Repairing broken pieces. If it is still green ware (not leather-hard), put damp paper towels on the broken pieces and leave overnight, then join together with slip of the same clay or add vinegar to the slip before joining. If fired (bisque) ware, use a thin coat of glaze in that area between the broken parts, and hope that when it is fired the glaze will hold the pieces together. If a fired piece broke into many pieces, repairs can be made with white glue, filling in holes with plaster of paris. Smooth the plaster with sandpaper and paint the entire piece with acrylic paint or spray paint.

Average Firing Temperatures of Clay: Large Cones

1855–2052 degrees F: earthenware: cone 06–02

1855–1971 degrees F: white talc: cone 06–04

1855–2205 degrees F: white sculpture raku clay: cone 06–5

1922–2014 degrees F: terracotta: cone 04–03

2205–2381 degrees F: stoneware: cone 5–10

2205–2269 degrees F: porcelain: cone 4–6

Grading

Because ceramics projects take so long and occasionally break after much hard work, many ceramics teachers grade as work progresses. One teacher grades one-fourth of the way through the project, halfway through, three-fourths through, and last, the finished product. Another teacher suggests grades in points: idea, 20 points; form, 20 points; construction, 20 points; decoration and glazing, 40 points. Criteria to consider are planning and good use of time, craftsmanship, following instructions, having the finished piece resemble the original idea, meeting a deadline, application of glaze, and appropriateness of decoration. You may wish to allow students to earn extra points by performing necessary chores.

GREEK POTTERY

Much of what is known about the Greek culture was recorded on its vases that were treasured and preserved. The styles and colors evolved over several hundred years and so enable modern scholars to determine when they were made. Some potters and painters became so well known that they signed their work (potters didn't always paint their own vases).

The Geometric Period (850–700 BC). Huge funerary vases were decorated in horizontal bands featuring the life of the departed, funeral processions, and beautiful bands of geometric ornaments such as zigzags, wavy lines, meander (Greek key pattern), checkers, and swastikas.

Orientalizing Phase (700–600 BC). Narrative subjects were battles, funerals, and pageants. Figures such as animals and humans were popular. Bands of spirals, circles, lotus, and leaf patterns were found only on handles, the foot, and lip. Figures were loosely arranged.

Gravemarker

Archaic Period (650–480 BC). Red- and black-figured ware had bands of design on the foot, neck, and lip. Vases were no longer used as grave markers because by then stone markers were being used. Pictures of mythological figures and stories were scratched into the red background.

Black figure ware, ca. 580 BC featured black slip painted on the figures, with background remaining red.

Red figure ware, ca. 530 BC shows black slip painted on the background, allowing much greater detail.

Classical (480–323 BC). White ground-ware vases were used primarily for funerals or wedding gifts. They were painted with red, black, and purple glazes and often showed scenes of ordinary daily life.

Lidded vessel

Lekythos

Gamikos

Amphora

Oinochoe

Volute Krater

Kylix

Pyxis Cosmetic Box

COIL-BUILT GREEK POT

Time needed: 20 fifty-minute classes

Materials: 3 pounds of clay per student, paper, plastic bags, paper towels, sponges, paddle (ruler or ¼-inch × 12-inch batten), scraper, X-acto knife, decorator wheel

Goal: Students research cultural traditions that influence style and decoration of coil-built vessels.

Goal: Students compare and contrast pottery needs in various times and cultures that have influenced shape, thickness, and decoration of vessels.

Objective: Students create a hand-built coil vase of uniform thickness complemented with a decorative surface that relates to an historical or cultural tradition.

Alyssa Wagner, Greek-inspired coil pot, 11 × 8 inches. Parkway West High School, St. Louis County, Missouri, teacher Marilyn Palmer.

FOR THE TEACHER

Building with coils is a universal art form, with people in each part of the world developing their own method of working and decorative style, depending on the type of clay and local tradition. Coils are usually about ¼- to ½-inch thick, depending on the size of the finished work.

Art History

Little would be known of ancient Greece if it had not been for beautifully painted vases on which the painter illustrated daily life, battles, and lives of the gods. When we see these vases lined up in museums today, we need to remember that they were cherished possessions: wedding presents or other special occasion gifts that outlasted earthquakes and wars. The vases ranged in size from six inches to six feet, with each vase shape serving a particular purpose, such as the *hydria* used to hold water or the *krater* used to mix wine and water. Huge vases used as grave markers were painted with the deceased person's life story, and it was not uncommon to find a hole broken in the bottom of a graveyard vase for wine to be poured in for the departed by mourners.

Vocabulary: symmetrical, profile, slip, coil, score, burnish, leather-hard

Preparation

Demonstrate for the students—show them how to make a base, how to roll out coils and attach them with scoring, slip (optional), paddling and scraping to connect and smooth the pot. When the vessel is leather-hard, they may also choose to burnish the pot with a rock or the back of a spoon to get a smooth sheen, a method used by Native Americans in the Southwest region of the United States. A rotating *decorating* wheel allows students to turn the pot easily to keep the pot symmetrical.

Alternative Project
Southwestern Pueblo Cultures Coil Pot

Building with coils is the standard method of Pueblo potters of the Southwestern United States. Each Pueblo has a specific method of decorating, incising, or firing that makes that Pueblo's pottery unique. Some Pueblos also specialize in modeling small figurines and animals or "storyteller" figures based on those originated by Native American Helen Cordero (1915–1994), of the Cochiti Pueblo. It may simplify this project if students select the style of pottery from one Pueblo to serve as inspiration.

Alternative Project
Coil-Built Vessel

Students can make a vessel of any diameter and height. Coils may be braided, coiled into small spirals to be used vertically, decorated with a pencil point, and combined with balls.

FOR THE STUDENT

It is *extremely important* to carefully wrap the clay at the end of each day to keep out air. If the clay begins to dry, place wet paper towels inside the plastic bag to remoisten the clay (not touching the piece itself).

1. Look online or through ceramic magazines and books to find pleasing shapes. Draw thumbnail sketches before beginning. Select your best drawing and enlarge it carefully, drawing side, bottom, and top views.

2. Draw an outline of the pot on tag board. Cut it in half vertically to get a *profile* pattern of the pot. If you cut this out and check it against your pot as it grows, you will manage to stick with your original plan.

3. Wedge at least three pounds of clay for a minimum of fifteen minutes. Roll some coils, starting with several fairly evenly sized lumps of clay. Place a lump of clay on cloth to roll out with your fingertips. Working from the center and going out to the

Barrett Litzsinger, stoneware, green-brown glaze, 8 × 10 inches. Instead of hiding the coils on this tall vessel, variety of form and shape is shown. Oakville High School, St. Louis County, Missouri, teacher Amy Kling.

Bird's Nest
Kelly Ries, stoneware, 9 × 7 inches. Varied cool colors would indeed make a comfortable nest. Oakville High School, St. Louis County, Missouri, Teacher Amy Kling.

edge, keep the coil moving. Use the palms of your hands to make the coil as even as possible. Cut the coils diagonally on the ends. You may roll a number of coils at one time, but keep excess clay covered with a damp paper towel or plastic while you are working.

4. Begin the bottom of the pot with a tightly rolled coil or a flattened piece of clay. To join one roll of clay to another, score both surfaces with a knife and coat them with slip. Omitting this step may leave holes in the vessel when the clay shrinks while drying. Unless coils are scored and smoothed together, they may fall apart when dry. Avoid using water on the outside to smooth clay, as it dries quickly and can result in cracks.

5. When the bottom is the size you want, start adding coils vertically. When a coil ends, add a new coil of the same thickness, cutting the slant in the opposite direction before scoring it and joining it with slip to the first coil.

6. A good working method is to place three coils on the pot, remembering to score and join them with slip.

7. Always make the first three coils straight up, as they will flare out naturally. For straight sides, place coils directly on top of one another. Later, if you want to make a slight curve, place coils slightly to the outside for an outward curve or slightly inside to curve inward. With practice, you will find it fairly simple to control the shape.

8. Take the time as you work to smooth the outside with the scraper. Support the inside with your hand and paddle the outer surface. The paddling will force out any remaining air bubbles. Alternate scraping inside and outside three times before adding the next three coils. The pot should be approximately ¼-inch thick.

9. Refer to your original sketch to see if you are following your design. When the pot has reached a height of at least nine inches, finish the top by scraping it smooth, then smooth with a damp sponge. There will be some shrinkage in height and breadth when the work is fired.

10. If you choose to add a handle, *pull* the handle from a cone of wedged clay by holding the clay in one hand, and pulling with the other to add strength to the handle. Use a sponge to add water as needed. Form it according to your design. Before you attach it, it may need to dry slightly to hold its shape. Place the top of the handle on the edge of a table, allowing the handle to curve over and hang free from the side of the table until it stiffens. Score the place(s) where it will be joined, attaching the handle(s) with slip.

MAKE IT WITH SLABS

Time needed: 7 fifty-minute classes

Materials: 3 to 4 pounds of clay per student, rolling pins (brought from home) or 1-inch dowels cut 12 inches long, 2 battens (flat sticks) per student (¼ inch thick × 1 ¼ inches wide × 12 inches long), rulers, canvas or burlap for rolling slabs, pointed knives, slip, wire screen (for adding surface texture), tag board

Goal: Students effectively use language of the visual arts to discuss similarities and differences in the use of practical ceramic items.

Objective: Students demonstrate creative adaptations with slabs to make items such as containers, tableware, decorative artwork, and lidded boxes.

Objective: Students use an innovative idea to enhance the surface of a pot with glaze, stain, or paint.

Swan Lady
Dexter Fletchall. This imaginative "jewelry box" with lid fulfills the assignment requirement for a slab-built lidded ceramic container. Lawson High School, Lawson, Missouri, teacher Helen Moore.

FOR THE TEACHER

Slabs are versatile, because the clay is plastic enough to drape on top of or inside an existing form. Slabs can be used flat to make tiles, but can be rolled as thin as ¼ inch and still be strong enough for the artwork to support its own weight when it has stiffened. Normally, the larger the form, the thicker the clay should be; ½- to ¾-inches thick is more than adequate.

Slabs have an almost infinite number of possibilities such as planter boxes (the clay should be at least ½-inch thick for a planter), a replica box of the student's own home, a tall rectangular vessel for flowers, a personalized desk set of pencil and letter holders, a decorative birdhouse, or a box with a removable lid.

To use slabs for tiles or low-relief works of art, remember to dry them slowly and evenly, as the slabs will curl otherwise. Keep them moist around the edges with damp paper towels until the center has had time to dry. Slabs should be rolled out on canvas or burlap for easy removal. If you have a slab roller, students will skip Steps 2 and 3 of the student directions.

Alternative Project

Draped Slab Bowl

Roll out a thin slab and drape it over a paper towel–covered form such as a bowl. Remove wedge-shaped slices to make "tucks." Score and add slip to join the cut edges, smoothing and scraping and trimming to make a perfect curved form.

Or you can hang a thin slab from a bowl suspended on something taller (for example, a tall coffee can filled with sand). Allow the excess clay to drape itself naturally, with uneven edges. Allow it to harden before removing it from the bowl and glazing.

Alternative Project

Four-Piece Place Setting

With careful preplanning, slabs can be combined to make a place setting for tableware. Students should draw the general idea for the shape and size of the individual pieces, then select forms (plastic containers and plaster molds on which to drape the clay slabs if curved sides are desired). For straight-sided pieces, they can make tag board patterns and tape them together as described here.

FOR THE STUDENT

Slab-Built Box Container

Make thumbnail sketches of the finished product. Choose the best one, then use a ruler to enlarge on tag board to make a model of your box. Tag board resembles clay in that it is stiff enough to support itself and hold a shape. Cut out the pieces of tag board and join them with masking tape. If the cardboard pieces fit together well, take them apart to use as patterns.

Draped bowl. This thin terra cotta draped bowl hung much as a woman's full skirt might because the form on which it was draped was tall enough so the clay hung freely. Parkway West High School, St. Louis County, Missouri, teacher Mary Ann Kroeck.

Henna
Jordan Slama, 5 × 5 × 5 inches. The handle on this colorful footed stoneware box repeats the decorative circular designs. The lid's opening is disguised by following the line around the geometric decorations. Oakville High School, St. Louis County, Missouri, teacher Amy Kling.

Dinnerware place setting. Ashlyn Mellon, Lawson High School, Lawson, Missouri, teacher Helen Moore.

1. Place a piece of burlap or canvas on the table. Then place two ¼-inch battens on either side, parallel and about 12 inches apart.

2. Use enough clay to avoid patching. Place a ball of clay in the middle and flatten it evenly by rolling it out with a rolling pin or dowel, resting the ends of the roller on the battens (sticks).

3. Lay the pattern on top. Cut straight edges with a knife, holding a batten or ruler beside the knife to get a good straight cut. Set the slab aside to stiffen while you continue cutting the other pieces for the box. It is better to assemble the pieces in one working session—but remember to wrap them well if they must wait overnight.

4. When all the pieces are cut, score the edges that will be joined together. Use slip on the joints. For extra strength, score the corners inside and outside horizontally after the pieces are joined, then smooth them again. Strengthen the corners by rolling a thin coil and placing it on the inside of the box, smoothing it onto each wall with your thumb or a small knife scraper. Use a scraper to clean the edges both inside and out.

5. If you want to make a flat top, make a pattern and cut the clay the same way as the rest of the box. Make a thin coil and place it on the underside of the lid approximately

My House
Jenny Vandas, white stoneware, 12 × 7 × 4½ inches. The flattened ball "shingles" make the removable roof on the house especially interesting. Oakville High School, St. Louis County, Missouri, teacher Amy Kling.

Birdhouse
Melanie Robben, white stoneware. The textured tree and leaves are effective yet subtle decorations on this "house" box. Oakville High School, St. Louis County, Missouri, teacher Amy Kling.

½ inch from the edges. Make a knob (handle) top. If you wish to make rooftop for a house, measure carefully and make a tag board pattern for it at the same time you are making the tag board model of the box.

6. Decoration may be applied in a number of ways:

Incise designs into the surface with a needle tool (or use a needle stuck into a cork for easy handling). Color inside the designs with underglazes.

Make extremely thin "worms" of clay to apply as decoration; score and use slip before applying.

Cut openings in the clay, carefully preserving the cut-out (positive) part to apply as a positive shape somewhere on the form.

Use various found objects such as stamps. Stamping is best done before joining, while the slabs are flat on the table.

WHEEL-THROWN POT

Time needed: 10 fifty-minute classes

Materials: potter's wheel (kick or electric), 2 to 3 pounds of well-wedged clay, water in small container, slop container, natural sponge, large sponge for cleanup, wire with toggles at both ends, needle tool or cork with needle inserted, loop tool (for finishing bottom of pot), plaster or Masonite bat

Goal: Students consider the relationship between the artist and the viewer as they develop skills in throwing on the wheel, asking questions of themselves about quality, form, and expression.

Goal: Students demonstrate ability to make a wheel-thrown pot that has uniform thickness throughout.

Objective: Students demonstrate skill in throwing a pot that has even walls, appealing form, finished top and bottom, and appropriate glaze.

FOR THE TEACHER

Few secondary schools have enough potter's wheels for an entire class to work on thrown pots at the same time. Although many high schools have a few wheels, it takes time and determination to learn to throw, and this project is best reserved for advanced students who have already learned other basic techniques. Set up a schedule that allows advanced or independent study students to go ahead and work on the wheel while other students are busy on another project. Students might also choose to come in after school and continue practicing until they've achieved perfection.

Preparation

Begin by demonstrating how to throw, going through the process step by step, including removing the pot and placing it on a bat to dry until the next day, when you will demonstrate how to trim the bottom.

There are as many methods of throwing as there are potters who throw, and all have developed personal techniques that work for them.

Ceramist Sandy Martin is finishing the top of a pot, using a natural sponge. She has chosen to leave decorative finger mark ridges on the outside of the vessel.

Sandy Martin is trimming the bottom of the pot, before removing it from the wheel.

Alternative Project
Pitcher

Make a pitcher from a basically vertical form, forming a pouring spout with a finger. Make a "pulled" handle by holding a rounded cone of wedged clay in one hand. Gently pull the clay with the other (dampened) hand, pulling it until it forms a long cone, thin at one end. When it is the length and size you want, cut it from the original cone and firmly set the upper end of the handle at a table's edge, allowing the entire handle to hang down until it has become firmer (you may have to place a wad of paper towels under it to form an *arch* until the handle becomes firm). Attach it to the pitcher by scoring the pitcher and the handle with slip. Sometimes the thumb marks that are used to attach it at the top and bottom are allowed to show.

Jan Sultz, teapot and pitcher. The graceful lines and thin walls of these thrown vessels reflect the skill of many years as a potter.

 FOR THE STUDENT

1. Wedge the clay *very* well for throwing on the wheel. If there is an air bubble, you may have trouble centering it. If your wheel will accommodate a Masonite bat on which you will throw, this will greatly simplify removing the pot and later cleanup.

2. Seat yourself in front of the wheel with your lap and knees well protected by an apron or cloth. The wheel must be completely dry. Throw the ball of clay onto the middle of the wheel with force.

3. Dip your right (or dominant) hand in water, remembering that both hands must be kept wet to avoid dragging the clay. *But* if you use too much water, the clay will become soggy. Use the sponge occasionally to clean excess water from the wheel and inside the pot.

4. Start the wheel, leaning forward, and place the nondominant hand (we will call it left from now on) at a slight angle and cupped around the ball of clay. Place the fingers of the right hand loosely over the first finger of the left hand so that the ball is almost enclosed by both hands. The clay will want to control you! To center the clay on the wheel, brace your elbows on your legs, pushing down, not allowing your arms to move.

5. Look at your hands. Are they staying in the same place? Use a thumb and lightly touch the top of the ball. Does the mark you made with your thumb continue to stay in the center? When your hands don't move at all and the ball of clay has lost its wobbly appearance, it is ready to open.

6. Place your right fingers loosely, almost vertically over the left fingers, with the right fingertips almost touching the wheel, allowing the left hand to control the pot. Place your right thumb in the middle, beginning to push down to the bottom of the pot (leaving ½ inch of clay between your thumb and the wheel). If the pot begins to wobble, take the thumb out and use both hands to contain the ball of clay and make it even again.

7. If the pot is stable as it continues to go around, enlarge the center. While bracing with the left hand, turn the right hand around to face the left hand and put two fingers in the pot and the thumb on the outside. Squeeze against the left hand, enlarging the opening, but still keeping the sides of the pot vertical. Remove the right hand and stabilize the pot again, making sure it is even. Look on the inside for air bubbles (they look like diagonal streaks). Use a needle to prick them.

8. Before pulling the clay upward, open the bottom of the pot to the thickness and width it will be when finished. Once the clay is pulled up, it is too late to do this step. To add a professional finish to the inside bottom, align the first three fingers of the right hand so that the middle finger is the same length as the others. Hold the fingers straight on the bottom as the pot goes around to make a circular pattern. Or, if you prefer, use a natural (elephant ear) sponge to gently smooth the inside bottom.

9. At this point decide about the shape of the pot. It can be drawn up vertically for a pitcher or vase or flared slightly to become a bowl. The angle of your hands determines the shape. The left hand supports the inside while the other hand gently pulls the clay up on the outside. Your two hands are separated only by a thin wall of clay and work together to form and maintain the shape of the pot. Some potters prefer to support the pot on the inside with the entire left hand while pulling the clay up with a knuckle or metal rib. If too much pressure is exerted, or if the fingers aren't wet enough, distortion can quickly happen. If you sense you are losing control, gently place both hands on the outside and stabilize the pot again.

10. The quality of a pot is often judged by its weight in proportion to its size. If you want the pot to be lighter than expected in weight, it must have thin walls and bottom. The walls shouldn't be much thicker than ¼ inch.

11. When the pot is the height desired, it will be necessary to cut off the top evenly, unless you have been extremely skilled. This can be done in one of two ways:

    a. Brace the elbows well and hold a wire taut with your hands about three inches apart. Spin the pot slowly and hold the wire in place at the lowest level of the top rim. As the pot goes around slowly, the excess will be sliced off. Remove it with thumb and forefinger.

    b. Use a needle tool and hold it horizontally (again bracing your elbows) and as the pot goes around, let the needle slice off the top. Use the needle tool to remove excess clay.

12. Use a sponge or your index finger and thumb to finish the rim.

13. To cut the pot from the wheel (or bat), spin the wheel slowly and hold the wire flat on the wheel and pull it under the pot toward yourself. If time permits, let the pot rest on the wheel an hour or so after it is cut, as it is preferable to let the clay stiffen somewhat before moving. If it is on a Masonite bat, remove the bat and pot together before cleaning the wheel.

14. To remove the pot (if you did not throw on a bat), place a plaster or Masonite bat in front of the pot, level with the wheel. Slosh water on the wheel in front of the pot and gently shove the pot from behind, touching only the bottom, and gliding it across the wheel onto the bat.

15. To finish the bottom of the pot, allow the pot to stiffen overnight until it is leather-hard. Put the pot upside down on the dry wheel, revolving the wheel slowly to make sure it is centered. Hold it in place with small wads of clay. Use the loop tool to make the bottom and sides of the bottom even. Finish the piece by simply trimming off excess clay. If the pot is thick on the inside, it can be made more attractive by trimming the bottom. Make a "foot" by leaving a ¼-inch wide rim around the outside of the bottom.

16. Thrown pots may be glazed after bisque-firing by dipping or pouring glazes.

Pablo Ruiz with Itch

Robert Arneson (1930–1992), 1980, earthenware with glaze, 87½ × 27 × 22 inches. The Nelson-Atkins Rockwell Museum of Art, Kansas City, Missouri. Photo: Jamison Miller. Art © Estate of Robert Arneson/Licensed by VAGA, New York, NY.

9

Sculpture and Architecture

Sculpture

Sculpture is an exciting class to teach, as students visualize a finished product and sometimes draw a specific idea. They learn to accept the changes that occur as the *material* sometimes dictates what can be done with it. In sculpture, they need to consider the artwork's appearance from all directions, which is a new experience for some. Throughout the ages some sculptors "drew" by creating a fist-sized *maquette* (a three-dimensional quick sketch made in clay or plaster) before refining and gradually enlarging it in stone or clay for later casting in bronze.

In a semester course you may be able to cover the major methods of sculpture: *modeling* (clay), *carving* (clay, wood, stone, fire brick, plaster, or Styrofoam), *casting* (paper pulp, plaster, or clay), and *assemblage* (mixed media and found materials). Most of the materials mentioned in this chapter are readily available and relatively inexpensive. School supply catalogs carry most tools and sculpture materials. Good sculpture materials may be found by the side of the road or through local manufacturers. Local businesses and families might be happy to donate unneeded scraps or "quality junk."

Flexibility, abstract reasoning, and imagination are developed as students make necessary adjustments. Sometimes unnecessary detail must be eliminated to achieve simplicity in form. Help students learn to accept that their best-laid plans may be subject to change. Pushing art students to experiment and take risks is also part of teaching them to become decision makers. Even if you do not teach a specific *sculpture* class, try to include at least one three-dimensional sculpture project in both beginning and advanced art classes.

You might notice in this chapter that the projects give general directions rather than specify a subject. Many of the materials such as stone, wood, and recycled materials are "found," and the shape and size of the *material* suggests what the end result might be. Challenge students to come up with creative solutions, whatever the material. Being open to change is a good character builder, and you will be amazed at students' ingenuity.

Letting Go of Home
Laura Gill, wood, foam core, and acrylic,
54 × 10½ inches. Parkway Central High
School, St. Louis County, Missouri, teacher
Cara Deffenbaugh. Laura's life-size figure
expresses beautifully the thoughts of a
senior ready to move on.

Gwyn Wahlmann, kimono, 2011. This garment, created from more
than one thousand bottle caps, is a wonderful example of creative
ingenuity and perseverance applied in the use of common
recyclable materials. © Gwyn Wahlmann.

Safety in the Sculpture Class

Before working with certain materials and techniques, you should go over safety procedures
and insist that students follow them. Demonstrate safe use of tools, and post safety reminders on or near equipment. It is imperative for the teacher to remain in the room during a
sculpture class, because some of the equipment has the potential to be dangerous if misused.
Students appreciate that the teacher cares enough about their well-being to insist they follow
safe practices.

Electrical or heating equipment. When students use electrical equipment such as a band
saw, drill, sander, or a torch or glue gun, they must push sleeves above elbows, wear
goggles, tie back long hair, and remove *all* jewelry.

Safety goggles or face mask. If there is the slightest possibility of something getting into
the eyes, the students must wear plastic safety goggles. A plastic mask should be worn if
something might fly off the material being worked.

Buddy system. Students should never work alone in a room (after school, for example),
but should have a buddy there also.

Plaster of paris. Plaster is a favorite, inexpensive material for many sculpture teachers, but the teacher must always be in the room when working with an active material such as this. This ancient material goes through a chemical reaction when mixed with water and becomes warm or hot as it sets. Students must *never* keep their hands fully immersed as the plaster begins to set. A hand cannot be removed after the plaster has set, except with sharp tools, and severe burns can result (this actually happened in a school in England). If you start with lukewarm water (not hot), you can avoid this problem.

Solvents and chemicals. Keep chemicals and solvents in a locked cabinet. Solvent-soaked rags must (by law) be in an enclosed metal container.

Noxious fumes. If working with anything that might pollute the air or leave a strong odor, do it after school so it will have time to dissipate overnight.

Carving safety. When chisels are being used for carving, secure the materials on a sandbag (3 × 6 × 12-inch heavy canvas bag filled with sand and sewn shut), C-clamp, or V-board (made by screwing two 2 × 4 × 12-inch boards at a right angle near the corner of a ½-inch × 30-inch-square piece of plywood). This may be clamped to a table or sat upon by the student while carving. Students must never hold something between their legs for carving, as chisels can slip.

Safety equipment.

CLAY SCULPTURE AND MODELING

Time needed: 5 fifty-minute classes

Materials: newsprint, pencil, 3 to 5 pounds of clay per student, canvas, decorating wheels, paper towels, clear glaze or acrylic paint, knives, wire, loop tools or spoons, paddles

Goal: Students plan and draw a creature that has both human and animal characteristics.

Goal: Students combine the most appropriate clay techniques for their design: carved, coil, slab, or thrown.

Objective: Students complete a human-hybrid clay sculpture that demonstrates a personal style and the ability to take risks to communicate an idea.

FOR THE TEACHER

This is where ceramic techniques can all come together: modeling, pinching, coiling, making slabs, carving away—all the techniques for forming clay may be used singly or in combination to make a piece of sculpture. This *fine art* form in clay serves no functional purpose but to be admired. Many sculptors use or combine other ceramics techniques to create inventive and amazing sculptures.

Vocabulary: modeling, classical, impressionism, expressionism, futurism, negative space

Art History

Classical figural sculptures in ancient Egypt, Greece, and Rome were usually by unknown sculptors. Michelangelo's (1475–1564) work in the Renaissance, in particular the *David*, is familiar to most students. Sculptures by the famous impressionist sculptor Auguste Rodin (1840–1917) had an unfinished quality and fresh way of applying clay to show the human form in motion. *Expressive* sculpture by Jacques Lipschitz (1891–1973) and Constantin Brancusi (1876–1957), and *futurist* sculpture by Umberto Boccioni (1882–1916) opened the way to a whole new way of looking at the human form.

Preparation

If this is the first ceramics project your students have done in secondary school, they will need some of the information (such as wedging and keeping clay moist) from the previous chapter on ceramics. Allow time to show examples of sculpture and for students to contemplate ideas and draw designs. They can develop an independent design or, as a class, might decide that they all would like to do something such as a figure in motion. Smaller sculptural forms may be carved or modeled from solid pieces of well-wedged clay.

One-Hour Exercises: Time Well Spent

A one-hour modeling exercise I have done that helps students free their minds to use abstract concepts is to give each student approximately one pound of clay. I then say, "You will have eight minutes to make a sculpture that reflects *anger.*" Time it carefully, and have them all put their small sculptures on the table, look at and discuss them, asking them to look for similarities and dissimilarities. Have them wad up the sculpture to make a new ball of the clay and again take eight minutes to make a clay interpretation of the word *calm*, then have another "compare and contrast" discussion. Two more emotions could be interpreted, such as *love* (no hearts or obvious solutions, please) and a word or emotion of their own selection. For this last one, when the sculptures are placed for discussion, the class should try to guess what the emotion is.

This exercise might be a good icebreaker at the beginning of a sculpture class or can be used as relief when students are between two long projects. It certainly helps them into see that abstraction can look pretty good when there is a concept behind it.

Alternative Project
Abstract Form

Model the solid form, then cut it open and hollow it out, putting it together by scoring and using slip-on pieces to be rejoined. It should not be thicker than one inch anywhere and should be open at the bottom to avoid trapping moisture inside.

Alternative Project
Maquette: Figure Sculpture

A small human-style figure can be made with an arrangement of three lumps, with the smallest lump on top. English sculptor Henry Moore (1898–1986) produced some very large bronze sculptures that often began with a small fist-sized model (maquette). His figures were often reclining, based on his drawings of figures sleeping in the London subways during World War II. He and colleague Barbara Hepworth (1903–1975) often featured holes in their sculpture to create fascinating *negative space*.

Alternative Project
Humanagerie

The two ceramic works shown here are from a ceramics exhibition for high school students at the St. Louis Artists' Guild, curated by William Perry, a teacher at the Central Visual and Performing Arts High School of St. Louis. Students were invited to submit sculptural ceramic animals with human characteristics. This is a challenge that most students would welcome, because there is no right or wrong and each individual's sculpture can be entirely different from that of other classmates. The history of art is filled with examples of human-animal combinations: the satyr (man-goat), harpy (woman-bird), centaur (man-horse), mermaid (woman-fish), and sphinx (woman's face–lion's body). As students select their "hybrid," help them decide the best ceramic method to use.

These small cast figures were first made in clay, then cast in acrylic resin by making plaster molds. The light-colored figures had white marble chips added.

Clayden

Micela Chalman. This owl-headed little boy was an entry in the Humanagerie exhibition for high school students at the St. Louis Artists' Guild. The art teacher and curator of the exhibition was William Perry of Central Visual and Performing Arts High School.

Pet Peeve (*front*)

Anna Shaw's sculpture is all too human, yet we know it is a cat. Hazelwood Central High School, teacher John Tiemann.

Pet Peeve (*back*)

Anna Shaw, Hazelwood Central High School, teacher John Tiemann.

FOR THE STUDENT

A combination of methods such as slab, coil, and modeling is appropriate for this sculpture.

1. Begin with an idea and sketches that show how the sculpture will look from at least two different directions. This piece of sculpture should be at least eight inches high (or at least eight inches wide). Make sure the sculpture is not thicker than one inch at any point and that you have a hole in the bottom to allow it to dry thoroughly before firing.

2. Wedge the clay thoroughly. Cut it open to make certain it has no air bubbles, then re-wedge.

3. This project will take several days, and it is important that the clay remain moist. Wrap it in dampened paper towels and plastic after each working session to keep it pliable.

4. You can make openings through the clay or hollow it out from the bottom to a thickness of no more than one inch to keep it from exploding during firing.

CERAMIC SCULPTURE PORTRAIT HEAD

Time Needed: 2 to 6 weeks of daily fifty-minute classes

Materials: newsprint, pencil, 3 to 5 pounds of clay per student (built with slabs), canvas, decorating wheels, paper towels, clear glaze or acrylic paint, knives, wire, loop tools or spoons, paddles. For a life-size head and shoulders *built on an armature* as the illustration here shows, it takes 20 to 35 pounds of clay.

Goal: Students apply knowledge of the proportions of the human face through measurement and drawing.

Objective: Students demonstrate mastery of skills and observation to make a clay portrait.

Objective: Students use subtlety, originality, and imagination to create an original clay portrait, perhaps including found material in a different medium.

Joy Is in the Journey
Shamus Higgins, terra cotta clay sculpture,
15½ × 13 × 11 inches. De Smet High School,
St. Louis County, Missouri, teacher Laurie Kohler.
This life-size portrait bust was made with 35
pounds of clay and hollowed by cutting off the
top of the head and removing clay to make the
bust ½-inch thick throughout (the clay that was
removed from the inside was later recycled). The
top of the head was replaced, and an opening
was made at the bottom to allow moisture to
escape. The artwork was painted with acrylic.

FOR THE TEACHER

Before the advent of photography, the sculptural portrait bust was a way of honoring someone. In many ancient cultures the head was given great importance. Although the student illustration shown on the previous page is almost life-size and uses a large amount of clay, the clay that is removed may be recycled. Viola Frey (1933–2004) and Robert Arneson (1930–1993) were ceramic sculptors whose oversize human figures and portrait busts are notable. Some contemporary sculptors create portrait busts—perhaps of baseball players and successful businessmen—on commission.

The method of construction described in the student instructions here is to form the head on an armature for easier handling. Art teacher Marilyn Palmer makes her own armatures by centering a 9-inch-high 2 × 4-inch board on a square piece of plywood.

Alternative Project
Portrait Head Using Slabs

Teacher Joan Larson has developed a method that uses less clay for a life-size head. Fill a 16- or 20-ounce plastic bottle with water and seal with the cap to become the armature for the neck. Find a large plastic bread bag and stuff it with small balls of newspaper. Take measurements of the subject's head and mold the stuffed bread bag to the same proportions, then secure with masking tape. The bottleneck should be slipped into the bag and taped. Roll out ¾- to ½-inch thick slabs of terra cotta clay in a slab roller or by rolling between two stacked ¼-inch battens on each side of the wedged clay and drape them over the armature. Join slabs by scoring and using slip. The slabs are used to complete the head, working in much the same method shown here when using solid clay. If a lot of clay is added, hollow out to no more than ¾-inch thick. The bottle is easy to remove, and the small balls of newspaper should be removed before tugging on the bag to get it out.

Vocabulary: armature, modeling, portrait bust, slip, scoring

FOR THE STUDENT

1. The reason for first drawing the head is to challenge you to come up with something unique. It takes time and imagination. The head may be from six inches high to life-size. Begin with an egg-shaped oval placed on a neck (and shoulders if you wish). From the beginning, consider something that is *not* made of clay that might be included as part of the sculpture after it is fired.

2. To work most effectively, put it on a decorating (turning) wheel on top of a stool placed *on* the table so the head is at your eye level. If you look down on it and your head is above it, it will look back up at you. After you have formed the (egg)head, join the head to the neck at a natural angle (shoulders need more clay), scoring and using slip.

3. Push in to form hollows for the eyes (remember—they are midway between the top and chin). If you are working with solid clay on an armature, you can hollow out the

eye sockets. Eyelids may be formed with two thin coils of clay, placing them in an eye shape, joined at the corners. Use a finger to smooth them at the top and bottom edges. A tiny ball of clay, slightly flattened, and added between these two *lines* can have a dot (the pupil) made with a pencil to give life to the image.

4. If the clay is perfect for working, you can form the nose by pulling out clay, remembering to indicate nostrils. Shape the cheeks and look at the face of a friend and really pay attention to how large the ears are. They are attached at the top just around the head from and parallel with the eyes (convenient for wearing glasses), arch above that area, and are attached at the bottom just opposite the bottom of the nose.

5. The ears may be made with a coil of clay that is shaped like a question mark. Score and use slip, smoothing them to attach. Put a ball of clay at the front of that coil, flatten, and smooth the front of it with your fingers.

6. Push the chin inward just below the lips and form lips by drawing the center-line of lips with a pencil. The line extends on each side to below the eyeball. Form the lips by pulling out the clay. If they are not full enough, add a coil of clay for the lower lip, smoothing it on the bottom.

7. When the piece is done, use a cutting wire to remove the facial mass from the cranial mass. Hollow out the inside with a spoon or loop tool until no area is thicker than ½ to ¾ inches. Score and rejoin the cut edges with slip. Remember that a hollow piece of sculpture must have an outside opening (a hole in the bottom), or moist air trapped inside will cause the piece to explode when it is fired. When you add hair, avoid adding a large slab or you may trap moisture between it and the back of the head. Instead use slip and add small amounts at a time.

8. The finish is up to you. If these are made of terra cotta, a reddish clay, they are effectively finished with shoe polish or polymer medium. Or they may be painted with acrylic paint.

CASTING WITH PAPER PULP (WHOLE-CLASS PROJECT)

Time needed: 5 fifty-minute classes

Materials: plastic containers of all shapes and sizes, collection of shredded paper, large container, Elmer's Art Paste, sieve, five-gallon bucket

Content connections: Science and social studies: environmental concerns

Goal: Students do long-range planning and work together to make a visual statement about waste and the need for recycling by accumulating necessary containers and discarded paper.

Objective: Students create an artwork using a *fiber art process* (paper pulp making) while using the resulting *cast* sculptures to communicate a message of concern about the environment.

Recyclable Is Not Always Recycled
Adam Long, size variable. Sculptor Adam Long created this sculptural installation by making paper pulp from bulk mail and fast food wrappers from an average household. Papers were sorted according to their original use and cast in common packaging items and plastic water bottles. Photo courtesy of the artist (www.AdamLongSculpture.com).

FOR THE TEACHER
"Recycling Is Not Always Recycled"

This paper *pulp* project, developed by sculptor Adam Long, results in a strong sculptural statement about the need to recycle. Working on a project like this helps students become aware of the accumulation of such materials in an average household and allows each student to gather his or her own bag of *stuff*. Students can store clean recyclable items at home in a grocery bag to be brought in later and shared.

Sculptor Adam Long, whose artwork reflects his lifelong quest to respect nature, says he takes advantage of modern technology by using a shredder and a kitchen blender to pulp the reclaimed paper.

Vocabulary: paper pulp, cellophane, Elmer's Art Paste, blender, papier mâché

Preparation

Start this project early in the semester to accumulate the scrap paper and plastic containers used for this particular papier mâché project. Students can shred the paper by hand or use a paper shredder at home, sorting the paper according to colors. The Elmer's Art Paste mixture can be made and used over a longer period of time than wheat paste. It keeps indefinitely in a closed container. Cleanup of dried, dirty containers can be done with vegetable oil and paper towels. To mix large amounts of pulp, use a *variable speed drill* and a *boring bit* or long *paint mixing bit* in a five-gallon bucket. Get an extra lid and make a hole in it for mixing to avoid splatter. Mixing of this type is best done outside.

Alternative Project
Bowl Made from Paper Pulp

Paper pulp can be formed into almost any shape. When the mixture handles easily, pat a coat of paper pulp evenly ¼- to ½-inch thick over a plastic wrap–covered bowl that is larger at the top than the bottom (the plastic wrap makes release easy). Remove the pulp bowl when dry and sand until it is smooth. The bowl can either be painted with acrylic paint or covered with small pieces of patterned wrapping paper, strips of colored tissue paper, or computer paper designs. I have seen beautiful scientific illustrations online that can be printed in black ink on white or colored paper to give a sophisticated look to this bowl. Apply the paper both inside and outside by dipping pieces into polymer medium and carefully smoothing to eliminate bubbles. The polymer medium acts as glue *and* varnish.

 FOR THE STUDENT

1. *Find the stuff and find the molds!* After you have done these two things, the rest is easy.

2. Spend several weeks accumulating *interesting* plastic molds: boxes from purchases ranging from doughnuts and light bulbs to scissors containers, water bottles, and curling iron boxes. Wash the containers if they are dirty and also keep the tops to complete the molds.

3. Collect paper that might be thrown away—things like receipts from cash registers, envelopes (including those with cellophane windows), fast food bags, flyers and letters, test papers, and scraps of construction paper. Do this at home, taking the time to sort items according to their prior use. If you have a paper shredder at home, shred the paper and sort it according to color.

4. *At school.* If your class agrees, you may sort some of the paper by color or by its purpose (fast food wrappers or cash register receipts, for example).

5. If your class has been saving construction paper scraps, you may use them to add color to some of the grayish paper that results from the ink-paper mixture.

6. To make paper pulp, fill a container to the top with shredded paper. Fill the container with warm or hot water and push the paper down so it is covered with water. Allow the mixture to soak overnight. Drain the water through a sieve, a piece of cloth, or an old pair of panty hose, squeezing the paper to remove excess water.

7. Get rid of lumps with your fingers and add Elmer's Art Paste, mixing it well with your hands.

8. Place this pulp in molds that have been sprayed with vegetable oil (to act as a release). Pack the containers tightly with pulp, and if you have a lid (such as those

in doughnut boxes), fill the two sides and round them off slightly before forcing them together (you may later have to do some trimming if you wish). To maintain the shape, plastic water bottles may need to be cut off about two inches up from the bottom and rejoined with tape when filled with pulp.

9. It will take a few days for the water to evaporate before you can remove the cast items from the molds.

SeventhYearProphecy
Adam Long, natural materials, including cicada shells. See also www. adamlongsculpture.com.

Revered
Adam Long, found natural material.

Matutinal
Adam Long, found natural materials.

PROJECT 9-4
CASTING WITH PLASTER (COOPERATIVE LEARNING)

Time needed: 5 fifty-minute classes

Materials: plaster, clay (1 to 3 pounds per student), shims (1 × 3-inch strips cut from heavy acetate or aluminum pie tins), 2 to 3 flexible plastic buckets, 1-gallon milk jugs with the top third cut off, petroleum jelly, 12 × 12-inch pieces of cardboard, hammer and screwdriver, tempera paint, finishing materials (milk, instant tea or coffee, shoe polish, charcoal, ink, polymer medium, or spray paint—in related colors), sandpaper

Goal: Students understand the process of working with a new material and take advantage of its unique properties to express themselves.

Objective: Students work cooperatively so each student will have a complete cast object.

Objective: Each student creates a finished work of art that incorporates complex ideas such as distortion, scale, and expressive content.

FOR THE TEACHER

Two schools of thought exist on using plaster in a sculpture class. One holds that it is a messy, almost uncontrollable, but necessary evil, and the other that it is an inexpensive, useful, and durable material. In truth, it is probably a little of each. Students enjoy the directness and action in

Student work, Hydro-Stone cast sculpture. This was first created in clay, with shims inserted into the clay so a mold could easily be separated into two parts. It was then oiled and coated with about a one-inch thick coat of plaster. When the plaster dried, the mold was separated, the clay removed, and the mold resealed. Hydro-Stone, a dense form of plaster, was poured into the empty mold, which was held upside down in a newspaper-stuffed box to keep it level. The dried Hydro-Stone was later coated with thin polymer medium to give it a glow.

Clasped Hands of Robert and Elizabeth Barrett Browning
Harriet Hosmer, 1830–1908, 1853, cast later, bronze, 8½ inches, St. Louis Art Museum, Gift of Mrs. Henry Cushman.

working with plaster and feel the pride of creation. They especially love to make castings of their own hands or feet.

Plaster of paris is made of powdered gypsum mixed with water and is a relatively inexpensive material that endures almost forever and has great potential for student work. It was in use in Syria nine thousand years ago.

The material can be stored for years, and is much less expensive to buy in fifty- or hundred-pound bags from a local building supply store. Odd as it may seem, clay and plaster are incompatible materials. If you try to recycle clay that will later be fired, even a tiny piece of plaster in the clay might cause the piece to explode in the kiln. The clay can be recycled, however, to make more forms for casting.

Preparation

Before students begin to make a clay sculpture for casting, make sure they understand the necessity to avoid using undercuts when they later make a mold for the sculpture. Draw undercut examples on the board to help them understand why plaster molds can't be removed without breaking.

Vocabulary

Mold. A sculptural clay form is encased in plaster or a similar material that hardens. When hard, this mold is opened, the clay is removed, the mold cleaned and greased, and liquid material is poured into the (often reusable) mold. Soft rubber molds also exist, but are expensive.

Negative space. The area that surrounds or goes through a piece of sculpture.

Plane. A flat area with edges on sculpture.

Release. Oil or grease that prevents a poured sculptural material from sticking to the mold.

Shims. Sturdy metal or plastic strips that are inserted into sections of a clay sculpture to facilitate easy removal of the plaster mold.

Undercut. Prevents removal of the mold, causing breakage of the sculpture.

Alternative Project
Hands

Students can make a cast of a hand, by casting only half of it at a time, allowing the plaster to set, and the next day greasing the flat sides of the mold, putting the hand into it, and completing the other half of the mold. Oil should be used on the hand to prevent plaster from sticking to the skin. This can be done on a plastic cafeteria tray or in a mold made in a shoebox (if necessary, one end can be cut down three inches to accommodate the arm). The two halves of the mold are rejoined as described in the student instructions in this project (numbers 11 through 13). Students should plan ahead for the position of the hand, keeping in mind that they can hold something or have wadded paper inside a fist to prevent plaster from making an undercut. Single extended fingers are likely to break off in the process!

Alternative Project
Plaster Gauze Body Part

Use plaster gauze on about half of one leg, allowing it to become firm before removing it. The next day, place the hardened plaster gauze where it was formed on the leg and add wet plaster gauze to the other half (up to the cast), allowing it to set. Remove it, and the next day join the two halves together. Or make and display only half of a body part on a board—a hand can look pretty good. Imagination reigns!

FOR THE STUDENT

Foot-Hand Tree
This work was a collaborative student effort, as students were challenged to come up with creative hand positions. Preplanning was necessary, as dowels had to be inserted into the hands and foot just as the plaster was setting. Photos were taken so all students involved would remember it, though only one kept the completed project.

1. Make a small, relatively *simple,* but interesting self-supporting sculpture (approximately 4 to 6 inches tall). It can have planes (flat surfaces), edges, rounded areas, and even holes.

2. *Avoid undercuts.* As you are forming the clay, think about making a cast from a two-part mold that can be pulled straight out from the sculpture without breaking. If you make a hole going completely through the form, a piece of shim must be put in the middle of it to allow the mold to be pulled straight out.

3. When the sculpture is completed, use a sharp pencil to make a thin line where the shims will be inserted to divide the mold. Use scissors to cut the shims (pieces of aluminum pie tins or sturdy file folder acetate) into 1 × 3-inch strips. Push each shim down into the clay sculpture to a depth of 1 inch, overlapping the shims to leave a continuous "crown" that surrounds the sculpture and extends 2 inches above the clay.

4. Use petroleum jelly or vegetable oil to lightly coat the piece of sculpture and the shims. This coating acts as a release to keep the plaster from sticking to the clay and shims. Place the sculpture on a square of cardboard at least 6 inches larger all around than the sculpture.

5. *Mixing plaster of paris.* Put warm water into a plastic container such as a flexible bucket. Plaster is normally mixed in proportions of two parts plaster to one part water. A half-full bucket of water is enough to make molds for two 6- to 8-inch sculptures. Add plaster slowly. Don't start stirring until the plaster has mounded in the center to break the surface of the water and has formed a "mountain peak" that

is above the water. To avoid bubbles, put your hand in the bottom of the bucket and use your fingers to gently mix the plaster and water, getting rid of lumps. Remove your hand from time to time, and when the skin on your hand is not visible because the plaster is the consistency of thick cream, it is almost ready. When the plaster is no longer shiny and your hand leaves a path as it is stirred, it is ready to make a mold.

6. Several people can make plaster molds at the same time if they work carefully as teams. When the plaster is at the right stage for making the mold, you often have less than one minute to work, so it is good to have a partner who will help you.

7. Take a handful of plaster and place it on the mold. Continue covering the sculpture with plaster until it is up to two inches thick all the way around, but with the tops of the shims still showing.

8. Clean as much of the plaster as possible out of the bucket and put the excess in milk cartons for carving. One teacher makes "splats" of plaster (by throwing a handful of plaster that would be wasted anyway onto a plastic cloth). Her students later carve the splats into flowers. Wash your hands in a bucket of water.

9. *Do not pour excess plaster down the sink. It will harden and clog the drain!* When the plaster has dried in the buckets, tap the bottom of the bucket over a wastebasket and flex it, and the plaster will flake off. The plaster will get quite warm while it is setting up because this is a chemical reaction. Allow the mold to set overnight.

10. Use a screwdriver or chisel and hammer to separate the two halves of the mold. Remove the clay and inspect the mold for holes. Use premixed patching plaster (spackling) to fill holes (or mix up a tiny bit of plaster in a cup). Dry the mold with a paper towel and remove most of the color left by the clay.

11. Coat the inside of the mold with petroleum jelly, including the flat surfaces formed by shims. Put the halves of the mold back together, cementing them by mixing a small amount of plaster to cover the outside of the mold along the crack (so liquid plaster can't leak out). Allow the mold to set overnight.

12. Cut off the top half of a plastic one-gallon milk container. Place the mold upside down in the carton, surrounding it with crumpled newspaper to hold the opening level. Mix the plaster or Hydro-Stone (a more dense variety of plaster) to pour into the mold. Allow it to dry overnight, then gently pry the mold apart to avoid damaging the sculpture. The mold may be reused a number of times.

13. Dry the cast sculpture using fine sandpaper to smooth off the casting seam or other rough surfaces. After the sculpture has hardened, it can be finished by staining it, spraying with clear shellac, or combining stains such as shoe polish and charcoal. Metallic power sprinkled into wet lacquer will make the piece resemble bronze.

PLASTER CARVING

Time needed: 2 weeks of daily fifty-minute classes

Materials: plaster of paris; ½-gallon cardboard milk cartons; paring or fettling knives; spoons; paper towels; plastic; newspaper; rounded files, rifflers, or rasps, sandpaper; 1 pint of milk for finish

Goal: Students show sensitivity to value differences, the use of negative space, and applied texture in carving in a one-color material.

Objective: Students complete a three-dimensional carved form, being aware of the limitations of the material.

FOR THE TEACHER

This subtractive method of working with plaster requires that plaster must be molded in cardboard milk cartons or a similar box prior to carving. The plaster is delicate when it is being worked on, but after it is dry will endure for a very long time unless it is dropped.

Art History

Introduce students to the work of sculptors such as Barbara Hepworth (1903–1975), Henry Moore (1898–1986), Constantin Brancusi (1876–1957), and Jean Arp (1887–1966), whose abstract work demonstrates simplicity of form.

Vocabulary: abstraction, negative space, planes, advance, recede, applied texture

Preparation

Try to have all of the sculptural blocks poured in the same day (so they are damp and students are able to begin carving at the same time). Cut the cardboard milk cartons to approximately six inches in height and have several students mix plaster in buckets at the same time. The plaster should be mixed to the consistency of cream, then poured. Tap the cartons on the tabletop to remove bubbles. Alternatively, the mixing can be done after school the day before you will begin carving. The plaster is easier to carve when damp. Students should have a drawing prepared to serve as a guide before mixing the plaster.

FOR THE STUDENT

1. Prepare a drawing that will give you a starting point for a carved sculpture. Remember that in carving you can also have *planes* (flat areas), edges, areas that *advance* (remove plaster around the area to get that effect), and areas that *recede*. This will be a project "in the round" and may eventually have a large opening that allows you to see through to the other side.

2. *Movement.* Even though the material you are using is hard, most sculptors try to suggest movement. Consider using curves or twisting forms to avoid a stiff-appearing sculpture.

3. *Balance and stability.* Tear or cut off the cardboard carton. While the plaster is kept wet, you can use a knife or spoon to shave away small amounts at a time, starting with the corners. Carving takes patience, and trying to take away large amounts may result in breakage. Keep turning the sculpture to make sure it is interesting from any view. For stability, sculpture is generally larger at the bottom.

4. *Negative space.* Look at the sculpture and see at which point you might make an opening that might go through to the other side. Use a knife that allows you to carefully work inside a piece without damaging the outside. The air around the outside of the sculpture and areas you can see through are considered *negative space.*

5. Keep the plaster damp until you have mostly finished with the carving by covering with damp paper towels and wrapping the sculpture in plastic to store.

6. When you feel you are nearing completion, allow the plaster to dry completely, then use sandpaper, working from coarse to fine. Rifflers (tiny shaped files) may be used to refine interior spaces. One teacher has students refine further by careful rubbing with a fingertip that is wrapped in a narrow strip of wet cloth.

7. Allow the piece to dry completely before adding a finish. The work can be left in its pure white state, stained, or painted, and protected by spraying with two coats of clear varnish.

Sculptural Carving with Stone or Wood

Although stone and wood carving takes an investment in time and tools, carving is highly satisfying to secondary school students. Half the students may choose to work in stone *or* in wood, so you can add to the collection of tools over time. The two techniques take approximately the same length of time. Students love both materials. The finishing (sanding) can be done at home to save class time. The hour a day for four to six weeks yields a sculpture students will likely always keep and have pride in. Carving develops the ability to analyze abstractly, while improving visualization skills. I advise you to always remain in the room during sculpture, as questioning is sometimes needed to guide students as they consider next steps.

The tools of stone and wood carving have changed little over hundreds of years. Specialized tools may be shared and gradually purchased as needed, as electric tools for sanding speed the process. Still, carving is a deliberate process, and doing work by hand is appropriate and satisfying. Students may never again have this much time to complete something of beauty, and it will *not* be thrown away or lost!

Safety reminders. If students use power or carving tools, you must be in the room with them. Make sure students know how to secure a work of art for carving to avoid wasting time and energy. Safety suggestions here and at the beginning of this chapter are not meant to scare you away; teaching sculpture is pure joy. You just want the students to be as aware of safe practices as you are.

HANDOUT

TOOLS, DEFINITIONS, AND BASICS FOR CARVING STONE

Definitions

Bruise. If a stone is hit by a chisel at a ninety-degree angle, it may rearrange molecules deep inside that will cause it to break; for this reason, chisels are held at an angle

Carrara. A quarry in Italy that is used today for fine marble, even as it was in Michelangelo's time

Carving. Removing material from a surface such as wood, stone, or plaster

Auarry. A place where sculpture materials are mined

Tools for stone carving. Clockwise from top left: canvas sandbag, hand drill, oil, sharpening stones, C-clamps, stone hammer, steel chisels in canvas bag, rasp brush, safety goggles, files, rasps.

Tools

Bush hammer. A metal hammer with a toothed surface for rounding surfaces

Chisel. Flat-bladed tool for carving, used with a mallet

Coping saw. A saw with a deep neck and fine blade; may be used for interior cuts

Face shield. Plastic shield to protect face from flying chips

Hacksaw. A saw with a thin blade for cutting stone

Hand drill. A hand-operated drill for making openings in stone or wood

Mallet. Soft iron hammer used with metal carving chisels

Pointing chisel. Used for preliminary carving

Sharpening slips. Stones of various sizes and shapes to use with oil for sharpening chisels and gouges

Toothed chisels. Chisels that come in various widths with jagged edges

Carving Materials

Alabaster. Translucent, soft material usually white or veined with gray; takes a fine polish

Balsa-Foam. Soft plastic foam easily carved with ceramic loop tools or knife

Carving wax. This wax may be carved with a knife for jewelry or small investment casting

Clay. Indian red, terra cotta, white art clay, stoneware, or sculpture raku clay with grog

Fire brick. Inexpensive beige porous brick, quite soft; may be carved with saws, rasps, or knives

Limestone. Porous gray or beige stone that is relatively easy to carve and finish

Marble. More difficult to carve, this material takes a high polish

Soapstone. Easy-to-carve stone that finishes to a high polish; gray, green, or off-white

Styrofoam blocks. These blocks may be carved with a heated blade or fettling knife

Finishing Tools and Materials

Paste wax. This waxy substance offers protection and will add a glow to the artwork

Rasps. Round, flat, and half-round iron tools with handles; for finishing prior to sanding

Rifflers. Small iron tools with shaped ends for reaching and finishing hard-to-reach areas

Wet-and-dry sandpaper. Sandpaper that is dipped in water for finishing stone; begin with 160 and finish with 600 grits per inch

263

PROJECT 9-6
STONE CARVING

Time needed: 4 to 6 weeks of daily fifty-minute classes

Materials: soapstone, alabaster, or limestone; chisel; goggles or face shields; hacksaw; hand drill; pointing chisel; bush hammer; rasps; rifflers; soft iron carving hammers; stone chisels; toothed chisels; wet-and-dry sandpaper

Goal: Students will become aware of movement and textural differences used for emphasis in sculpture.

Objective: Students will use tools safely and effectively to complete a work of sculpture that demonstrates a personal, expressive concept.

FOR THE TEACHER

The best stones for student carving are limestone, soapstone, and alabaster. These may be purchased through art supply catalogs or building suppliers. If students choose to use stones they find at a landfall, suggest they hold them at chest height and drop them. If the stone breaks—find another. Warning: make sure they understand that this technique applies only to *found* stone, not something they paid for.

Limestone carving, student work. This two-inch thick piece of limestone was a scrap obtained from a stone supply business.

If stone is easily carved, it is also easily broken. Tell students to always carve at an angle, never to hold the chisel straight up and down. The stone may have been bruised at some point and may have a deeply hidden fault. Remind them to always keep chisels pointed away from the body, turning the stone so they are always aiming toward the side. If they use cutting or power tools, an adult must be nearby.

Remain in the room when students are

Limestone carving, student work. The thickness of a piece of stone doesn't limit an imaginative student.

carving, not only for safety, but also so that you can discuss options with them if an artwork breaks. Broken pieces can be developed individually to produce a mounted set. They can also be repaired by drilling a ⅜-inch hole in each part and inserting a dowel or metal rod using epoxy glue (such as a heavy nail with the end cut off). Joints can be almost perfectly filled with stone dust mixed with glue.

The stone limits what can be done, and the student will want to do drawings of possible solutions. Or a three-dimensional *sketch* can be done by forming a piece of clay roughly the

264

same shape as the stone and then subtracting clay. Most purchased stone is rectangular in shape, but *found* stone has a high point and a low point, and sometimes a good starting point is to leave some high points in place. Often no particular subject seems to present itself, and the student decides to do an abstraction, simply shaping and smoothing the stone, making planes and edges, and giving movement to the form to draw the eye around on all sides. Even though the student may not have had a person in mind when carving, these sometimes come to resemble the human form.

Let students know that the tendency of most people when they see sculpture is to want to touch it. For this reason it is desirable to give a smooth finish to a piece. People rarely are moved to touch something they know will not feel good.

Safety note. Students must always wear safety goggles when carving stone to avoid stray particles. They should stand while carving, with the stone resting on a sandbag or soft, rolled towel. If they are dry-sanding, they should wear mouth and nose mask to avoid breathing particles of dust.

Art History Connection

Students should be introduced to the classical sculptures of Greeks and Romans and artists of the Renaissance. The movement shown in sculpture is a principle you would like them to understand, even though their sculptures will of necessity be simpler. It is pretty awe-inspiring to them to know that they are continuing a tradition that goes back over two thousand years, using similar tools and materials. This is a good time to bring up the fact that the arts are a reflection of the times. Literature, science, religion, the political climate, and philosophy influence the arts, even today.

Alternative Project

Fire Brick Sculpture

Students will create a sculpture from refractory fire brick (purchased from ceramic suppliers or online). This roughly $4\frac{1}{2} \times 2\frac{1}{2} \times 9$-inch material is porous, similar to stone, but much more easily carved. It may be shaped with a saw, rasps, and coarse sandpaper. Bricks can be glued together to make larger pieces. It will never be really smooth because of its porosity. Remind students that as with soap sculpture that they might have tried as youngsters, they can't try to remove all the material at once. *Safety note: It is recommended that students wear masks when using rasps to avoid inhaling the dust.*

 FOR THE STUDENT

Study the stone, then make sketches of your carving to get you started. Or it might help to shape a small piece of clay in proportion to the stone and "take away" from it to get ideas. If you've ever carved a bar of soap, the same rules apply to stone carving—take away a little at a time and work all over it, not just one side. If you try to take away too much at once, you run the risk of breaking it.

Making decisions is often the most difficult part of carving. Sometimes you may spend a day just making decisions, then carve for six days straight. Be open to change. Sometimes the material will not do what you want it to, but instead will dictate what you do.

1. Always carve toward the side and hold the chisel at an angle. If the chisel is perpendicular to the stone, you run the risk of fracturing it. Work over the entire surface, sculpting all surfaces before you totally finish one area.

2. Begin roughing out the sculpture with the pointing tool. Place the tip at an angle against the stone, then tap it with the stone hammer, watching the point and guiding it down or sideways as you hammer. The point and hammer become extensions of your hand as you work. Use tools such as a pointer, toothed chisel, bush hammer, and smooth chisel before getting rid of the tool marks.

3. With the point, make a number of parallel grooves. They will be shallow at the start, but become deeper at the finish of the stroke. Then cross-hatch with the chisel at angles to the grooves. This creates texture that you may choose to leave unpolished in some places. Begin with the largest toothed chisels and finish with the finest.

4. To round large areas and remove excess material, tap gently with a bush hammer. Use flat chisels, then a stone rasp for smoothing. Begin polishing when the stone has been shaped and smoothed as much as possible with metal tools. If your artwork is large, you can use an electric drill with a sanding disk for polishing, but wear a mask and do it outside, as it produces a large amount of dust.

5. To make a deep indentation such as a neck, carve this area last, as thinner areas will make the piece more delicate. Use a hacksaw to cut to the desired depth. Chisel toward the saw cut (or a hole you have drilled with a hand drill) from each direction to avoid bruising the stone. Remember to always support the stone underneath with a firmly rolled towel or sandbag so you are not hitting toward an area that could break because it is not supported.

6. Use wet-and-dry sandpaper for finishing stone. Work from coarse (160 grit) to fine (400 to 600 grit). When the stone is wet, you can see what it will look like when the finish is done. Take the time to do this step properly; you will be glad you did. Rub paste wax on the surface and buff to bring out a glow.

7. Mount the artwork on a stone or wooden base by drilling a hole in the bottom of the sculpture slightly larger than the size of the screw you will use. Use a counter-sink drill bit to make a recessed hole in the bottom of the base to avoid scratching a table with the screw. Fill the hole in the sculpture with white glue and wood chips, allowing it to dry before you screw the base onto the sculpture.

HANDOUT
TOOLS, DEFINITIONS, AND EQUIPMENT FOR CARVING WOOD

Definitions: Wood Carving Basics

Grain. Grain in wood is what makes it beautiful—chisel *with* the wood's grain to make it easier; when the grain varies, the chisel will go deeper, rather than rising to the surface; adapt by carving from a different angle

Roughing out. Removing the extraneous material from a carving surface prior to refining

Slice cut. A chisel will naturally rise from the wood if you are cutting with the grain

Stop cut. If you need to cut toward an area to make it narrow, hold the chisel vertically and hit straight down; then you can use the chisel to cut toward this slice from more than one direction; any stop cut should be supported underneath with a sandbag or towel

Tools

Bent gouge (spoon gouge). Has a spoonlike end; available in deep and shallow

Bent knife. The blade is bent almost at a right angle

C-clamp. Can be used to hold a piece of sculpture or the V-board onto a table

Chisel. Flat-bladed tool for carving, used with a mallet

Coping saw. A saw with a deep neck and fine blade; may be used for interior cuts

Gouge. A carving tool with a rounded blade; gouges come with ⅛- to 1-inch tips

Holding tools. Vises and clamps or V-board

Palm-grip carvers. Handles are rounded, and the blade is short; suitable for wood relief

Parting tool. A V–shaped tool used for cutting lines and corners

Salmon bend gouge. The entire blade is like a scoop

Skew chisel. The end of a skew chisel is angled; a bent skew chisel has a spoonlike curve at the end

V-board. Two 2 × 4 ×12-inch pieces of wood at right angles, screwed about 2 inches in from the corner of a 30-inch square of ½-inch plywood

Vise. An adjustable clamp for a workbench that will hold wood for carving in place

Whittling knife. A knife with a short blade, sometimes at a right angle for whittling

Wood carver's adz. A long-handled, double-edged, axelike tool for roughing out a log

Wood chisel. Wood- or plastic-handled steel tool for carving

Wood mallet. A specially shaped tool for pounding on chisels to remove wood; often made of lignum vitae, the hardest wood of all

Finishing Tools

Rasps. Round, flat, or half-round tools with handles; used for finishing prior to sanding

Rifflers. Small iron tools with shaped ends for reaching and finishing hard-to-reach areas

Sandpaper. From rough to fine

Steel wool. Used to refine even further than sandpaper or may be used between coats of varnish

Tools for wood carving, clockwise from top left: V-board, saw, oil and sharpening stones, C-clamps, file brush, wood files, chisels in bag, hardwood mallets.

WOOD CARVING

Time needed: 4 to 6 weeks

Materials: wood (preferably hardwood), sculpture tools, sandpaper and steel wool, vises and clamps or V-board, varnish, oil, paste wax, stain, or shoe polish

Goal: Students demonstrate safe use of carving and electrical tools.

Goal: Students plan ahead an approach to carving by working all around, examining first to make changes, then sculpting. Sometimes the approach is one-third thinking, two-thirds carving and finishing.

Objective: Students complete a work of sculpture, finishing and mounting it for display.

Cat
Student work, 12 × 12 inches, walnut. The grain of a hardwood such as walnut makes a piece that will always be treasured by the sculptor. Parkway West High School, St. Louis County, Missouri.

Portrait Bust
Student work. This 16 × 10-inch wooden bust might be male or female, although the bark left in place as hair gives it a slightly more feminine look. Parkway West High School, St. Louis County, Missouri.

FOR THE TEACHER

Wood can be purchased from manufacturers or lumberyards. Kiln-dried lumber is desirable because it has already lost its moisture. Seasoned firewood is okay, but seasoned oak is *very* difficult to cut. Trees are classified as either hardwood or softwood. Hardwoods are trees that have leaves, such as maple, birch, cherry, hickory, walnut, ash, oak, and elm. They are preferable because they are generally finer-grained, heavier, harder, denser, and usually finish beautifully. Softwoods (those with needles such as pine, fir, cedar, balsa, and redwood) are easier to carve, but tend to split and do not normally have a beautiful grain.

Work closely with the students, questioning them, pointing out good things that are happening, and giving suggestions. Try to help students avoid rigidity (such as might be seen in a cigar store wooden figure) by encouraging students to work all over the piece, to twist, or give movement.

FOR THE STUDENT

Make a number of drawings (from all sides) before you begin to sculpt. As you work, you may need to just sit and look at the piece from time to time, deciding where to make adaptations to your original design. Don't attempt to develop one area completely, but work first on one area, then another, to achieve overall unity. Keep your tools sharp by using oil on a sharpening stone.

Devise a way to hold the wood in place without it slipping each time you hit it or you will be wasting your effort with each stroke. Here are some things that work:

- Use sandbags or a rolled towel.
- Use a C-clamp attached to the edge of a table.
- Make a V-board of two 2 × 4 × 12-inch pieces of wood at right angles, screwed about 2 inches in from the corner of a 30-inch square of ½-inch thick plywood. The V-board can be held in place by clamping it to a table, pushing it against a wall, or by sitting on it.
- A wood vise will hold the work firmly, but you can't keep turning it and the sculpture becomes one-sided.
- Place one side of the wood against a wall.

1. Basically the right hand (or left, if you are left-handed) is producing a forward thrust of the cutting edge, while the left hand controls the chisel. Hold the chisel at an angle loosely in the left hand, with the flat side up and the bevel (slanted edge) against the wood. Make a *slice cut* by holding the mallet in the right hand and hitting the edge of the chisel with enough force to drive it into the wood. If you are doing this correctly, "with" the grain, the chisel will naturally rise to the surface and the area you sculpted will be smooth. If the chisel continues to go deeper, you are cutting against the grain. Turn the wood the other direction. Many sculptors prefer to leave the chisel-marked surface unfinished.

2. Constantly reassess what you are doing. Be receptive to changes that the material almost forces you to make, as they may improve your original idea. If you need to make a deep cut into the piece, it may help to use an electric or hand drill to make a hole to the depth you want. Then chisel toward the hole, turning the piece often. Another technique is the *stop cut*, made by holding the chisel vertically and hitting it into the wood so you can chisel from all angles to make an indentation. *Safety note:* use power tools under adult supervision and with great caution.

3. When you are afraid that one more change will "ruin" the form, it is time to finish the piece.

4. Finishing tools are used to refine. Use rasps first, working from coarsest to finest. To smooth with a wood rasp, grasp the rasp at both ends and smooth the wood all over. To get into hard-to-reach areas, use small rifflers, pointed files, or electric drill accessories. Sandpaper is also worked from coarse to very fine, until the wood has attained a glow and is smooth all over.

5. When the wood is so smooth that you're sure nothing further can be done, dip your hand in water and wet the entire surface. When it has dried, you will find that the water has "raised" the grain and it needs further sanding with superfine sandpaper. Do this step at least twice before finishing.

6. The final finish is necessary to protect wood from dirt. The trend is to leave the material as natural-looking as possible, and this can be achieved with paste wax or linseed oil.

7. Attach the piece to a base to achieve both physical and visual balance. The base should never dominate the sculpture it supports, and it should be finished to enhance the sculpture.

PROJECT 9-8
ASSEMBLAGE (GROUP PROJECT)

Time needed: time variable

Materials: the background will depend on the weight of the scrap materials

Goal: Students will be involved in a classroom critique that demonstrates an understanding of the potential for art to be an agent of change in contemporary society.

Goal: Students work in groups to plan for either a monumental group project or an individual sculpture for each to make that could contribute to a display of related artwork from others.

Objective: Students contribute time and effort to work(s) of art using a variety of media to express and communicate their point of view.

FOR THE TEACHER

Many sculptors have become famous for the use to which they put found materials. Assemblages by 1950s artists Robert Rauschenberg (1925–2008) and Robert Indiana (1928–) included wood, metal, plaster, and other materials. Rauschenberg included a stuffed goat standing in a tire on a mattress in one of his assemblages. Louise Nevelson (1899–1998) was famous for her assemblages of scrap wood, while Deborah Butterfield's (1949–) life-size horses are found in museum collections all over the world.

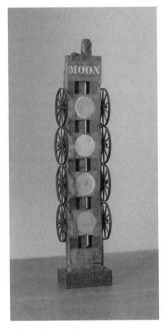

Moon
Robert Indiana (1928–), 1960. Wood beam with iron-rimmed wheels, white paint, and concrete, 6½ feet × 17⅛ inches × 10¼ inches, including base. Philip Johnson Fund. The Museum of Modern Art, New York, NY, U.S.A. Digital Image © The Museum of Modern Art/Licensed by SCALA/Art Resource, NY© ARS.

Metal wall assemblage, 12 × 5½ feet. This was a semester-long project on which art students worked between other projects. Everything was attached to ¾-inch plywood that was spray-painted silver. Copper scraps were donated from a factory. Other found items were large metal factory wheels, a cast-iron sewing machine leg, an unknown number of nails, even scrap silverware. The entire piece was spray-shellacked when finished to protect it from rust. The district's facilities people acted as a technical resource to help plan for the eventual hanging (holes were drilled before starting the assemblage). Parkway West High School, St. Louis County, Missouri.

Butterfield sometimes used metal from destroyed mobile homes, sticks, and scrap metal for the originals, which were later cast in bronze.

Preparation

A three-dimensional assemblage can be made of almost anything, including materials thrown away by local factories or scrap items from home. Let students know right away that they should start looking around their homes for items they can use. Artists throughout time have utilized whatever was available, sometimes sticking with one material, but frequently combining them. Materials that can be used are cardboard, metal, or Styrofoam packing material. One word of advice: if after a few days of moving materials around, things don't seem to come together, it may be necessary to get one person (perhaps the teacher) to put together a workable design for the entire construction to pull it together.

Alternative Project

Box Sculpture

An assemblage on a small scale can be made in a shallow box (preferably wood), inspired by Joseph Cornell (1903–1972). Cornell combined a wide variety of coordinated found items within one box. These boxes often had a theme that included a printed map or an artwork photocopy pasted on the back. Students should be told to think about a theme or title for the box, as that may help them in their search for odds and ends. Paper items may be attached with spray mount or polymer medium and three-dimensional items with a glue gun. Appropriate boxes can be purchased at a hobby store, though a found box may be more challenging. Plexiglas cut to size will protect the assemblage. WebMuseum shows many wonderful reproductions of Cornell's work at www.ibiblio.org/wm/paint /auth/cornell.

 FOR THE STUDENT

1. Sometimes after you have found all the "stuff" that you plan to use in an assemblage, it takes time to arrange it. Multiples of one item (such as wheels or jar lids) arranged in a pattern might be a starting point.

2. The sturdiness of the background will determine how you are going to assemble stuff on it. If it is plywood or something from which you will suspend items, what will work? Screws? String? Nails? Glue? While you have the entire thing lying down when you are working on it, consider how it will look when hanging on a wall.

3. Arrange and rearrange until you are satisfied, then attach items. While you are doing this, if you are lucky you may have a brainstorm of something else that will be the finishing touch. You may end up painting a portion or spray-painting the entire assemblage. Louise Nevelson's large wooden assemblages were always painted in a single color: black, white, or gold.

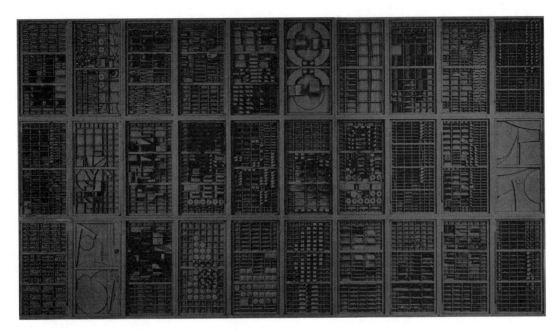

End of Day, Nightscape IV
Louise Nevelson (1899–1938), 1973, painted wood, 101¼ × 183¾ × 7 inches. The Nelson-Atkins Museum of Art, Kansas City, Missouri, gift of the Friends of Art. Photo: E. G. Schempf. A.R.S. Artists' Rights Society.

Architecture

Sculpture and architecture were grouped in this chapter because (from the aspect of teaching students) they have many similarities. Sculptors and architects both create three-dimensional form, and both attempt to push available materials beyond their normal limits—think of Frank Gehry's (1929–) sculptural buildings or Frank Lloyd Wright's (1987–1959) Guggenheim Museum.

Architects are also often involved in creating sculptural objects, public art installations, fountains, applied designs such as stained glass windows, and practical items such as chairs.

Hermitage
Andrew C. Rubin, acrylic, 30 × 24 inches. Students can become aware of architecture in any class. This painting employs the use of perspective and demonstrates sensitivity to nuance in mixing acrylic paint. Ladue High School, St. Louis, Missouri, teacher Daniel Raedeke.

POSTER BOARD BAS-RELIEF ARCHITECTURAL ORNAMENT

Time needed: 3 days of fifty-minute classes

Materials: 1 sheet of 6-ply poster board per student, cutting knives, scissors, white glue, brass two-tone tooling foil (brass on one side, silver on the other) or thin copper tooling foil, old ball-point pen (no ink), black fine-line marker, white copy paper

Goal: Students participate in class discussion, reflecting about how culture, time period, and other issues are reflected in the ornamentation of buildings.

Goal: Students describe similarities and differences between architectural ornamentation of two cultures or time periods (for example, art nouveau and art deco).

Objective: Students select a culture or time period for inspiration in designing and carving a clay architectural ornament.

FOR THE TEACHER

Architectural bas-relief ornamentation was used in the past to enliven the facades (fronts) of buildings that might otherwise be considered a bit boring. Today such ornamentation may even be found in professional baseball parks, with architects avoiding sameness in a wall by using a bas-relief portrait of the team's mascot. Among others, famous architects Louis Sullivan (1856–1924) and Frank Lloyd Wright (1867–1959) continued this long tradition of creating bas-relief ornamentation for skyscrapers and residential designs. Traditional ornaments found on buildings included portions of human and animal shapes and were often combinations of leaves, curving lines, and geometric shapes. Inside buildings, architects also designed elevator doors, doorknobs, and other details that were coordinated with the building's outside designs.

Vocabulary: viewfinder, façade, bas-relief, ornamentation, acanthus leaves, pilaster, column, frieze

Preparation

This design is based on cutting lightweight mat board, but two other bas-relief projects are listed here as alternatives using sculpture techniques found earlier in this chapter.

If instead of using colored aluminum foil you choose to use thin *copper* foil, liver of sulphur may be painted on to add depth. After everything has darkened, burnish raised surfaces with fine steel wool to create highlights.

Alternative Project

Architectural Detail: Art Nouveau or Art Deco Carved Clay Detail

Students can make carved bas-relief (low relief) art deco (1920s, 1930s, and 1940s) or art nouveau (ca. 1890–1910) architectural wall ornaments or tiles. Inspiration will come from designs based on the Mayan culture such as those at Rockefeller Center, featuring stylized panthers, eagles, and other animals. These must dry slowly to avoid warping. Keep the outside edges damp by wrapping them in paper towels until the center is dry, then allow the outside edges to dry. Art nouveau (new) designs are often based on natural forms.

Alternative Project
Architectural Building Ornament Carved in Plaster

The base for carving can be made by pouring plaster into a square or round cake tin, to a depth of 1 ½ to 2 inches, removing it while it is still damp, then carving one side of it with a sharp instrument. It should be kept moist until the carving is complete. When dry, it can be sanded smooth. (Refer back to Project 9-4 for information on working with plaster.)

Ornament from the Scoville Building, Chicago, Illinois
Louis Sullivan (1856–1924), 1884–1885, 19 × 53 ½ × 9 ½ inches, made by the Northwestern Terra Cotta Company, Chicago, Illinois. St. Louis Art Museum, Gift of the General Services Administration.

FOR THE STUDENT

1. *Find abstract designs.*
   With a cutting knife, cut a *viewfinder* (1 ½ × 2-inch opening cut into the center of a piece of copy paper). Use the viewfinder to go through old magazine pages to isolate abstract designs. Be alert for variation in lines and shapes, and designs that show differences in value.

2. When you find a design you like, draw around it with ball-point pen and cut it out. Make at least ten of these cutouts. Select three of these and draw them in black and white. Select one to enlarge onto newsprint in a 9 × 12-inch size, making it interesting with variations in detail, perhaps based on drawings or patterns you designed earlier.

3. The newsprint designs will be scribbled on the back with pencil and transferred to the poster board. The poster board must be cut out carefully with an art knife. Always remember to keep a magazine under the poster board as you cut to protect the table. *Safety note:* You may need to repeatedly cut in one place to go through the poster board. Use caution, and always keep your hands behind the blade. If it should slip and your finger is in front of the blade, you will have a nasty cut!

4. This composition will consist of several layers of poster board going from the bottom layer, a plain 10 × 12-inch base. Subsequent layers will be design details, and it may take several days of careful design and cutting. Layer 2 will be quite large, filling

most of the space and touching some edges. Layers 3 and 4 will have considerable detail. After the layers are cut out, they will be glued together.

5. After all the pieces have been cut out and glued together, this bas-relief will be covered with tooling foil, starting with a piece of foil 12 × 14 inches. It is necessary to center the foil. Use a smooth instrument such as the flat nonink end of a ball-point pen to push and stretch the foil to cover the crevices of the cardboard base. Continue working from the center until the design on the base is easily seen on the foil and it is as smooth as you can make it. You can also use plastic tools to "puff up" the tooling foil in some places (stretching it) to give varied depths to the design.

6. Fold the excess foil to the back of the poster board. If you use aluminum foil, the front can be covered with india ink and allowed to dry. Steel wool can then be used to buff the highlights. This can be mounted on a piece of black construction paper for display. Title your artwork.

PROJECT 9-10
PUBLIC ART: CALL FOR ENTRIES

Time needed: 2 to 3 class periods

Materials: pencil and paper, camera, computer access

Goal: Students identify trends in art and discuss how the time period and local culture influence works of art designed for a specific place.

Objective: Students determine in discussions what might be appropriate for use in a public location in their own town and make a written proposal or model for a work of public art.

FOR THE TEACHER

Many cities are inviting artists of all ages to respond to a call for entries for public art. In some cases it might be a mural design that reflects the culture of the neighborhood. Urban transit systems issue calls for entries for designing art for subway or above-ground stations, even the exterior of a bus! St. Louis Metro Transit offered a curriculum kit for teachers to involve their students in such designs. Usually a call for entries offers specific guidelines about size, materials, and deadlines.

Public sculpture is found all over the world in the form of fountains, sculptural portraits, and, in modern times, abstract and realistic sculptures. Many cities now require builders and developers to set aside a "percent for art" (usually 1 percent) to erect artwork either in front of the new building or nearby. Many cities have sculpture parks, and temporary or permanent abstract sculptures are seen in the hearts of large cities. Some, such as the five-story-high bronze horse head by Picasso in Chicago, are permanent installations.

Bird
Laura Ford, 2007, 130 × 50 × 75 cm, edition 2 of 5, plus two artist's proofs. Citygarden, St. Louis, Missouri, © the Artists and New Art Centre, Roche Court Sculpture Park, London, UK.

Two Rabbits
Tom Classen (Dutch, 1964–), 2004, painted bronze, 87 × 61 × 55 and 63 × 68 × 45 inches, Citygarden, St. Louis, Missouri.

Art History

The Internet abounds with information about public art in various large cities, and many artists have made it their life's work. Christo (1935–) and his wife, Jeanne-Claude (1935–2009), are known for wrapping "gates" in New York's Central Park in orange cloth. Both he and Andy Goldsworthy (1956–), whose public art is often temporary, record their work through photographs. Other well-known examples of public art are Claes Oldenburg's (1929–) *Spoonbridge* in Minneapolis and Antony Gormley's (1950–) *Angel of the North* in Gateshead, England.

Vocabulary: public art, maquette

Preparation

Ask students where they have ever seen public art. These students may be the future patrons who challenge their local government to make the city more interesting. Help them become aware of their surroundings and the possible impact they can make in their surroundings by becoming involved.

Ask students to give a definition of what they think *public art* is. If they were to select a piece of public art for their town, ask where it should be placed and what purpose it would serve. Ask whether graffiti or "street art" might be considered public art and whether the artist intends it to be art or is merely writing a name to "claim" a neighborhood. Would passing motorists consider it ugly, as trash is considered ugly, or might they admire it? In a few cities in South America, some of the art painted on highway underpasses or subway walls is commissioned and of such high quality that it is greatly admired by viewers.

Alternative Project
Sculptural Installation (Group Project)

Students are challenged to work with partners to create a temporary sculpture of found materials along a country road, a riverside, or beach, leaving a moment of surprise for passersby. If there is not an opportunity to do this as a class, they can record their "public art" by taking a photograph or making a drawing.

Alternative Project
Draw, Photograph, and Write

Students are requested to record the historic buildings in their town for a book or digital slide presentation. These could be vernacular architecture (barns, silos, stores, grain elevators) or the oldest houses. The book will include photographs, written interviews from older and new residents, research as to the founding of the town, and drawings of people and buildings to "flesh out" the book. At least a first edition of the book can be assembled, or chapters can be published on the school's website.

Alternative Project

Call for Entries: Bus Shelter

In one city, artists are asked to design an artistic bus shelter for that town's public transportation system. Design a shelter that has seating, is not too deep (so passersby can walk around it), and is covered on three sides for wind protection. It should be graffiti-proof, easy to maintain, and open enough in appearance that people feel sheltered yet not vulnerable. Be sure to make it a work of *art*.

FOR THE STUDENT

Many calls for entries for designs for public art require that the artist conform to a budget and that the artwork will go in a specific location and be of significant size. This is mostly a brainstorming activity as you look around your city for possible locations. Draw or take photos of a building, train station, or traffic corner that could accommodate a piece of public art. Another possibility is to find your neighborhood on Google Maps, satellite view, enlarging and looking around for empty lots or parks that would be seen by passersby.

Select one of the possibilities listed here and first do thumbnail sketches of possible solutions to the problem.

- Use a program such as Photoshop to develop a graphic design solution using the photograph you took of a possible location. Draw your public artwork and install it on a different layer, merging the two. Consider size, lighting, angle, and installation needs to fit the existing photo.

- Design a cardboard maquette for the entrance gates of your local zoo. The sculpture can be of painted sheet metal or Cor-Ten steel (which is allowed to rust naturally).

- The local Children's Hospital wants colorful sculpture to make its entrance more inviting. What can be done to make the exterior look less forbidding to children who might have to be admitted?

- An old street overpass bridge must be replaced. It needs lighting and should have attractive entrance ramps. Create decorative bas-relief decorations that relate to a specific art style such as classical, art deco, or baroque.

- A square block has been given to the local university to use as a dog park where dogs are allowed to run free. You've been asked to design a fence, plantings (trees or shrubbery), and seating areas, waste containers, and sculpture.

10

Careers in Art

Art teachers know what a thrill it is to do what you love while earning a living at it. You can help a young person consider future goals by introducing career-based projects for students to explore. Projects about careers offer a different approach to teaching a standard art curriculum while responding to current emphasis on offering career options to high school students. The projects in this chapter introduce a variety of media and address the teacher's need to cover the elements of art and principles of design. Each project contains explicit directions and illustrations.

Time to Start Thinking about a Career

By the time students are in secondary school, many are thinking about what they might like to do with their lives. Students who have taken several art classes and have a love for it may be considering a career in the field of art. You can support the student by providing information about art careers and schools and assisting them as they develop a portfolio. Although most of your students will go on to other careers, these projects provide opportunities for personal and meaningful exploration for all. Adults in many different fields of work find time to enrich their lives through continued involvement in the arts.

Role-playing. To give "reality" to the projects and to emphasize that artists will often be working to please a client, try playing different roles such as "art director." Art teacher Ron Jennings in the St. Louis, Missouri, school system (a former commercial artist) announces to students that they are being paid for the work they do and that they should share their planning (rough designs) with him before they go on to the next step. Another time you might prefer to be the "client," or the "buying public." Other roles you can play include museum visitor, fine art collector, competition judge, home builder, sports enthusiast—whomever the artist might be trying to please.

Testosterone
William Gant, graphite and ink, 15 × 30 inches.
Parkway West High School, St. Louis County,
Missouri, teacher Peggy Dunsworth.

Boat Engine
Kelly Blaskow, charcoal, 15½ × 15½ inches. Kelly's work
demonstrates that charcoal lends itself to beautifully
rendering exactly what is seen. Careful attention to value
makes this a work of art as well as an illustration. Oakville High
School, St. Louis County, Missouri, teacher Brian Crawford.

Architecture
- Model builder
- City planner
- Interior designer
- Landscape architect
- Marine architect
- Theme park designer
- Architectural writer
- Environmental architect

Art Education
- Art therapist
- Artist in residence
- Community arts
- Grant writer
- Historian
- Museum educator
- Researcher
- Art teacher, K–12

Artisan/Crafts
- Blacksmith
- Bookbinder
- Ceramist
- Fiber artist
- Furniture maker
- Jewelry designer
- Metalsmith
- Sign painter
- Woodworker

Art Services
- Art director
- Artist's agent
- Gallery director
- Appraiser
- Consultant
- Critic
- Auctioneer
- Art supply sales

Design
- Exhibits
- Floor coverings
- Floral designer
- Housewares
- Interior designer
- Packaging designer
- Textile designer
- Toy designer
- Window displays

Digital Media
- Advertising
- Animator or cartoonist
- Digital photographer
- Game designer
- Mobile design
- Weather graphics
- Website designer
- Paste-up artist

Fashion Design
- Color consultant
- Clothing designer
- Art director
- Consultant
- Editor or writer
- Illustrator
- Merchandiser
- Handbags or shoes
- Patternmaker

Fine Arts
- Courtroom sketch artist
- Fine art copyist
- Mural artist
- Painter
- Police sketch artist
- Printmaker
- Sculptor
- Photographer

Graphic Design

Outdoor advertising

Calligrapher

Font designer

Graphic designer

Greeting card designer

Logo designer

Print layout designer

Sign painter

Household Design

Tiles, wall, and floor design

Bedding design

Dinnerware design

Furniture design

Paperware design

Party decoration design

Rug design

Textile design

Illustration

Advertising

Animation

Automobiles

Botanical

Catalog

CD and DVD covers

Children's books

Editorial

Fashion

Scientific and medical

Industrial Design

Airline equipment

Automotive

Color consultant

Factory layout

Heavy equipment

Package design

Renderer

Safety equipment

Sports equipment

Tool designer

Museums

Art historian

Art photographer

Conservator

Curator

Educator

Exhibition designer

Lecturer

Museum director

Photography

Aerial

Architecture

Cinematography

Commercial

Crime scene

Fashion

Medical illustrator

Photography teacher

Photojournalist

Portrait

Publishing

Book designer

Editorial designer

Illustration

Art writer

Art research

Art book copy editor

Art critic

Art historian

Magazine designer

Theater

Art director

Costume designer

Lighting designer

Makeup artist

Program designer

Puppet maker

Set designer

Special effects

PROJECT 10-1
PORTFOLIO

Goal: Students maintain personal artwork over time for a personal portfolio.

Objective: Students present a portfolio of personal work either online or in actuality. This may demonstrate an area of concentration or show evidence of mastery of several different media.

FOR THE TEACHER

Students can benefit a great deal by going to portfolio reviews that take place in universities throughout the country. Art teacher Joan Larson recommends encouraging students to go to reviews as juniors or in the senior fall semester, so they will have time to fill in gaps such as more drawings from observation. The portfolio should show what the student has learned in recent years. The artwork can be photographed digitally for a web page or online portfolio, but the actual artworks should be matted and ready for presentation at a portfolio review. It is not a good idea to send actual artwork to one specific location because it may be needed for an exhibition before it is returned.

Information about national Portfolio Review days may be found on the Internet at www.artinstitutes.edu/career-services/portfolio-review-schedule.aspx.

Teacher Marilyn Palmer annually plans a field trip for students in advanced studio classes to see designers at work in a business setting. Students observe designers who are working on ads, signs, and magazine spreads and who are also closely involved with photographers. She highly recommends this experience for students who are learning about careers in art.

Advanced students may be looking for scholarship opportunities, and you can help them learn to use the Internet to search for contests and scholarships online.

FOR THE STUDENT

Actual Portfolio

- Include approximately twelve to twenty artworks of your best and most recent work that show your unique viewpoint.
- The work should include original drawings from observation, such as landscape, still life, or figure drawings. Avoid working from photographs. If the resource was your own photo, it may be included in the portfolio.
- No copies of published work, ever!
- Professionalism should be shown in presenting artwork that is matted, clean, and free of smudges.
- Include a current sketchbook (or photocopies of a few pages) or sketches that show how an idea was developed from the initial sketch to final project.
- Photograph sculpture from more than one angle and avoid shadows.

- There should be less emphasis on classroom assignments and more on independent work. If you have a special interest, such as painting or sculpture, this could be an "area of concentration."
- Select artworks that demonstrate mastery of at least one medium and competency in others.

The Digital Portfolio

Each art school or university has different requirements. Follow these as closely as you can. If you change resolution, work from a "copy" of the original work, keeping the original digital image untouched.

- To send higher-resolution images, save a JPEG at 150 PPI (pixels per inch) and copy to a CD or USB flash drive (publishable quality is 300 PPI).
- To send an online portfolio, use 72 PPI screen resolution with a minimum height or width of 1,000 pixels, high quality.
- Include a document that has your name, address, phone number, and e-mail address. List the artwork, giving the title, the year the artwork was done, size, and medium, to correspond to the numbers on the photos of the artwork.
- If you send a CD, write the date, your name, phone number, and e-mail address on the disk.

If you send a flash or thumb drive, tape a mailing label with your address onto the drive with postal tape.

CAREER IN ARCHITECTURE: ARCHITECTURAL SCALE MODEL

Time needed: 6 to 10 days of fifty-minute classes

Materials: 14-ply poster board, chip board, or foam core; metal ruler or yardstick; X-acto knives; tape; white glue; drawing paper; ¼-inch graph paper

Goal: Students discuss problems that must be solved by an architect to comply with contemporary rules and customs of society.

Objective: Students solve a specific problem through the use of organizational principles and functions.

Objective: Students submit a scale model of a building that takes into consideration the varied needs of the people who use it.

Museum scale model. Beth Bennett made this as a student at Parkway West High School, St. Louis County, Missouri. This two-story model was created for an honors art history class on mat board covered with paper. Beth cut out reproductions of favorite paintings and arranged them by gallery on both floors.

Careers in Architecture

The architect of today, unlike Thomas Jefferson and George Washington, who were so-called gentleman architects, must have a university degree and be licensed from an accredited school. In addition to the design of homes, schools, shopping centers, and hospitals, there are many other fields open to the architect, such as urban planning, interior design, landscape design, furniture design, remodeling, and renovation.

In addition to designing a beautiful structure, today's architect is also responsible (in cooperation with specialists) for air conditioning, heating, and ventilation; energy efficiency; choice of interior and exterior structure and building materials; meeting zoning laws, building codes, and fire regulations; providing access for the disabled; and considerations of environmental impact. The creative person with an ability to communicate with clients and builders and the ability to work either independently or with a team will find this a rewarding career.

FOR THE TEACHER

This project gives students an opportunity to build a three-dimensional structure and encourages them to *think* like an architect. Museums are a challenge for today's architects, as they often try to visually join new additions to old art museums.

Art History

The "built environment" has left civilization with enduring evidence of earlier civilizations, going back more than five thousand years to artisans who built amazing architectural features such as columns and carvings in the Ajanta Caves in India.

One of today's best-known architects, Frank Gehry (1929–), is quoted as saying, "Throw away the T-square in favor of the computer." He disregards the use of conventional shapes and materials in his rule-breaking buildings seen throughout the world. Architect Frank Lloyd Wright (1867–1959) designed the Guggenheim Museum in New York and broke with tradition in this upward-spiraling building. Wright was best known for his Prairie Period buildings, each of which takes advantage of its particular site, blending long, low lines with flat terrain. He said, "A doctor can bury his mistakes, but an architect can only advise his clients to plant vines."

Vocabulary: scale, chipboard, foamcore, poster board

Preparation

Although a model building can be made from a variety of materials, 14-ply cardboard or foamcore both work well for this project. However, students may want to use a material such as textured sheet plastic, corrugated hollow plastic, or just plain cardboard.

Alternative Project

Terra Cotta Pueblo-Style Building

Students can make a building in terra cotta clay by making and joining small boxes, side by side or stacked on top, appearing much the same as Native American pueblos. Keep in mind that the structure must fit inside the kiln for firing, so it cannot be very large. Walls can be ¼- to ½-inch thick. Instructions for box construction may be found in Project 8-7.

This needn't be glazed, though shoe polish or polymer medium can be used as a finish.

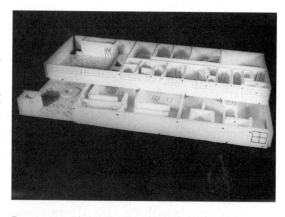

Foamcore scale model. Dawn Citrin made this as a student at Parkway West High School, St. Louis County, Missouri. This foamcore museum is held together by metal brads. Dawn included meeting and reception rooms, disabled access, a grand hall entrance, and bathrooms. She attached a list of artwork that would appear in the galleries.

Alternative Project

Souvenir Clay Building

Many cities that have a famous structure such as Paris's Eiffel Tower, New York's Chrysler Building, Athens's Parthenon, and Rome's Colosseum sell small souvenir models of them. Students can make a clay souvenir model that will easily fit in the hand (4 to 5 inches high). If the model will be fired, it should be hollowed out so the walls are not thicker than ½ to ¾ inch. The building can be either glazed and refired or painted with acrylic paint.

The City
Peter Grippe, American (1912–2002), 1946, terra cotta, 18½ × 25 × 15 inches. This terra cotta "city" of strong geometric shapes brings to mind the building processes of Native American pueblos such as Taos. Mildred Lane Kemper Art Museum, Washington University, St. Louis, Missouri. Elizabeth Northrup McMillan Fund.

FOR THE STUDENT

To build an architectural model, you will need to do some research. Decide what purpose your building will serve. It could be a model for a house or office building, a museum addition, or firehouse (or you choose a theme). Keep the model itself no larger than 10 × 15 inches on the base so it will fit on a base no larger than 12 × 18 inches and still have room for landscaping.

1. After deciding on the purpose of the building, make a few *small* quick sketches from more than one view. If this building will be open to the public, consider how people who have walking disabilities will enter and where you might put an elevator and bathrooms. If it is an office building, there might be a reception area and offices, vending machines, or lunch room. If this were a museum, you would perhaps plan a coat-check room, museum store, educational rooms, display galleries, and offices.

2. Draw the sides of the building on graph paper to the exact dimensions, perhaps using a scale of ¼ inch equal to 5 feet.

3. It is better not to try to cut out entry doors, windows, and decorative details, but instead draw them on the walls before joining all the pieces together. If using mount board, the corners can be glued together and reinforced inside with white or clear

tape. If using foamcore, attach corners and walls using metal brads (tiny nails) to go through both pieces.

4. When the model is complete, it can be left unpainted or, if you prefer, you can add color. Often no roof is added so people can look inside the model, particularly if you have finished the inside. Some inside rooms can have wallpaper added by using digitally printed patterns or wrapping paper. If you are doing a museum, you can select work by favorite artists to display inside the galleries.

5. When the model is finished, it can be landscaped with fake trees or bushes, and human figures can be added to give some idea of scale.

PROJECT 10-3
CAREER IN ART THERAPY: MANDALA

Time needed: 1 to 2 fifty-minute classes

Materials: 12 × 18-inch drawing paper, compasses, ruler, eraser, black construction paper for display, black fine-line markers, colored pencils, circular objects such as lids

Goal: Students research the history of techniques used to create mandalas in different times and cultures.

Objective: Students create a design reflecting knowledge of the elements of art and principles of design and using meaningful personal symbols.

Careers in Art Therapy

Art therapists are trained in both art and therapy. They work with children, adolescents, and adults of all ages individually or in groups. They work at a variety of locations such as schools, hospitals, prisons, mental health centers, corporations, nursing homes, and in private practice. The therapist may work closely with a number of other professionals such as psychologists or counselors to help the client express a problem and work through it. In art therapy, the art *product* of a client has less importance than the *process*. Dr. Judith Fowler, art therapist and art department chair of Missouri State University, says, "When people can't speak of something, they can draw it."

FOR THE TEACHER

In this project, a circular mandala is used as an example of the work done by some art therapists as they work with clients. This project is ideal for students, as they can express private thoughts, yet create a beautiful work of art. Symbols they use may be meaningful only to themselves.

History

The mandala circle is found throughout the world and is considered in some cultures to have soothing, mystic powers. In the Far East, large mandala circles (often within a square) are interpreted in colored sand on a floor by a group of monks, following specific guidelines. These sand mandalas are not meant to be permanent and are destroyed within a few days. Mandalas are also interpreted in opaque paint on silk as wall hangings.

Preparation

Although there are many guaranteed great ideas to complete a circle design using a compass and ruler, the purpose here is not the end product, but the *process* of the student expressing personal feelings. As always, if you have time, do one of these for yourself. It truly is soothing. However, it can be daunting for students if you show them your example before they start the project, as some students try to please you by imitating what you have done. Students may want to talk with you about some event that they have depicted. Try to schedule time later for a private conversation if you sense a student would like to discuss it with you.

Alternative Project

I Wish I Hadn't Done That

This should not take more than one class. Everyone experiences events that he or she wishes had been handled differently. It might be a phone call, a misunderstanding between friends, a scrap with a brother or sister, or any one of life's daily human interactions. If students are not comfortable drawing figures, they can draw a geometric shape of different sizes to symbolize those involved. Students will show an incident that occurred that they wish they could change. When that is finished, ask them to take out a new piece of paper and draw the event as they would *like* to remember it. If students are intrigued with this idea, they can privately perfect the drawings.

Alternative Project

Geometric Mandala

Another option for making a mandala is to put a compass point in the center of the ten-inch circle and make consecutively smaller concentric circles. You can make geometric figures using even divisions and a different set of designs or colors within each ring. If you choose to make a mandala of this style, it can be done on black paper rather than white. Whether you use black or white paper, color intensely and carefully.

 FOR THE STUDENT

In creating a mandala, you're going to recall your life's journey so far, noting special events and people in your life through the use of symbols, colors, and writing. You may choose to share some of the symbolism with friends, but it isn't necessary, and the symbols can be meaningful only to you.

1. This process will be easier for you if you first write a list of places you have lived, family celebrations, people you have known and admire, small items you have saved because they were special to you at the time (such as a rock you found in a stream, a photo, or a ring). This can be "stream of consciousness" writing, just letting words tumble out as one word reminds you of another. From this list you will gather ideas that you can use in creating a personal mandala.

2. Draw a ten-inch circle. An authentic mandala often starts in the exact center and features several circular designs of different sizes. Use either a compass or small round items (lids, for example) to trace around.

3. You can join the circles together by *taking a walk with line*, often writing a word or phrase as it occurs to you. You can write a single word within a circle or completely fill it with information about an event in your life. Or put a symbol of something you love inside one.

4. When you are satisfied, cut out the circle and mount it on black or gray paper.

CAREER IN FASHION DESIGN: WEARABLE ART

Time needed: 5 days of fifty-minute classes

Materials: ink and watercolor, 11 × 14-inch poster board, cloth swatches, glue, fashion magazines, scissors

Goal: Students identify and describe clothing trends and discuss how the relevant place, time, and culture are reflected in wearable art.

Objective: Students complete a design for wearable art that may be inspired by a specific historical period or culture.

Careers in Fashion Design

Some fashion designers' names, often seen as motifs on their designs for clothing and accessories, are more readily recognized by young people than the names of famous artists in other fields. High-fashion designers have their own firms, but the bulk of designing is done anonymously for the broader apparel industry. Designers are involved in all aspects of design, production, and marketing. It takes large numbers of assistants, production managers, fashion marketing specialists, coordinators, patternmakers, and sample makers to launch seasonal lines. Designers stay current in their use of color, materials, and international fashion trends through travel, the Internet, reading, and attending fashion shows and social events. Historical references in fashion are frequent inspiration for people in the design field. The term *fashion* indicates that change is necessary, and updating is constant. Many contemporary designers have branched into designing interior furnishings and lines of bedding. Designers are as involved in presentations and fashion shows as in actual designing.

Fine Print

Kiri Mason, newspaper and paint, life-size. This student aims to be a fashion designer, and this life-size ball gown, made of ordinary newspaper with a woven, folded newspaper bodice and painted color "trim," is evidence of patience and creativity, two traits of most designers. Whitfield School, St. Louis, Missouri, teacher James Daniels.

FOR THE TEACHER

The project will be a combination of drawing, painting, and collage, as these "clothing designers" select a particular client base for whom they will create an ensemble. Have a discussion about a few "name designers" whose designs (or knock-offs of their designs) some of the students wear. Discuss this project with them and be clear about your expectations.

Ask students to bring in fashion magazines from home if they happen to have them, or suggest they go online to get information to share about a designer whose work they see in the stores. Much information is available online using search terms such as *fashion illustration, designer's logos, presentation board, fashion brief, fashion knockoff,* or *famous fashion designers.*

Vocabulary: presentation board, knock-off, brief

Alternative Project
Fashion Illustration

As part of this project, urge students to develop a unique style for drawing the human figure. Many fashion illustrators exaggerate aspects of the human figure, with extremely long legs and small heads or cartoonlike figures.

 # FOR THE STUDENT

This project is for you to create a "presentation board" that will include drawings of a model or models wearing something you have designed and at least one or more sets of color swatches. If these are sports clothes, indicate the sport by including sports gear or a background. Your name or initials should be included on the clothing or accessories.

1. As a designer you will make your own "brief" to create one outfit and accessories for one specific season and for a specific gender or age group. Remember that you are designing for contemporary people, but your *inspiration* is from another culture or time period. Your outfit might be ski or snowboarding apparel, helmets or headgear, a formal gown or tuxedo for senior prom, a new top to wear with jeans, or "Sunday best" clothes.

2. Select one item from each of the groups listed, just to help narrow your choice.

Season	Gender	Age of Client	Culture or Inspiration	Time Period
Spring	Female	Adult	African	Medieval
Summer	Male	Teenage	Asian	Victorian
			Aztec	1930s
Fall		10–12	Egyptian	1920s
Winter		6–10	Native American	1960s
Tropical		2–6	Russian	1990s

3. When your selection is made, research to see what the clothing of that time period or culture looked like. Photocopy or include drawings from your resource to add to the presentation.

4. As you research in fashion magazines, make sketches of several poses that you can later "dress" to show your design. Notice details on clothing of the chosen era to use for your design. Keep these drawings, as you may refine them later to be part of a presentation board.

5. Here are some suggestions that you might use on a presentation board:

   - Name your collection using your own name.

   - Show more than one view of how your design looks on the human figure.

   - You can show decorative detail such as a pocket or your name appropriately sized for the garment it is on.

   - Include swatches (sample pieces of fabric or printed wrapping paper). If you see a pattern in a magazine (at least 4 × 4 inches), it can substitute for fabric.

CAREER IN COMMERCIAL ILLUSTRATION

Time needed: 5 days of fifty-minute periods

Materials: illustration board (or canvas board), drawing pencils, ink, eraser, drafting tape, brushes, acrylic gel medium, acrylic paint or gouache (opaque water color), woodless colored pencils

Goal: Students compare and contrast the impact of electronic media in the field of commercial illustration and discuss how this affects visual artists.

Objective: Students complete a "commercial illustration" that demonstrates problem-solving ability and time management, both valued career skills.

Careers in Illustration

Illustrators are fine artists who can express an idea by doing what they love best—drawing, painting, and creating other forms of art, while making a living! Yet unlike a fine artist whose work is sold to collectors or through a gallery, an illustrator must depend on clients such as publishers or advertising agencies. The work is not usually hung on a wall, but seen in final form as a printed commercial illustration.

There are many specialized fields of illustration such as sports, editorial illustration, medical, children's books, and fashion. Most illustrators obtain training and degrees in fine arts and are capable of creating almost any form of illustration ranging from developing a logo or license plate to an advertisement for a concert. Competition is keen, but there is always room for a person with ideas or a unique style.

Illustrators may begin with original photographs or drawings, then transform them by painting, computer manipulation, using airbrush, combining in a collage, or making a cartoon. Artists may do a completely digital illustration using a vector-based drawing application. Although hand-lettering is still a useful skill, the computer allows the illustrator to be more productive. A website allows the artist to display work for potential clients to see.

Although much work can be completed on the computer, the love of drawing and the ability to think quickly by sketching ideas are important skills. Clients may want to see a quick sketch of an idea on the spot!

Vocabulary: gouache, political commentary, overlay

FOR THE TEACHER

Commercial illustrator and professor Bill Vann (Willam Vanhoogstraat, 1940–2011) shared this project with colleagues to demonstrate that you don't have to solve all your problems at once, but may produce artwork that is ready to be commercially printed by taking it a step at a time.

Hernandez Swinging
Bill Vann was famous for his sports illustrations. You know this was a home run ball. Courtesy of the Vann family and Robert J. Shay.

Soccer
Bill Vann. This lively action picture features the logo of a famous St. Louis firm, as well as the St. Louis background, while showing a moving soccer ball. Courtesy of the Vann family and Robert J. Shay.

Alternative Project
Children's Book Illustrator

A number of book illustrators such as Eric Carle and Kathryn Falwell often use cut paper collages to illustrate their books for children. Students may prepare their own paper for collage with ink or acrylic paint. When they have written a short story appropriate for children of any age they choose, they can use cut paper both inside and on the book's cover. Thumbnail sketches will help them develop ideas, selecting the one that best illustrates their "title." This same project can be done using fadeless paper and ink or colored pencil.

Alternative Project
Political Cartoonist or Caricaturist

Students make several facial drawings of a political figure, then find a national or international incident and make political commentary that would be appropriate on a daily newspaper.

Alternative Project

Digital Graphic Signage

Students demonstrate use of computer skills to design appropriate entrance signs. They should select one of the following: a mall entrance; a coffee shop; university complex (indoors and outside); a parking garage; restrooms; a zoo; or visual symbols for an airport, train station, or the next Olympics.

FOR THE STUDENT

You don't have to solve all your problems at one time, but instead work step by step to completion. Decide on an idea for your illustration. It can be something to do with sports (snowboarding, uniforms, or athletes in action), fashion (shoes, purses, or dresses), editorial (political satire), or a CD cover idea based on one of your photos. Get used to doing drawings of actual shoes, purses, or clothes.

1. After making a few small thumbnail sketches, make a final pencil sketch on good tracing paper. The sketch does not have to be large. It can be enlarged to the desired size in a copy machine onto quality paper. Ink the sketch itself for visibility. This sketch will gradually evolve into a finished painting with lettering.

2. Apply gel medium with a brush all over the inked drawing, allowing it to dry before also using gel medium on the back for gluing it in place on illustration board (or other heavy backing). The gel medium acts as both sealant and glue.

3. Illustration is usually done with opaque paint such as acrylic or gouache. Colors can be used straight from the tube or mixed, working from dark to light.

4. When the painting is dry, add finishing touches with colored pencils.

5. This work of art, the illustration, is usually the beginning of the job. If it is an advertisement, an overlay with the name of the product and other text will be necessary to complete it.

6. You may prefer to scan your original drawing into the computer, working in layers to enhance the drawing by adding color and texture, adding image adjustment layers, filling in the background, and adding lettering.

7. Keep the computer file in layers so that if you show the work to a client and suggestions are made, you can go back and make changes. One temporary layer can be made that allows you to show how the finished layer would look when all the elements are brought together.

PROJECT 10-6
CAREER IN INDUSTRIAL DESIGN

Time needed: 5 days of fifty-minute classes

Materials: paper, pencils, colored pencil, acrylic, gouache, or tempera paint

Goal: Students apply what they have learned about careers in industrial arts reading, research, and discussion.

Objective: Students create an original design of an object to be manufactured.

Careers in Industrial Design

Industrial design has become a major career field since the early twentieth century, when it was recognized that hiring a designer might make it easier to manufacture and sell mass-produced goods such as toys, appliances, cars, and mobile devices. The Bauhaus movement in Germany stressed good design with its dictum, "Form follows function."

Designers often work closely with engineers, architects, physicians, sports figures, and manufacturers when developing new ideas or innovations. They influence design in everything from toothbrushes, trucks, and appliances to signs, packaging, and movie sets. Rapidly changing technology and manufacturing needs offer great potential. Industrial designer Arnold Wassermann says, "Between now and 2050, we will redesign the world."

An industrial designer should be creative, inquisitive, inventive, and self-disciplined, with the ability to meet deadlines. He or she should have good communication skills and demonstrate the ability to work with others. Much of the work today is completed on the computer, although the ability to quickly sketch an idea and follow through with a rendering assists in "selling" an idea.

FOR THE TEACHER

Choosing the object to draw may be the most difficult part of this job for students. It may speed the process to bring machine parts and a few old household appliances. It might also help to review information about showing value differences with pencil and pen. Students can do two small 8 × 8-inch drawings: one of the object as is and one as they would redesign it.

Alternative Project
Design a Unique Perfume Bottle

Some glass perfume bottles are such perfect designs that they are instantly recognizable, eventually becoming collectors' items. Students, of course, name the perfume, using some portion of their own names and make the bottle design fit the scent they intend to put in the bottle. They may have to do some writing first to decide how they can best describe the scent for advertising. A package design to complement the bottle would be an extra little touch.

299

Alternative Project
Automotive Design

Students can consider themselves as industrial designers for a large automotive firm. It is time to revise the current design for a new model to come out within five years. Using clay, students can create a model car of the future, giving it a name. If it will be fired, it is necessary to hollow the clay so no area is thicker than ¾ inch. Otherwise the design can be "immortalized" by photographing or drawing it first in pencil, then colored pencil.

Alternative Project
Design a Bicycle Rack

As more people ride bicycles, the need for safe places to lock and leave them has increased. Some cities and campuses rent out bicycles that may be left in a bicycle rack for the next rider.

Alternative Project
Redesign an Ordinary Object

Students create a new design or a series of designs for an ordinary item such as a skateboard, hairdryer, curling or straightening iron, cell phone protector, or keychain. Famous designers make these ordinary things look new and exciting each year. This can be a group project, with designers challenged to use seasonal colors.

City bikes. Oslo, Norway, rents bicycles by the twenty-four-hour period for people to get from one of their one hundred bike "stations" to another. As cities become more crowded, the need for secure bicycle racks has grown, and these racks might as well be imaginatively designed.

FOR THE STUDENT

Picture yourself "building a better mousetrap." Industrial designers do this when they take an ordinary manufactured item and, sometimes working closely with engineers and the manufacturer, make it more beautiful, streamlined, or functional.

1. Look around your home for an object such as a cell phone, desk phone, desk lamp, clock, camera, snowboard, or other practical item. The more complex the object is, the more interesting it will be to draw. If the object is too large to bring in (such as a bicycle or stroller), take a photo and work from the photo.

2. Place the object on a sheet of paper and use pencil to draw the object as realistically as possible, including shadows. When using pencil, try to shade with the strokes going the same direction, showing differences in value.

3. For a second drawing of an object that serves the same purpose, let your imagination soar, trying to streamline and simplify the object. Thank about

What its purpose is

Who will buy it

How to color it to make it appealing

What materials can be used to make it

How it might be packaged and sold

Why it needs to be redesigned

What process might be used for manufacturing

Where your name, as the developer or designer, can be used

4. When the pencil drawing is complete, it can be colored with colored pencil or acrylic paint.

CAREER IN PHOTOGRAPHY: PHOTOGRAPHY SPECIALTY

Time needed: 5 to 7 days of fifty-minute classes

Materials: digital camera, tripod, photo floodlights, white reflector cards (14-ply mat board, 22 × 30 inches)

Goal: Students describe meanings of artworks by analyzing how specific works relate to historical and cultural contexts.

Objective: Students select a photographic genre to illustrate, turning in at least one photo in that career specialty.

Careers in Photography

Photography is a competitive field. A large percentage of photographers are self-employed. In addition to the ability to make outstanding photographs, it takes good business skills and a genuine interest in working with people to be able to sell yourself. The photographer must take responsibility for the details of running a business such as purchasing equipment and supplies, billing, scheduling, taking the photos, and marketing. There is always room for self-motivated, imaginative, patient individuals who love what they are doing and are good at it. The Internet has changed the distribution of photographs, with photographers maintaining their own websites and making their work visible to anyone. Their photos can be easily sent online anywhere in the world. Computer expertise is a necessity.

Many photographers specialize in one area such as advertising, photojournalism, fashion, industrial, or medical photography. It is best to get as much formal education in the field as possible for a good career start.

FOR THE TEACHER

Photography Specialty (Group Project)

This project allows students to work as professional photographers in several of the specialized fields in photography. Few photographers work solely by themselves, but have assistants to help with lights, check results on a laptop (most work today is digital), and in general make it easy for the photographer to concentrate on lighting and composition. The class will get the most from this assignment if all the photography career specialties are discussed. The students research and get examples of the work done by photographers in the field they choose to investigate.

If at all possible, invite a professional photographer to visit your classes and demonstrate portrait studio lighting arrangements. Otherwise it is helpful for you to demonstrate several different lighting possibilities for portraits and three-dimensional objects.

Vocabulary: high key (mostly light), low key (mostly dark), key light, backdrop, main light, fill light, bounce card

FOR THE STUDENT

For this assignment you will select one of these photographic specialties and take a photograph to represent it. A one-page typed essay detailing the preparation for a shoot and some related jobs for a specialized or general photographer can be displayed next to your "assignment." If possible, find examples by someone famous in this specialty. If you work with one or more partners to explore this assignment, you can make a digital slide show or someone in the group can explain (not read) the report.

Medical illustrator: body parts. Show human anatomy by shooting close-ups of feet, hands, elbows, knees, necks, and faces.

Fashion photographer. Fashion consists of not just men's, women's, and children's clothing, but also sportswear, shoes, handbags, hats, and jewelry. Use props or locations that complement the fashion you have chosen to photograph.

Food photographer. Take photos of food being prepared or a table set with food on it.

Photo journalism: breaking news. This can be an action photo (sports), a photo that illustrates a special season of the year, business news (the groundbreaking for a new mall), an "accident" (staged), or a theatrical production.

Portraiture. Consider that you have been hired by a specialty magazine for a cover portrait. Select one of the specialties for this magazine: musicians, sports enthusiasts, snowboarders, computer geeks, chess players, cooks, jazz enthusiasts, dancers, or animal lovers. In addition to your photograph, design a cover sheet, including a magazine title and text appropriate to the specialty.

Product photography (advertising). Make pictures of cell phones, computer equipment, art supplies, industrial equipment, cars, or anything else that people might buy if you photograph it interestingly enough.

Wildlife photographer. If you have access to a telephoto lens, use it. If you've ever tried to photograph a pet, it sometimes seems as if every animal is "wildlife." To get your wildlife photo, photograph a pet, wait patiently at a backyard birdfeeder, go to your nearest nature preserve, or try the zoo.

Crime scene photographer. The crime scene will have to be staged, such as a robbery, murder, or fight. Avoid breaking school rules or frightening anyone. Appropriate dress for the medical personnel, police officers, and onlookers will make it interesting.

Architectural photographer. Most architectural photography shots are taken indoors with a wide-angle lens and natural light to record as much detail as possible. If a window is in the background, the interior may appear too dark. Make adjustments by opening the lens. Try such shots at different times of the day.

Lucy Right, fashion shoot. This group of photos could well have been done for a fashion magazine, showing different aspects of the same person with dramatic lighting. Oakville High School, St. Louis County, Missouri, teacher Joan Larson.

BIBLIOGRAPHY

Atkinson, Jennifer, Holly Harrison, and Paula Grasdal. *Collage Sourcebook: Exploring the Art and Technique of Collage.* Minneapolis, MN: Quarry Books, 2005.

Ayres, Julia. *Monotype: Mediums and Methods for Painterly Printmaking.* New York: Watson-Guptill, 1991.

Barron, Gill. *Acrylic Secrets: 300 Tips and Techniques for Painting the Easy Way.* Pleasantville, NY: Quarto, 2009.

Berry, Robin. *Watercolor Secrets: Over 200 Tips and Techniques for Painting the Easy Way.* New York: Reader's Digest, 2012.

Brown, Kathan. *Ink, Paper, Metal, Wood: Painters and Sculptors at Crown Point Press.* San Francisco: Chronicle Books, 1996.

Camp, Jeffrey. *Paint.* London: Dorling Kindersley, 1996.

Castleman, Riva. *Jasper Johns: A Print Retrospective.* New York: Thames & Hudson, 1986.

Diehm, Gwen. *Simple Printmaking: A Beginner's Guide to Making Relief Prints with Linoleum Blocks, Wood Blocks, Rubber Stamps, Found Objects, and More.* New York: Sterling, 2000.

Gair, Angela, and Ian Sidaway. *How to Paint: A Complete Step-by-Step Guide for Beginners Covering Watercolours, Acrylics, and Oils.* London: New Holland, 2005.

Giddings, Anita, and Sherry Stone Clifton. *Oil Painting for Dummies.* Hoboken, NJ: Wiley, 2008.

Golden, Alisa. *Unique Handmade Books.* New York: Sterling, 2003.

Halliday, Frank. *Watercolors in a Weekend: Landscapes.* Cincinnati: F & W, 2003.

Horejs, J. Jason. *"Starving" to Successful: The Fine Artist's Guide to Getting into Galleries and Selling More Art.* Phoenix: Red Dot, 2009.

Horowitz, Ellen G. *Digital Image Transfer: Creating Art with Your Photography.* New York: Sterling, 2011.

Hughes, Ann D'Arcy, and Hebe Vernon-Morris. *The Printmaking Bible.* San Francisco: Chronicle Books, 2008.

Hume, Helen. *The Art Teacher's Book of Lists,* 2nd ed. San Francisco: Wiley, 2010.

Hume, Helen. *The Art Teacher's Survival Guide for Elementary and Middle Schools,* 2nd ed. San Francisco: Wiley, 2008.

Johnson, Cathy. *Watercolor Pencil Magic.* Cincinnati: North Light Books, 2002.

Kahn, Wolf. *Pastels by Wolf Kahn,* 1st ed. New York: Abrams, 2000.

Kane, Annette. *Being Bold with Watercolor.* New York: Sterling, 2006.

LaPlantz, Shereen. *Cover to Cover: Creative Techniques for Making Beautiful Books, Journals, and Albums.* Asheville, NC: Lark Books, 1995.

Leslie, Clare Walker. *Drawn to Nature: Through the Journals of Clare Walker Leslie.* North Adams, MA: Storey, 2005.

Leslie, Clare Walker. *The Art of Field Sketching.* Dubuque, IA: Kendall Hunt, 1995.

Leslie, Kenneth. *Oil Pastel: Materials and Techniques for Today's Artist.* New York: Watson-Guptill, 1990.

McDonald, Quinn. *Raw Art Journaling: Making Meaning, Marking Art.* Cincinnati: North Light Books, 2011.

Meyer, Allyson Bright. *The Complete Idiot's Guide to Altered Art.* New York: Penguin, 2007.

Mittler, Gene A., and James Howze. *Creating and Understanding Drawings.* Mission Hills, CA: Glencoe, 1989.

Raynes, John. *The Ultimate Drawing Course.* Cincinnati: North Light Books, 2002.

Robinson, David. *Soho Walls: Beyond Graffiti.* New York: Thames and Hudson, 1990.

Rubin, Susan Goldman. *Delicious: The Life and Art of Wayne Thiebaud.* San Francisco: Chronicle Books, 2007.

Seggebruch, Patricia Baldwin. *Encaustic Mixed Media: Innovative Techniques and Surfaces for Working with Wax.* Cincinnati: North Light Books, 2011.

Shay, Bee. *Collage: Experiments, Investigations, and Exploratory Projects.* Minneapolis, MN: Quarry Books, 2010.

Simblet, Sarah. *Botany for the Artist: An Inspirational Guide to Drawing Plants.* New York: Dorling Kindersley, 2010.

Spring, Justin. *Wolf Kahn: An Artist's Travels,* rev. ed. New York: Abrams, 2011.

Terry, Kayte. *Paper Made.* New York: Workman, 2012.

Tourtillott, Suzanne. *Making and Keeping Creative Journals.* New York: Sterling, 2001.

Yanagi, Sori, ed. *The Woodblock and the Artist: The Life and Work of Shiko Munakata.* Tokyo: Kodansha, 1991.

INDEX